MW01122323

THE LANGUAG.

The Language of English Studies

A Handbook for Advanced Students of English

John Dent-Young

The Chinese University Press

© **The Chinese University of Hong Kong** 1994

All Rights Reserved. No part of this publication may
be reproduced or transmitted in any form or by any
means, electronic or mechanical, including photocopying,
recording, or any information storage and retrieval
system, without permission in writing from
The Chinese University of Hong Kong.

ISBN 962–201–648–0

THE CHINESE UNIVERSITY PRESS
The Chinese University of Hong Kong
SHA TIN, N. T., HONG KONG

Printed in Hong Kong by Nam Fung Printing Co., Ltd.

CONTENTS

_I_NTRODUCTION

The purpose of these notes on English grammar, style and usage is to increase your sensitivity to different varieties and uses of English (among them your own), to help you develop the kind of English you need for writing basic assignments on English language and literature, and to lay the foundation for good written papers and examination answers in advanced English studies.

My aim is also to draw your attention to special problem areas in writing technique, style, grammar and usage. My approach is, I think, a mixture of prescriptive — telling you how I think you should write — and descriptive — describing how people, including students, often do write and the effect it may have on the reader. Because my advice is unlikely to be new to you (most students feel they have heard too much about English grammar already), I hope to make you see why some grammatical and stylistic choices may be better than others, or even obligatory, by relating them to meaning. Some of my grammatical explanations may be quite personal, but their aim is to encourage you to see grammar not as dead rules but as the tool-set which shapes what we can say about things or events and defines what we can do with the language.

I assume that you are likely to be studying English at an advanced level and that your course of study includes, or will include, the study of both English literature and linguistics, with English itself as the language you are required to work in. I also make certain assumptions about the kind of work you will be expected to do in your study of literature and linguistics: for example, that you will be asked to consider various kinds of _text_, to talk about these texts and write about them. I could also express this by saying that you will be asked to *discuss* the texts, which could mean either talking or writing about them. It is important to be able to recognize differences between different texts you are asked to discuss.

Varieties of English

You will be asked to discuss some texts as literature. These are likely to be short stories, poems, novels and plays. You may also be asked to *identify* certain linguistic phenomena in some texts, which may be literary texts (stories, poems, plays), or may be news reports, newspaper articles, advertisements or any other form of written English. The *detailed examination* of written language can contribute to your knowledge and understanding of both literature and linguistics.

You will probably also be asked to consider the way people speak and the fact that people speak differently: different people speak differently, because of regional or educational differences, and the same people speak differently on different occasions, because of varying requirements of formality or friendliness. These are facts that hold true for your own language as well as English. The study of a foreign or second language should lead to an interest in language, in general, and both should heighten your awareness of the subtlety and complexity of your mother tongue and of the uses to which it is put.

Spoken language is a little more difficult than written to observe directly, but it is possible to make recordings from the radio and TV or from actual lectures or conversations. For the purpose of study it is generally necessary to write down (*to transcribe*) this spoken language. Different ways of speaking will also be represented in some of the written texts you study (for example, in the dialogue of plays and novels) and may constitute an important part of their meaning.

You may also be asked to consider the relation between language, literature and culture. In this case you will be examining the way people think of themselves, the assumptions they make, the sort of things they are interested in and the way any of these features may vary between people with different cultural or linguistic backgrounds. You will be asked to consider who you are and the extent to which who you are depends on the language you speak and the culture you feel you belong to.

Most of the following grammatical and stylistic points are relevant to any of the writing you will be doing, but there are some which especially concern writing on literature. We will deal with those first. Serious discussion of literature is generally called *literary criticism*. I shall present a very simplified view of literary criticism because I think it will help you if you start off looking at it in this way. The essential skill involved is supporting what you say by evidence from the text. If you acquire this skill of finding support in the text for your observations and judgements, it will serve you equally in linguistic analysis.

Finally, this is a text not for study but for consultation. I hope that you can find useful items in it when you need them. The appendices list a number of useful structures and problem expressions. The examples in the text all relate to problems which have occurred in the writing of Hong Kong students.

Many of the examples I have used relate to discussion of the following literary texts:

Anton Checkov's "A Wicked Boy" and John Collier's "The Chaser" (in *75 Short Masterpieces*, edited by Roger B. Goodman, New York: Bantam Books, 1972); E. M. Forster's *A Room with a View and A Passage to India*, John Fowles' *The Collector*, William Golding's *Lord of the Flies*, Graham Greene's, "The Invisible Japanese Gentlemen", Ernest Hemingway's, "Cat in the Rain", George Orwell's, *Nineteen Eighty-Four*, G. B. Shaw's *Arms and the Man* and *Pygmalion*.

You do not need to know these texts in order to read this book; they are simply texts which students often have studied, and the examples are merely intended to illustrate problems that students have in writing about texts.

What you will need to do, however, if you want to improve your formal English writing, is develop the habit of checking the words and construc-tions you use in good dictionaries and works on English grammar and consulting style manuals on the proper style and layout of research papers. Here is a list of books you may find useful for this:

Dictionaries:

Collins Cobuild English Language Dictionary. London: Collins, 1987. This is a particularly useful dictionary because of its simple explanations and good authentic examples from contemporary English sources.

Longman's Dictionary of Contemporary English.

The Oxford Advanced Learner's Dictionary.

The Shorter Oxford English Dictionary, 2 volumes. Interesting information on the history of English words, where they come from and when they were first used.

The Oxford English Dictionary, 12 volumes. The full version of the above. Not something you would buy yourself, but it is usually available in a reference library and is something every student of English literature and cultural history should know about.

Longman's Pocket Roget's Thesaurus, Longman's Dictionaries. A thesaurus groups together words with similar meanings and is a very useful tool for any writer. Often you know there is a word that fits what you want to say but you can't remember it. You search your mind till you find a word that has some part of the meaning you want even though it does not fit perfectly. If you look this word up in the thesaurus, you will probably find the word you want listed under the same heading.

On grammar and style:

Collins Cobuild English Grammar, London and Edinburgh: Collins, 1990. Like the dictionary, this is based on authentic examples of contemporary English and is non-technical in its explanations.

Collins Cobuild Student's Grammar. This contains practice exercises that go with the Grammar. There is also a range of Collins Cobuild books on specialized aspects of English like phrasal verbs or the language of reporting.

A Students' Grammar of the English Language, Greenbaum and Quirk, London: Longman, 1990. A rather more technical study of English grammar, with some unfamiliar terms, but thorough and systematic.

A Practical English Grammar, A. J. Thomson and A. V. Martinet, Oxford: OUP, 1983. A convenient short, non-technical survey of English grammar.

The MLA Style Manual, Walter S. Achtert and Joseph Gibaldi, New York: The Modern Languages Association of America, 1985. This is very useful for questions of layout. There is a shorter version on writing research papers.

There are also many useful practice books on English grammar by authors such as L. G. Alexander and Michael Swan.

1

WRITING ABOUT LITERATURE

There are many different kinds of literary criticism, each with its own way of approaching literature, but we will not worry about this here. Certain conventions are common to all writing about literature. The best introduction to criticism is for you yourself to practise writing about specific literary works.

1.1 The general aim

Your first aim in writing about a work of literature is to discuss or *comment on* the work itself.

What this means is first that you must read the work, and then, when you write, that your aim should NOT be to discuss yourself, your family, your friends, your likes and dislikes, your moral sense, or the nature of man. In other words, *comments* like the following are not much good because they are irrelevant to your chief aim:

- ✗ This poem is about war. I think war is a terrible thing because of all the suffering that it causes, often to innocent people.
- ✗ When I first read this poem I felt deeply moved. It made me feel how much suffering there is in the world.
- ✗ The subject of this poem, war, is a very important one because war is one of the scourges of mankind. There have been many wars since the earliest history of mankind right down to the present day, when we have wars in the Middle East and in many other parts of the world.

✗ The theme of this poem is war. I am a Christian, and I think war is wrong, so for me this is not a good poem.

What sort of comment then should you make? How should you begin?

1.2 Preliminary stages

The first thing is to read and, if possible, talk about the work.

1.2.1 Reading

Let us suppose you are going to discuss a story. You begin, obviously, by simply reading the story (reasonably fast, so that you do not lose interest). But you can help your understanding if, as you read, you ask yourself questions:

(a) Why does the character do this?
(b) Why does the character say this?
(c) Do I like this character? Am I supposed to approve of this character?
(d) What does this word mean?
(e) What does this sentence mean?
(f) Why has the author written this story?

Your questions may be of different kinds: some of them may be related to knowledge you lack (e.g. a word you do not know) and can be answered quite quickly by consulting a dictionary or another reader; others may be questions that the author deliberately raises, which may or may not be answered in the work itself. The second kind are particularly important because they can probably lead you towards the story's meaning. You may also have some questions which refer to what is not in the story (did the hero and the heroine really live happily ever after?). This last kind may be interesting, but the only useful information we can get from them is the fact that the author does NOT tell us the answer and presumably did not consider it important (though this in itself may be illuminating, because it may point to some important difference between this story and others).

It is a good idea to make notes while you are reading. Note down anything that you do not understand, anything that you find surprising, exciting, or interesting, and anything you particularly like. Note down your important questions.

1.2.2 Discussion

When you have finished reading, you should if possible discuss the story orally with others who have read it. This is the time to raise any questions that you have not been able to answer by yourself, and to try out any ideas you have formed of what the story means and of what is important in it. You should also compare with the others your general impressions: do you find the story interesting, illuminating, exciting, profound, amusing, boring? Listen to what other people say and ask them why they say it.

Remember that at this stage questions are as useful as answers. Do not feel that you have nothing to contribute to the discussion merely because you do not understand the work you have read. The opposite, in fact, is true. The most important part in this preliminary discussion is played by those who can identify what is difficult, what aspects of the work demand some kind of explanation. But you can also contribute just by questioning the views of others. If someone expresses an idea, test it in your own mind to see if you agree. If you do not agree with the idea, or if you do not fully understand it, ask the speaker for further explanation or ask them to identify something in the text which supports the idea.

1.2.3 Your own experience

In these preliminary stages it is useful to measure what you read against your own experience of life: do you think people behave this way, do you think life is like this? Do you think life could be like this? In fact all the comments in 1.1 which we said are irrelevant in writing, may be helpful at this stage. You *should* ask yourself if you like what you are reading, you *should* compare it with what you know or think about the subject. There *should* be a relation between literature and what you know and think about life, including any religious beliefs you may hold.

But when you come to write formally you will need to omit most of what goes on in these preliminary stages. It is useful for creating understanding and involvement with the work, but not suitable for a written paper. If you are not careful to make this distinction, you will end up with a paper which discusses the ideas which were already in your mind (your *preconceptions*), rather than discussing the story, poem or play you are supposed to have read.

The ideas that come to you when you read a literary work are often described as your *response to* the work. What we have to consider now is how to turn your first response, which may be made up of irrelevant ideas because you are not looking closely enough at the text and because you are misled by preconceptions, into a relevant, well-reasoned piece of writing. Such a piece of writing, which amongst other things says or implies what you think the work means, is often referred to as an *interpretation.*

1.3   What to write: your opinions

Your aim is to express your opinion about the work: this includes saying what you think it means. You do not have to be an expert to do this; all you have to be is a reader. And there is no need to feel apologetic about your opinion. Provided you read carefully and base your opinion on what you read, you cannot be wrong (I shall contradict this later, but for the moment we will let it stand).

You want to express your opinion as firmly as possible. Do not, for example, write:

> ✗ In my opinion, but I may be wrong, I think perhaps this story may be about something to do with old people, to a certain extent.

Instead of this, try to make a firm statement about the work:

> ✔ This story is about the problems of growing old.

Notice that there is no need to say anything about this being your opinion, since it is one of the conventions of this kind of writing that everything you put down *is* your opinion, unless you explicitly say that it is a fact or someone else's opinion.

But suppose your opinion is wrong? I said just now that you can't be wrong. What I really meant is that you can't be completely wrong. In fact, some opinions are better than others, because some opinions fit the text better. So what you are trying to do from the very beginning, when you read and start to discuss the work, is to find things to say about it which can be supported from the actual words in the text. Opinions must be tested all the time against the words of the text, and when you write them down they must be supported by references to the text so that your reader can also test them.

The opinion you form about what a work means is often referred to as an *interpretation* of the work. There is controversy about interpretations, but I think we can say this: that there is always the possibility of more than one interpretation, but that some interpretations are better than others and some interpretations are definitely wrong because they are contradicted by the words of the text, or because they result from a simple misunderstanding. The important point for you to note is that it is possible to base a good essay on an interpretation which your reader (your teacher) disagrees with.

Think about what I have just said. It is a natural consequence of the fact that there can be more than one interpretation. It means that the object of studying literature is not to find a set of "right" answers to a specific set of questions. There are various ways we could try to say what the object of studying literature is, but for the moment let us say that the main purpose of your writing about it is to practise forming and supporting opinions. If your opinion is clearly expressed and well supported you have written an acceptable essay, even if your interpretation of the work is based on a misunderstanding.

I will discuss how you support your opinions in a moment, but first I want to recapitulate and offer some advice on the language of expressing opinions.

1.4 The language of opinion in speech and writing

Here I want to consider some ways in which you can make the expression of opinion sound professional and convincing.

1.4.1 Expressing your own opinion

It is generally useful to try and sum up what you think about a work in as concise a form as possible, ideally in a single clear sentence. Such a statement, since it needs to be supported by an analysis of the text, can provide you with the impetus for a whole essay. Suitably elaborated it can form a useful opening paragraph which will establish what the rest of the essay needs to explain:

> This story is about the problems of growing old. The protagonist passes from a mood of disillusion and despair to a joyful acceptance of reality as a result of a chance meeting with a former enemy.

Notice that here the opening sentence could stand alone as a brief summary of the whole work. The second sentence is also a summary of the whole story but gives us more information about how it is constructed (*the protagonist* means the main character). Further statements might be made about any outstanding features of the story (background, subsidiary characters, humour, for example), but it would probably be a mistake at this point to say much more about what is meant by *a mood of disillusion and despair* and *joyful acceptance of reality*, because you will be doing this in the rest of the essay. Probably in the second paragraph you will start to describe the protagonist, and you will do this in such a way as to bring out the way his mood changes between the beginning and the end of the story, and the reasons for this change.

(You may find as you struggle to develop your original idea that the original idea itself changes. You may find when you read what you have written that it does not support the original idea but raises some quite different ideas. If this is the case you should go back and re-write your opening so that it does summarize what you now want to say.)

In the later paragraphs you will provide supporting evidence, but in doing this you will also continually be making judgements: about what you think the characters feel, about why they act the way they do, about the significance of certain events, and even about the meaning (in this context) of particular words. There is one useful convention that will help you in expressing these judgements: the assumption that as a reader you represent other readers and can therefore describe your response to the story using the pronoun *we*:

> ✔ *We* feel a strong sympathy for Miranda, because her suffering comes about through no fault of her own.

A statement like this means that you think the story has been constructed in such a way that *any* reader can be expected to feel sympathy for Miranda, so you are not just describing a personal response but making a judgement about the way the story is constructed.

> ✔ What *strikes us* immediately is that there seems to be no relation between the title and the action of the story.

Here, too, though you seem to be describing the actual process of reading, you are making a judgement: any reader (you believe) can be expected to notice and be puzzled by this feature that you have noticed.

> ✔ At first sight *we might think* that this story is simply a romantic view of love.

Again, you are saying that anyone might think this. This particular opening, of course, also hints that a main purpose of your essay will be to correct this false first impression.

It is also often convenient to use *we* when you are trying to describe information provided by the text:

> ✔ At the outset of the story *we are told* that the protagonist is young and pretty.

Notice here that the verb, *tell*, is being used to describe what is communicated to us in or by the text. In this case we need not worry whether it is the text that tells us, or the author, or something else. The vagueness of the passive is actually quite useful (but see 3.3.1b and 5.4 for cases where such vagueness is unacceptable).

Other similar expressions: *we learn on the first page / from the character's own words that …*; *we discover that …*; *we see that …*; *we realize that …*; *we may wonder why …*; *we may feel that …*.

1.4.2   Other people's opinions

The difference between expressing your own opinion and expressing someone else's is important. It can be illustrated like this:

> Jane Austen is a major English novelist. (= I think this)

> According to the critic, F. R. Leavis, Jane Austen is a major English
> novelist. (= Leavis thinks this)

Other people's opinions must be labelled. There are many other ways to
label an opinion as someone else's. You can, for example, be much more
vague about whose opinion it is:

> *Most people agree* that Jane Austen is a major English novelist.
>
> *It is generally agreed* that Jane Austen is a major English novelist.

You must be careful, though, to make sure what you say is reasonable. If
your reader does not like Jane Austen, he can be made quite angry by a
statement like: "Everyone agrees that Jane Austen is the world's greatest
novelist." You should also be careful NOT to use the impersonal or passive
forms to introduce an opinion of your own: a statement like "It is considered that this work is a failure", is not valid on its own. Your reader will
assume that you are referring to other people's opinions, not your own, and
will want to know which particular critics hold this view.

You can also be quite specific about where you found an opinion:

> ✔ In his book, *The Great Tradition*, F. R. Leavis argues that Jane Austen is
> one of the great English novelists.

It is seldom enough, however, to state someone else's opinion. Even if
almost your whole paper were made up of a list of other people's opinions
about a work, you would still need to give reasons why in your opinion
those other people are right (if they all agree), or why some are right and
others wrong (if they disagree). When in writing you quote the view of
some authority it is either because you agree with it and it supports the
opinion you are trying to express or because you disagree with it and want
to argue against it.

1.4.3   Qualifying your own opinion

So what is really important is the statement of your opinion, and I have
recommended you to state your opinion firmly, if you can. But in oral
discussion this may sound rude (a more precise word is "brash"), so in
speaking, people tend to offer ideas in a more tentative way:

It seems to me that this point is quite important.

I think/feel this point is quite important.

I'd say this point is quite important.

I am inclined to think this point is important.

I would like to suggest that this point is important.

Could we say that this point is really rather important?

In my view/opinion this point is important.

As far as I can see, this point is important.

I wonder if we could say that …

Now although these forms should generally not be used in writing, you may also in writing feel a need to soften or *qualify* your statements (to qualify a statement means to make it more tentative, less assertive, less aggressive). Generally in writing this should be done impersonally:

It seems reasonable to say that …

There is reason for believing that …

It seems possible to argue that …

There is evidence to support the view that …

There are many other ways to qualify a statement (see 4.5 Emphasis and qualifying). But do use your judgement — it is always desirable to express an opinion as strongly as you can, so you should not automatically weaken every statement you make by adding *to a certain extent*. The reason why you qualify a statement is fear: you are afraid that someone is going to read what you have written and say: "Nonsense! This is not true!" It is good to be cautious, but sometimes it is more interesting to be brave!

1.5 Supporting your opinions

Comments that you make about a work of literature should be supported by evidence from the text. This involves referring to either the words or form of the text or something which occurs in it — some aspect of the story, for instance. Experienced writers can weave this evidence into their writing in a great many different ways, but I shall point out a few basic ways that you will probably need to use.

Evidence from the text can take the form of direct quotation — of words, phrases, sentences or longer passages (see 2.4) — or it can take the form of a reference to something in the text. This reference can be to a single word, or it can involve a paraphrase of some part of the story or even a summary of the story's whole structure.

Whatever it is, the quotation or reference must have a purpose: it must be used to support a *point* you want to make about the meaning, style or structure of the work. You should not quote just to show you have read the work (though that is a secondary effect of quotations which has a certain value in examinations). Nor should you just retell the story (unless you have been asked for a summary).

1.5.1   Support without direct quotation

When you follow a comment with evidence there is often no need to explain what you are doing:

> ✔ In this scene Amanda strikes us as bossy. She repeatedly uses imperatives and she seems to be critical of everything Tom does.

We can easily see that the second sentence provides support for the first. You could however make the relation explicit:

> ✔ In this scene Amanda strikes us as bossy. *This is largely a result of* her repeated use of imperatives and her critical attitude towards Tom.

> ✔ The enterprise which Higgins embarks on could have a serious effect on his own life. *We know this from* the title, because in the original Greek myth Pygmalion falls in love with the woman whom he creates as a statue.

You will notice that in both the examples above, the evidence is represented by a noun phrase: "her repeated use, the title". It can be a little more complicated when the evidence is in the form of a whole sentence. Suppose you want to link more clearly the following sequence, showing the second sentence as evidence for the first:

> Amanda is excited at the prospect of a visitor. She repeatedly questions Tom.

In this case you could turn the second sentence into a noun phrase: "her repeated questioning of Tom." But it is often quite awkward to do this, so the other way is to use *the fact that* or *the way (that)*:

> Amanda is excited at the prospect of a visitor. *We can see this from the way* she repeatedly questions Tom.

Notice now that the order of comment and evidence can be reversed:

> Amanda's repeated questioning of Tom shows that she is excited at the prospect of a visitor.

Here the evidence (Amanda's behaviour) is followed by a deduction about Amanda's state of mind.

1.5.2 Paraphrasing the text

Try to do this in a neutral way. Do not use any unusual terms that are in the text unless you wish to make a point by doing so. For example, in *The Glass Menagerie*, Amanda refers to her past boy-friends as "gentlemen callers". From her point of view, Jim is also a "gentleman caller". But from our point of view, Jim is just a visitor, whom Tom has invited to dinner. So unless you are trying to paraphrase from Amanda's point of view, it would be better to refer to Jim as "visitor":

> The only actual event in the play is Jim's visit in the last scene.

> If Laura cannot work, the only hope is that someone will marry her. This is why the visit of the "gentleman caller" takes on such importance in Amanda's eyes.

The quotation marks in the second example show that "gentleman caller" is not your term but someone else's (your reader is expected to know or guess that it is Amanda's). In using the term, you are quoting a small part of Amanda's point of view. The fact that Amanda uses it tells us a great deal about her personality and her view of life, so you are making a point about Amanda's character by using her words here.

1.5.3 Achieving your purpose

I have taken it for granted that in writing about literature you must have a purpose and should be trying to prove something, because this is true of all academic writing. It is also true that for judging what you write a major criterion is whether or not you express and achieve some clear purpose.

The purpose of any academic writing is often defined for you by a question: that is to say, your purpose is to answer the question. But sometimes you have to invent the question yourself, so one of the things you need to discover is what kinds of question are worth asking and answering in the form of an essay or paper. Literature papers can be written about very small and detailed questions or about broad general issues: you may write to prove that Shakespeare in *Macbeth* uses many words that are associated with the idea of darkness, or to argue in favour of a particular view of the function of literature. But the most basic kind of purpose is to explain what you think a work means, to offer an interpretation of the work. At this basic level, your writing is to be judged by whether you can express convincingly what you think a work means. An important point about this is that it should be what *you* think, not what someone else thinks, even if that other person is a famous critic, or your teacher. Of course you can *agree with* the famous critic (or your teacher!), but you have to give reasons for agreeing.

What makes the expression of your view convincing is mainly the support you provide from the text. But students often seem to forget that quotations and references to the text are only helpful if they support some point the writer is making. Unless you have been asked to write a plot summary there is no value in just retelling the story. A possible exception is when you want to make some point about the plot, to say, for example, that it is very complicated. But even here you should aim to show the complications of the plot as economically as you can.

I have talked a good deal about *making a point, making some point*, and so on. To say that what you write should always aim to *make some point*, is just another way of saying it should have some purpose. The reader's reaction to poor writing is often to want to say "What is the point?" or "I don't see the point." This kind of response means something like "I understand what you are saying, but I don't see *why* you are saying it." It should remind us that there is more to understanding or expressing a meaning than just knowing and using words.

1.6   Evaluation

For many people the ultimate aim of criticism is not just to analyse but also to evaluate: to decide if a work is valuable, important. Since all art involves some element of entertainment, the basis of evaluation is whether the work is interesting and enjoyable. But this is not just a question of whether or not you find the work easy to enjoy at the moment. In fact it may be reasonable to suppose that the greatest enjoyment comes from something that is not immediately easy to understand and that the most interesting work is the one which people can continue to find meaningful even centuries after it was written, even though changes in the language add to the difficulty of understanding it.

1.6.1   Expressing appreciation

Supposing you admire a work, how can you express this in your writing? Direct statements about your feelings are too self-centred and direct statements about the writer's skill tend to sound patronizing:

✗ When I started reading this story I found it so exciting I couldn't sleep till I had finished it.

✗ Ernest Hemingway is a skillful writer and he successfully creates the character of the old man.

Comments like these are not very much help in formal writing about literature, though you might find them, or something like them, in journalistic book reviews.

It is not particularly helpful either to talk explicitly about techniques — the word has no precise meaning:

✗ Ernest Hemingway *skillfully uses many techniques* to express the meaning of this story.

This is not much more helpful than saying "Ernest Hemingway used a pen to write this story", or "Ernest Hemingway wrote this story in words". The word "technique" is really quite meaningless until you describe what you mean by it. The proper way to praise a work is by concentrating on the specific qualities you find in it. If you describe these with enthusiasm, you will be making it quite clear that you admire the writer's skill:

> ✔ Hemingway's powerful use of understatement, combined with the open-endedness of his story, leaves us to work out for ourselves exactly what is wrong in the relationship.

Admittedly it is difficult to find words which can pin down a story's effect in this way. If you do not feel confident enough to make statements like the above, stick to describing the story closely:

> ✔ We sense that there is something wrong in the relationship. But Hemingway does not exactly tell us this. A sense of boredom and frustration is created by the atmosphere — a rainy day which makes it impossible for them to go sightseeing — and by the trivial nature of their conversation. In these circumstances the cat seems to represent something more than just a cat.

Here, you are in fact describing Hemingway's technique and the fact that you describe it so carefully implies that you think it good. This kind of writing may not be particularly elegant but it is honest and will eventually lead you to a greater understanding of the story.

A useful tip is that you can sometimes model part of your own writing on some aspect of the text you are discussing. For example, if your point is that the plot is exciting and suspenseful, try to create a miniature version of the suspense and its resolution, perhaps just in one sentence. If you are discussing a story by the end of which the protagonist has reached some kind of new understanding, you can first describe the character in his or her unenlightened state, and then mention the factors leading to the change and the resulting state. By following the original order of events you give your reader something of the excitement of gradual discovery conveyed by the original story. This may sound obvious, but it is surprising how often students fail to provide any order for the information they give about a story.

1.6.2   Evaluating use of language

Literature and linguistics come together in the close analysis of language use. Generally speaking, however, linguistics is mainly interested in establishing the facts about language use, whereas literature is concerned with finding out why certain patterns of words and meanings excite us so much that we call them great literature.

Students are usually well aware of this, and tend to make statements like the following:

> The poet uses figurative language to express his meaning more vividly.

Such statements may be true but they are not very helpful. What we want to know is *how* the use of figurative language can make meaning more vivid. Sometimes students adopt a more objective approach, one that you might think is more suitable for linguistic analysis:

> Figurative language is used in this poem.
> The poet uses the image of a bat and the image of darkness.
> The poet uses many abstract nouns.

These statements, assuming they are correct, are perfectly reasonable, but also not very helpful. What we want to know is what or how the figurative language contributes to the poem's meaning.

What sort of statement should you try to make?

Most of the tasks you are set will involve the analysis of specific texts. Even if you are not given specific texts to write about, you should find them before you try to make statements about a writer's use of language. The next step can be approached in two ways, but they really come to the same thing: you can first decide what you think the text means, and then try to find what aspects of the language are important in conveying that meaning to you, or you can first decide what aspects of the language seem to call attention to themselves, and then try to decide what they could mean. In practice you will almost certainly work on this problem from both ends simultaneously. Your aim is to produce statements more like these:

> ✔ The poet uses the image of the bat to convey a sense of blindness and darkness. This helps to shape our understanding of the communication gap between the husband and wife.
>
> ✔ The use of double negatives suggests the speaker's uncertainty and expresses his idea that it is very difficult to be both truthful and kind.

Notice that there is generally no need to say that the writer's use of language is skillful. If you can show that it contributes importantly to the meaning, then you have strongly implied that it is skillful.

<u>1.7</u>   Author, narrator, speaker, persona

If a story, poem, or play can be regarded as a form of communication, then the message communicated is the meaning of the whole story, poem or play, and not any particular sentence that it contains. It is risky therefore to make comments beginning "The author says that ...", followed by a statement extracted from the text. In the case of a play this is quite obvious, since everything in the play except the stage directions is spoken by one of the characters. It is not so obvious in stories, though most people recognize that in first-person narrative the "I" is an invented character rather than the author himself or herself.

It is important when you make statements about a story to be clear whether you are referring to something *in* the story, or to the writer of the story. Credit for the whole story, for its overall meaning, structure and technique, and for its success (or blame for its failure) belongs to the author or writer, who can also be referred to by name. But the things which happen in a story and their implications, are motivated either by chance or by the behaviour and intentions of the characters; they can be discussed more or less like real events, in terms of why they happen and what they mean *within* the story. The same can be said of everything the characters say and do. Even when a comment on events or characters seems to be made by the author, the safest policy is to ascribe it to "the narrator".

The same applies to poems, but unfortunately there is no simple obvious word to avoid saying "The poet says that ...". The usual convention is to talk about the *speaker* or the *persona*. *Persona* means mask, and its use to describe the speaker of the words in the poem comes from the idea that a poet puts on a mask when writing poetry; the poet, that is to say, is deliberately creating a personality in the poem. Thus the poet aims to express true feelings by *imaginatively* creating the situation of the poem, which is not simply a record of something that happened (like a news report).

1.7.1 Persons and persona

The word *persona* is not really part of the ordinary vocabulary of most English speakers and it can sound quite awkward and pedantic if you use it too much, so it is worth remembering that there are statements you can legitimately make about the poet, and others you can make about people in general.

the poet the person whose name is probably printed at the foot of the poem. A real person, living or with a known biography, who has certain views on life, and some special writing skills.

the persona the invented personality created in the poem, whose ideas and feelings we deduce from the words of the poem.

a person, people ourselves, the readers, and all the real people the poet knows or knew, and all the people the poet imagines, so long as they are not the imagined speaker of this poem.

> ✗ In the poem called "Grandfather", the *persona* aims to express his sense of the gap which exists between the *persona* and someone of a different age.

This can be written as

> ✔ In the poem called "Grandfather", the *writer* aims to express his sense of the gap which exists between *people* of different ages.

1.8 Plagiarism

I have insisted on the importance of expressing your opinion on the texts you read or the questions you discuss. I have also said that even when you quote other people's opinions you will be giving your own opinion as well, simply by accepting or rejecting what those people say. But students sometimes use other people's opinions as a substitute for the work of thinking out an opinion of their own; that is to say, they write down what other people have said as if they had thought of it themselves. This is known as plagiarism, and in the academic world it is equivalent to theft. Although you can't go to prison for it you will be rightly penalized if you do it knowingly and if you are caught.

The more important reason for avoiding plagiarism, however, is that it wastes your time. If when you write you don't do the work of forming your own opinion, you are performing a useless exercise that will not increase your knowledge or train your mind.

It is also worth knowing that plagiarism usually can be detected: it is difficult to fit someone else's writing into your own because their style is different. Also, since plagiarists are not thinking for themselves, they usually copy material which they do not understand and cannot relevantly introduce or explain. The result is a piece of writing which would not in any case be commended because it is incoherent or irrelevant.

1.8.1   Why do students plagiarize?

It is possible that students sometimes plagiarize through modesty: they think their own opinions are not good enough. They feel when asked to give an opinion that it is better to go to experts and copy down what they say. It is NOT. Experts can provide you with stimulating ideas, but they cannot do your thinking for you.

Students may also plagiarize through misunderstanding of the rules and inability to distinguish what is and is not plagiarism. They see that in advanced academic writing, in the essays published in journals and the papers delivered at conferences, for example, a great deal of use is made of other people's opinions. Certainly, scholars discussing a subject need to take into account what others have thought about the subject. And this is something students should learn to do, although their principle aim is to use these secondary sources (a primary source is the poem, novel, play, etc; a secondary source is what some critic has written about the poem, play or novel) to help them form their own opinions. It is entirely respectable to use secondary sources so long as you acknowledge them, which means giving the name of the book or other source from which you have obtained an idea. Unfortunately students sometimes forget or are too lazy to do this.

The rule therefore is very simple. You can always use someone else's idea provided you say where you got it from; this is usually done in a footnote at the bottom of the page or at the end (but see any good handbook on writing research papers for the accepted methods, which vary slightly in different disciplines). You can use someone else's words provided you put them in quotation marks and say whose words they are. It is important to remember however that you still need to give your own opinion of the material you quote or refer to, and explain its relevance to your topic. You will get no credit for simply mentioning the views of authorities without saying anything about them.

1.8.2   What is and is not plagiarism?

The problem remains that it may not always be clear what is and is not plagiarism. Let me give an example.

It would be plagiarism if you wrote without quotation marks and without saying where they come from the following words about *A Room with a View*: "Light in touch it may be, but it is very far from lightweight; indeed it is as cunningly organized and complex a novel as any he wrote". It would be plagiarism because those words can be found in the introduction to the book (E. M. Forster, *A Room with a View*, London: Penguin, 1990) and were written by Oliver Stallybrass. It would also be very foolish, because the sentences have a carefully balanced and relatively unusual structure and it is very unlikely that they would sound like an appropriate expression of *your* thought.

In the same introduction you can find: "Holmbury St. Mary is only two or three miles south of Abinger Hammer ..." Should you repeat that, without acknowledgement, you would not be plagiarizing because it refers to two English villages and the distance between them is a fact which anyone can verify. The only question that might be asked is why you should think it worth mentioning this fact.

Or, to put it another way, for any new and unusual view credit or blame belongs to the person who first puts it forward. If you read somewhere that *A Room with a View* is a novel, you can say the same yourself without acknowledgement. If you were to read somewhere that, contrary to popular opinion, *A Room with a View* is really not a novel but an epic poem or an advertisement for soap powder, you would be unwise to repeat that as if you had simply thought of it yourself.

Let me go back to the quotation from Oliver Stallybrass's introduction and see if it can be legitimately used without actually quoting it. If you try to paraphrase the idea in more ordinary language, you may get something like this: "*A Room with a View* may seem to be quite a simple novel, but in fact it is very carefully organized." Ask yourself if you agree with this and if you could have thought of it yourself. Does the novel in any way seem simple to you, and do you believe it is carefully organized? If your answer is yes, there is really no need to worry about saying where the idea comes from, because anyone could think of it. However, there is no point in writing the idea down if you do not provide support. What you need to do is show in what way the novel may seem simple, and in what way it is carefully organized; the second point is more important than the first. You could include the first in your first statement: "*A Room with a View* may seem to be just a simple story about a love affair, but in fact it is very carefully organized ...." You will have to continue by giving examples of its careful organization.

Plagiarism should not be a big problem in the beginning stages of studying literature. Provided you refer closely to the text you are discussing and make an honest attempt to give and support your own opinion about it, there is little chance that you will plagiarize. It will not really matter if what you say has been said by someone else. The much more important point to bear in mind is not to repeat ideas which you do not understand. There is little value in mechanical, uncomprehending repetition, even if the material you repeat comes from your lecturer.

2

SOME BASIC TECHNIQUES

From now on my comments will mostly apply to any kind of writing you do, though what I particularly have in mind is still the discussion of texts, whether from a literary or a linguistic point of view.

2.1 Names and titles

There are some easily avoided mistakes which can greatly damage the professional appearance of your writing.

2.1.1 Books

Use underlining or italics to distinguish titles of books. Be especially careful where the title is a person's name, because failure to distinguish titles from names can lead to confusion:

> The protagonist of Shakespeare's *Macbeth*, is, not surprisingly, Macbeth.

Try to get names and titles right, i.e. do not misspell them, or miss out words in a title (except when you use reasonable abbreviations for long titles because you need to repeat them many times) or add words to the title.

Check whether there should be an article:

The Glass Menagerie / Pygmalion

Do not use the definite article unless it is part of the work's title, i.e. do not refer to the *Pygmalion*.

There are two common ways of referring to a work's title:

> The title of this story is "A Wicked Boy."
>
> The story is entitled "A Wicked Boy."

(Note there is no *as* after *entitled*.)

You can also say, somewhat informally, "The story is called 'A Wicked Boy'." But not "The title is called ..."

2.1.2   Authors and famous people

Refer to authors, critics or linguists by their last name (with or without first name, or initials):

> T. S. Eliot says ...
>
> Eliot says ...
>
> According to Virginia Woolf ...

Do NOT use first name alone for authors. Authors are treated with respect. Characters in a story can be referred to by their first names alone (they are your friends!), or in any way the author refers to them. But spell their names correctly.

Similarly, use last name (with or without title, first name, initials) for public figures: "President Bush", "George Bush", or "Bush"; "Diana Ross"; "Michael Jackson". People like filmstars are usually known by first and last name, and so usually are women, though some feminists also recommend the use, as for men, of last name only, in order to remove what they see as a form of discrimination (e.g. "Woolf", rather than "Virginia Woolf").

We know that authors write books, so the word *written* is redundant (unnecessary) when you refer to the writer and book together:

> In *Pygmalion*, by George Bernard Shaw ,...
>
> Shaw's *Pygmalion* is a comedy.

A pronoun can be substituted for the name to avoid repeating it when the author is the subject of consecutive sentences, clauses or phrases:

> In *Nineteen Eighty-Four* Orwell attacks totalitarianism. *He* paints a grim

> picture of the future, in a world where even the freedom to love has been suppressed.
>
> In *his* last plays, Shakespeare seems to take a new direction.

But this does not apply across paragraph breaks; repeat the name if you are starting a new paragraph:

> Another way in which Shakespeare differs from his contemporaries is ...

Assuming this is the start of a new paragraph, it is best not to use *he*, even if the last paragraph was about Shakespeare

2.2 Referring to texts

You will frequently find yourself having to make references to texts you are asked to analyse.

2.2.1 Naming the text

In the most general terms, any piece of writing can be called *a text*. All texts also are examples of *discourse* — sentences joined together meaningfully, and the close linguistic study of texts is generally known as *discourse analysis*.

A literary text can also be called *a (literary) work*:

> *Hamlet* is *a* difficult *work*; no one has yet produced an entirely satisfactory interpretation.

The total literary output of a writer, say Shakespeare, can be referred to in two ways:

> The *works* of Shakespeare (a physical object, a book).
>
> Shakespeare's work is distinguished by its brilliant use of language.

In the second example above, *work* is used as a non-count noun to describe the content, the ideas, rather than the physical object.

However, when you have to name the text you are examining, it is best, if you can, to use a more precise word. You should certainly NOT refer to everything as *the passage* (This term, *the passage*, is used by examiners and language teaching books because they generally use *excerpts* or *extracts* from longer texts to test comprehension.). If you are doubtful, ask your lecturer to tell you the correct term for any text you are asked to discuss. Here are some of the terms you may come across:

a story   *a short story*

a novel   *an excerpt from a novel, a chapter from a novel*

a poem   *a stanza, a verse, a line, an excerpt from a long poem*

a play   *a tragedy, a comedy, a farce, a melodrama*

an article   *a newspaper article, a news report, a feature article*

an editorial / a leader   *an interview, an advertisement*

a report   *an essay, an extract from an essay, etc.*

a letter   *a biography, an autobiography*

a radio programme   *a radio play, a talk-show, a commercial*

a film / a movie   *a documentary, a cartoon*

a TV play   *a serial / a soap (-opera), a TV commercial*

Note that these are count nouns (see Chapter 6). It is wrong therefore to write *a piece of poem, a piece of advertisement*.

There are however some related non-count nouns with more general meanings which cannot be used to refer to specific examples unless you add something like *piece of*: e.g. *a piece of writing, this piece of prose*.

Generally it is best to use the most specific term. An exception is that when you refer to two different works together, for example, a novel and a play, you must use a more general word: *these two works, these two texts*.

Some of the more technical words for literature have count and non-count equivalents, so you can choose whichever is appropriate for what you want to say (i.e. non-count for a general statement, count for a specific comment):

Non-count	**Count**
poetry, verse	*a poem*
fiction, narrative	*a novel*
drama, tragedy, comedy	*a play, a tragedy, etc*

For example:

> *Poetry* is not necessarily difficult to understand. Some poetry is quite simple and straightforward.

> In this essay I shall compare two *poems* with the same title. They differ in that the first poem is quite traditional, whereas the second does not rhyme and has no easily recognizable form.

The first is a general statement. The second refers to specific texts.

2.2.2 When, and when not, to begin *In the story* ...

Once you have made it clear what work you are writing about, do not begin sentences with *In the story* ..., *In the play* ..., etc. This gives us no useful information. Do, however, find ways to identify the exact place in the text where a quotation or reference can be found, so that your reader can check what you say about it (see 2.2.3).

An exception to this rule about not beginning with *In the story* is when you are comparing, say, a film and a story. Then you might well need to say things like:

> In the story ..., whereas in the film ...

It is worth noting that adverbial phrases which you place like this at the beginning of a sentence often have this kind of contrastive function. Compare: "*At first sight* this appears to be.... *But on closer examination* we find ..." or "*On weekdays* my life is quite boring.... *But at weekends* ...."

Another reason for mentioning *the story* is that you might wish to stress how some feature occurs very frequently in the text:

> Throughout the story the author stresses the importance of the environment.

This does carry useful information. If you are discussing a story and you tell me that the author does something, or the characters do something, I shall know without being told that they do it *in* the story; but I shall not know, unless you tell me, that they do it *throughout* the story.

2.2.3   Locating a comment, reference, example or quotation

You often need to identify the part of the work you are commenting on, or from which you are taking an example.

If you are certain your readers are using the same edition (i.e. when you are working with a prescribed text) you can use page numbers for this, but note the preposition: ***On** page 22, we find* ...

Some literary texts are divided into named parts: *act* and *scene* for some plays, *chapter* for novels, *line* and *stanza* for poetry, etc. (But note the preposition is usually *in*: *in chapter three, in the fifth act, in the third line.* Also, note, *in the newspaper, in the advertisement,* but *on TV, on the radio.*) If such words are not available, you may be able to use general terms like *at the beginning (of)* ... or *at the end (of)*....

Often however it is necessary for this purpose to use paraphrase of events in the story or topics dealt with in the poem:

> In Miranda's diary, *when she is describing her first meeting with G. P.,* she says ...
> When Wordsworth describes his memory of the daffodils, he says ...

> (There is in fact a special term for what you write in a diary: you could say, "In her *entry for* October 15th Miranda writes ...")

A useful term here is *scene,* which can be applied to stories, novels and films as well as plays to describe any kind of occasion when something happens:

> In the scene where / when George first kisses Lucy, she is apparently overcome more by the beauty of nature than by any feeling for the young man.

> (But spell *scene* correctly, please.)

In this method of locating your comments by paraphrase, you should try to give the most relevant features of the context (most relevant, that is, to the point you are making). This contextualization actually serves a double purpose: besides enabling your reader to check the text, it helps to explain the point you are making by providing a context for it.

Having established the point in the story to which you are referring, you can identify further references to it with *at this point (in the story)*, or *at this stage*. We could continue the last quotation with one of these:

> *At this point* she has no idea that she is going to fall in love with him.
>
> *At this stage* she is still very inexperienced and does not understand her own feelings at all.

You may have noticed that I have been using the useful word, *point*, with two distinct meanings: (1) significance, purpose (see 1.5.3); (2) moment in time, or place in a text.

It is also often possible to use *here*, especially in referring to part of the text you have quoted or identified. For example, when you want to comment further on a passage you have just quoted:

> Tomorrow and tomorrow and tomorrow,
> Creeps in this petty pace from day to day,
> And all our yesterdays have lighted fools
> The way to dusty death. . . .
>
> *Here* Macbeth expresses a pessimism which is scarcely surprising, considering that he must now see how hopeless his position is.

2.3   Giving examples

You may want to support a comment on the text with an example:

> Higgins treats Liza very unreasonably and repeatedly insults her by referring to her as if she were an object. *For example*, in Act II he tells Mrs Pearce to "put her in the dustbin", and elsewhere he refers to her as "a baggage".

2.3.1   *For example*

Normally this introduces a new sentence, though it doesn't necessarily come first in the sentence; it could come after the prepositional phrase, or in the complement, or at the end of the complement:

> In Act II, for example ...
>
> In Act II, he tells Mrs Pierce, for example ...
>
> In Act II, he tells Mrs Pierce to "put her in the dustbin", for example ...

Note that there is NO PLURAL of *for example*, or *for instance*, even if you give more than one example.

You can introduce an example even more explicitly by starting your sentence with *An example of ... is ...*

> It is clear that Higgins' treatment of Liza is totally inhumane. An example of his neglect of her rights as a human being is the way he speaks of her in the third person when she is present.

Note that an example is *one* case which represents *many*; for convenience you mention only one, or a few, but you are really saying that there are plenty of others you could mention. Therefore it is *an* example rather than *the* example; the definite article would suggest that there is only one, in which case it is not properly speaking an example. Students are too inclined to introduce their examples with *The best example of this is*, which rather suggests that you can't think of many good ones. A much more emphatic introduction is *A clear example of this is....*

Of course, *the* will apply to repeat mentions of a previously given example:

> Let us look again at the example I quoted before....

As with other kinds of support, it is not always necessary to introduce an example explicitly:

> Higgins treats Liza very inhumanely and repeatedly insults her by referring to her as if she were an object. In Act II, he tells Mrs Pearce to "put her in the dustbin":

The reader can easily see that the second sentence is an example of his referring to her as if she were an object.

2.3.2   Introducing an example with *like* or *as*

Like can be used to introduce an example (see 2.6.3) but normally only when the example is a noun phrase added on to the previous sentence. It cannot introduce a sentence:

> Some people are absurd because they live in a dream-world, *like* Amanda in *The Glass Menagerie*.

> Some people are absurd because they live in a dream-world. *For example*, Amanda, in *The Glass Menagerie*, seems unable to come to terms with the fact that the world of her youth no longer exists.

> Some people are absurd because they live in a dream-world, as Amanda does in *The Glass Menagerie*.

You could not use *like* in the second of these because the example is a complete sentence.

(There are alternatives, however. *Like* can be followed by a noun with a relative clause: "... they live in a dream-world, like Amanda, *who* seems unable to come to terms with ..., etc.")

As tends to be used when verbs rather than nouns are being related, as in the third example above. When *as* is followed by an adverbial phrase both subject and verb can be omitted, *as* in my last sentence and in this one.

2.3.2a   *Just as*

You should avoid automatically adding *just* to *as*. You should only use *just as* for special emphasis. *Just as* is useful in comparisons when equal weight is given to both sides of the comparison:

> ✔ Lucy discovers herself when she recognizes her true feelings about George Emerson, *just as* Raina discovers herself when Bluntschli deflates her ego and forces her to recognize that her noble sentiments are false.

You should beware of using *just as* followed by a noun:

> ✗ Lucy undergoes a process of self-discovery, just as Raina.

You can rewrite as either of the following:

> Laura, like Raina, undergoes a process of self-discovery.
>
> Laura undergoes a process of self-discovery, just as Raina does.

Like is also used to introduce comparisons, and I shall deal with this use below in 2.6.3. The two uses of *Like and As*, introducing examples and introducing comparisons, seem to overlap.

For problems with *Like* at the beginning of a sentence see 3.3.1c below.

2.3.3   Introducing examples with *such as*

Such as can introduce examples (usually more than one) which are nouns, and should if possible follow immediately after the more general noun which tells us what they are examples of:

> ✔ We face many serious problems, such as inflation, a rising crime-rate, and environmental pollution.

Note that the examples ("inflation", "a rising crime-rate", etc.) can all be called *problems*. The examples should all have meanings which can be included within the meaning of the first noun, in much the same way as *dog* and *horse* are included within *animal*, as hyponyms. In the example given above you can test that *such as* is correct by making sentences like "Inflation is a problem", "A rising crime-rate is a problem", etc. You should not use *such as* to introduce a sentence example:

> ✗ Higgins treats Liza very rudely, such as he calls her "a baggage".
>
> ✗ They face many serious problems, such as they do not have enough food and water and the war makes it impossible to harvest any crops.

Both these examples should be rewritten in two sentences, introducing the second with *For example* (if you think it necessary to label it as an example).

2.3.4   *Etc., and so on*

In order to underline the fact that the examples you give are only a small proportion of the actual cases, you can end your list of examples with *etc.* or *and so on*. Generally, however, you should not use *etc.* in formal writing.

Etc. is supposed to imply that there are many more items which you are not going to mention because it would waste time. But people sometimes use it to give that impression, when in fact they cannot think of any more items to list. This is NOT a valid way to use it.

Another point is that an example is, by definition, only one item out of many, and is named to represent many other items. Little is gained therefore by using *etc.* If anything, it may give the impression that you are too lazy to think of anything more.

The actual meaning of *etc.* is "and other things", so it is quite incorrect to write "and etc."

Occasionally you might find *etc.* used satirically, to imply that a statement is too boring or too obvious to be worth finishing. Byron parodies the opening of a classical poem in this line from Canto III of his long narrative poem *Don Juan*:

> Hail, Muse! etcaetera. — We left Juan sleeping ...

Here *etcaetera* (the spelling is an alternative one) is used to make fun of such openings, implying that they are so well-known and boring that the reader can easily finish this one for himself.

2.4 Quotations

Instructions about the layout of quotations can be found in *The MLA Style Manual* and other similar reference books. The general rule is that short quotations should be integrated in your text, and longer quotations (more than two lines of verse) should be separated from your text, indented and single-spaced.

Here I want to draw your attention to a few common problems.

First a quotation should make a definite point. It is necessary therefore to introduce it and if it is a long one it may be necessary to comment on it afterwards.

2.4.1   Introducing quotations

If you are going to separate the quotation from your text, it is best to end the preceding sentence with a colon. Before quoting you should have made it clear what point the quotation is meant to support and you should provide some context for it or say where it comes from:

> Fred is not completely naive, nor is he unaware that there is something abnormal about his kidnapping of Miranda. Right at the beginning of the novel, when he is describing how he used to dream about Miranda, he speaks of times when seeing her go out with a boyfriend made him jealous:
>
>> Those were the days I let myself have the bad dreams. She cried or usually knelt. Once I let myself dream I hit her across the face as I saw it done once by a chap in a telly play.

The purpose of this quotation is to show that Fred is aware, or partly aware, of his own abnormality. It should be followed by further explanation, emphasizing the sadistic impulse it reveals — something Fred is evidently not aware of.

With short quotations, integrated in your text, the important thing is that they must fit grammatically. The easy way to make sure a quotation fits is to quote a complete sentence, or part of a sentence which can stand on its own, and introduce it with *says*:

> From the beginning, Fred associates his interest in Miranda with his butterfly collecting. Describing how he felt whenever he saw her, he says, "Seeing her always made me feel like I was catching a rarity …".
>
> (Note that Fred's use of *like* is not quite standard English: the more standard form would use *as if*.)

But if for example you want to quote only part of a sentence, you will have to incorporate it in a sentence of your own:

> In her diary entry for November 9th, Miranda says that Fred is one of the kind of people she hates, the people who have "this hatred of the unusual, this wanting everybody to be the same."

Here two noun phrases are quoted and they follow quite grammatically after the verb *have*.

Problems may arise with verbs and pronouns in the text which do not fit your sentence. This can be dealt with by changing them to appropriate pronouns or tenses, which you put in brackets, but the simplest way is to get rid of awkward joins by making the quotation either longer or shorter:

> ✗ Shakespeare in this sonnet asks whether he should "compare thee to a summer's day."

Rewrite as

> ✔ Shakespeare in this sonnet asks: "Shall I compare thee to a summer's day?"

By making the quotation a complete sentence, you avoid awkward doubts about who *thee* refers to.

> ✗ The speaker in Robert Frost's poem decides not to stop in the woods and watch the snow because "I have promises to keep".

Rewrite as

> ✔ The speaker in Robert Frost's poem decides not to stop in the woods and watch the snow because he has "promises to keep".

By shortening the quotation, you avoid the clashing pronoun: *The speaker — I*. But you retain the interesting and slightly mysterious phrase *promises to keep*.

An even more basic solution, of course, is not to quote at all, but to paraphrase the passage. It is always worth asking yourself if a quotation is really necessary. (see 2.4.2)

If you are quoting poetry you should reproduce it exactly, in the same format, unless you incorporate it in your text. If you incorporate it, you should indicate line breaks using a slash: "Robert Frost writes 'But I *have promises to keep,* / And miles to go before I sleep …'"

Short introductory phrases can sometimes be useful for discussing things that are said by the writer or the characters:

✔ According to Amanda,...

✔ As Amanda says,...

✔ As we learn in the second act,...

Do NOT put these in the passive: "as said by Amanda" sounds awkward and gains no advantage. (see 3.3.1b and 5.4.4)

Note that the present tense is used here, as with other comments on literature. But you would probably use the past tense if you were quoting a statesman or other historical figure:

As Napoleon said, or is reputed to have said ...

Either present or past may be used in the case of political ideas expressed in writing: *As Marx says / said.*

It is possible when quoting a real person to say "Napoleon *once* said". This means that you cannot remember on what occasion he said it. But you cannot use *once* like this when quoting a literary character (see also 8.3.2). It is an important part of literary quotation that you know and indicate the context of the quotation.

2.4.2   When are quotations necessary?

How do you decide if a quotation is necessary? Essentially this is a question of whether there is something special about the actual words used. If the idea is important but the words in which it is expressed are quite ordinary, it is more sensible to use paraphrase rather than quotation. Only use quotation when the ideas or words are relatively unusual or interesting or when the idea is so difficult that is important to consider the exact words in which it was originally expressed. Consider the following comment on *The Glass Menagerie*:

✔ Amanda talks a great deal about "gentleman callers".

Quotation marks are needed because this is Amanda's special term and it plays an immensely important part in her view of life. You could, I suppose, paraphrase it roughly as "boy-friends" or "young men", but that would miss the point (the point is that Amanda still imagines herself to be living in an elegant society where it is too ordinary, too vulgar, to speak of "boy-friends").

Another example would be the quotation from the Robert Frost poem in 2.4.1, where an important part of the poem's meaning hinges on how we interpret "But I have promises to keep".

2.4.3 Wrong ways of using quotations

Do not end a quotation at a point where the grammatical structure is incomplete, or where stopping will change the meaning of the passage you are quoting.

To illustrate this I shall have to use some more difficult quotations, but I hope the point will be clear since it is quite an important one. For example, the following quotation in an essay on the poetry of W. B. Yeats is not helpful:

> ✗ Yeats is referring to death when he says: "Nor know that what disturbs our blood. ..."

This is unhelpful because the sentence quoted is unfinished. It should be: "Nor know that what disturbs our blood / Is but its longing for the tomb." Without the second half of the quotation, we cannot verify the writer's statement that Yeats is referring to death.

The problem arises of course mainly in connection with poetry that has a lot of run-on lines — where the sentence is not finished at the end of the line.

Breaking the quotation in the wrong place can produce complete nonsense. For example:

> In "Youth and Age" Coleridge writes: "This body that does me grievous wrong, / O'er aery cliffs and glittering sands ..."

This distorts the meaning. It makes it sound as if Coleridge means that the *aery cliffs, etc.* are where his body does him grievous harm.

Actually the quotation should be: "This body that does me grievous wrong, / O'er aery cliffs and glittering sands, / How lightly then it flashed along".

This means approximately that "This body flashed along lightly over aery cliffs, etc."

The real problem is that when you quote improperly like this, it is most probably because you have misunderstood the syntax of the poem. So beware! Rather than showing how much you know, a quotation can actually show how much you don't understand!

Another good principle is not to use more than one quotation at a time. If you have more than one which is important, introduce each one separately. If your point is that something is repeated often in the text, either paraphrase the moments when it occurs or try to make the quotations very short and integrate them in your text:

> ✔ Higgins insults Liza repeatedly. He describes her as "deliciously low", refers to her as "a baggage", tells Mrs Pearce to "put her in the dustbin" and threatens to "throw her back into the gutter". He treats her more like an object than a human being.

Also do not try to build long quotations consisting of more than one sentence into the middle of your own sentences. For example the following is very awkward:

> ✗ Though Mrs Moore has faith in universal love and brotherhood, which she believes to be the will of God: "Because India is a part of the earth. And God has put us on the earth to be pleasant to each other. God … is … Love….", (*A Passage to India*, p. 70) the British colonial administration in India falls short of achieving a genuine relationship between the subjugator and the subjugated.

This can be corrected by removing *Though*, putting a full stop after the quotation, and then beginning with something like: *However* … or *Nevertheless* …

> ✔ Mrs Moore has faith in universal love and brotherhood, which she believes to be the will of God: "Because India is a part of the earth. And God has put us on the earth to be pleasant to each other. God … is … Love…." (*A Passage to India*, p. 70). *However*, the British colonial administration in India falls short of achieving a genuine relationship between the subjugator and the subjugated.

2.4.4 Quotation marks

Quotation marks have several different purposes. They are used, of course, to identify quotations. They are also used to isolate words or phrases in two rather different ways. Firstly they can be used to identify words that you are *discussing* rather than *using*: that is to say, you want to say something about the word itself, and if you didn't put quotation marks round it the reader would try to read the word's *meaning* into the sentence:

✔ In Liza's speech, both "haven't" and "isn't" are expressed by "ain't".

You will have noticed that I have mostly been using italics (e.g. *italics*) to show that I am discussing a word, not using it. This is a matter of convenience: since a great deal of this book is devoted to discussing words, it would look clumsy if I used so many quotation marks.

Secondly, quotation marks can also be used to suggest that you do not much like a word. In this case the implication is that someone else uses this word, but you do not agree with that person, or do not accept their use of the word:

✔ The trouble was caused by "trade-unionists".

This means that someone says that the trouble was caused by trade-unionists, but you think it is not true or at least not proved. You would not need the quotation marks if you began your sentence with "The government claims" or "According to the government ...", though you might still use them to stress your doubts about the official view:

✔ The government claims that the trouble was caused by trade-unionists.

✔ The government claims that the trouble was caused by "trade-unionists".

Another way to cast doubt on the validity of a word is to use *so-called*. But do NOT use this together with quotation marks:

✗ She is very proud of her so-called "success".

A similar effect of showing you disagree with a description is obtained with *self-proclaimed*, which literally means this is how the person sees himself or herself, and implies that you do not agree:

✔ Imelda Marcos, the self-proclaimed saviour of her people, says ...

Thirdly, you use quotation marks if you are using a word in a new or special sense, or if you have just invented the word yourself.

I do not think, however, you should use quotation marks merely to show that you are using a colloquial expression. You should decide for yourself whether it is appropriate or not to use colloquial expressions in your writing. Sometimes even in formal writing a colloquial expression can be valuable to achieve some kind of shock effect. In such cases, do not use quotation marks or you will spoil the effect.

Notice also that in fiction a writer sometimes gives a special meaning to a word or uses it with someone else's meaning and does NOT use quotation marks. You will find a great many examples of this ironic use of words in Forster's *A Room with a View*, and in the novels of Jane Austen. It usually means that the author is slipping into the viewpoint of one or more of the characters, and you have to read with great care because you are not meant to take the word at face value. An example from *A Room with a View* is where in the first chapter Mr Emerson's kind but straightforward offer is described as "brutality" — a way of describing it which is possible only from the absurdly refined point of view of the conventional middle-class English at the *pension*. The effect of this irony, to make the middle-class English seem absurd, would be destroyed by the use of quotation marks, just as the effect of a joke can be spoiled if the person telling it laughs too much himself.

2.5   Talking about the use of words

In both literary and linguistic analysis you will need to talk a good deal about words, and it is important to have the right vocabulary and structures for doing it.

2.5.1   Talking about what someone or something means

The two verbs, *mean* and *refer to* are used somewhat differently. I am not concerned here with the important technical difference between meaning and reference. But even in ordinary language there is a difference: *to mean* is usually followed by a clause rather than a single noun, unless it is used in precisely defining a word:

> Here the poet is *referring to the contradiction* between appearance and reality.
>
> What the poet *means is that there is* a contradiction between appearance and reality.
>
> The word "Japanese" here *means* "people from Japan". The word "invisible" *usually refers to* something or someone that cannot be seen, but here the author *is referring to* some people who are very easy to see.

Notice the grammatical structure with *refer* is quite straightforward: a word *refers to* a thing (active voice); also a person can *refer to* a thing or a person (active voice). In this meaning of *refer to* there is usually no reason for a passive.

When you discuss the meaning of a word, you generally use singular agreement, even if the word is plural:

> "Watchers" *refers* to some people who are watching.

The reason is that you could also write this as "The word 'watchers' refers to some people who are watching." Of course, if you discuss the meaning of more than one word, you use plural agreement:

> Here "I" and "you" *refer* to the poet and his father, respectively.

An exception to the rule of singular agreement is in a sentence like the following which is more or less a paraphrase or explanation of the text rather than a discussion of word-meaning:

> Here the "watchers" *are* some people who are watching.

Note the preposition in the following, which is another way of asking about the meaning of a word:

> What does the writer mean here *by* "watchers"?

Note also that when you are discussing how a writer uses a word, it is best to put the word in quotation marks and use no article. Without the quotation marks there can be ambiguity:

> ✗ Higgins uses baggage to describe Liza.

Higgins does not use baggage, he uses "baggage", or "the word 'baggage'".

On the other hand, if you are talking about symbolism or imagery you probably have in mind not the word but the thing it represents, so you do not need quotation marks. Compare the following two examples:

> The writer introduces the image of *the dove* because *a dove* is a symbol of peace.
>
> "*Dove*" means the same as "pigeon".

The first sentence is about the thing, the second about the word. Note also that in the first sentence the singular count noun, "dove" has to be used with an article (see 6.1), but when you discuss it as a word, you do not need the article.

It may occasionally be useful to say that something is not a proper word of English:

> Is there *such a word* as "chobble"?
>
> No, there is *no such word as* "chobble". It does not appear in any dictionary.

2.5.2   Referring to people and addressing people

There is a clear distinction between referring to people and addressing them. If you address someone, it means you are speaking *to* them; if you refer to them, you are speaking *about* them:

> In Shakespeare's *Julius Caesar*, Mark Anthony *addresses* the crowd as "friends, Romans and countrymen".
>
> Bluntschli *refers to* the man who led the cavalry charge *as* a fool who ought to be courtmartialled for it. He is not aware that he is *addressing* the man's fiancé.

A number of other verbs are more or less synonymous with *refer to* in this context, but the constructions vary:

> Bluntschli *describes* the man who led the cavalry charge *as* a fool.
>
> Bluntschli *speaks of* the man who led the cavalry charge *as* a fool.
>
> Bluntschli *calls* the man who led the cavalry charge a fool. (NB no *as*).

2.5.3 Substituting and replacing words

Another valuable way of analysing the use of words is to consider what words can be substituted for a word used in a text, but the verb *to substitute* can itself cause some problems:

> In this context *we can substitute* "trapped" *for* "prison-like" without changing the meaning.
>
> The speaker describes the situation of the Chinese as "prison-like". In this context, *we can replace* "prison-like" *with* "trapped" without changing the meaning.

Notice the important difference. You *substitute* something new for something old. You *replace* something old with something new. The same difference exists in the passive: something new *can be substituted* for something old, or something old *can be replaced with / by* something new.

> In this context, "trapped" can be substituted for "prison-like".
>
> In this context "prison-like" *can be replaced by / with* "trapped".

2.5.4 Words for words

Be especially careful to note which words describing language are count nouns and which are non-count nouns (see Chapter 6). Beware also of the count nouns which are collective in meaning.

a language   this refers to the national languages of countries, e.g.

> French, English, Chinese, etc. are different languages.

language (non-count)   this refers to the general phenomenon studied by linguistics. It also refers to different ways of speaking or varieties of language, or registers, e.g.

> informal language, technical language, figurative language.

You cannot say "the poet uses many figurative languages." *A* language cannot be figurative.

an expression   this is a most useful expression (!). It refers to any small piece of language, and saves you the trouble of deciding whether it is a phrase or a word, etc. It can be useful in describing differences in language: *technical expressions, informal expressions, colloquial expressions, etc.* Using *expression* will save you from the mistake of trying to use *language* as a count noun: "the poet uses many figurative expressions".

a sentence   for proper definitions of a sentence, and all the problems involved in trying to define it, you will have to study quite a lot of linguistics, but for our purposes let us say that a sentence has to have one main verb and has to end with a full-stop or at least a colon or semicolon.
This is a working definition of a sentence, necessary for producing acceptable formal writing.

a subordinate clause   any part of a sentence introduced by a word like *that*, *who*, or *although*, and containing a finite verb (not a participle or infinitive).

a phrase   a group of words which is not a complete sentence because it lacks either a subject or a finite verb, though it may contain a participle or an infinitive, e.g.

> ran to the bus-stop, a member of the English society, students attending lectures, in order to graduate

(Again, this is a working definition of clause and phrase, not a linguistic definition).

an utterance   an utterance is anything that someone says. It may or may not be a sentence; since there are no punctuation marks in spoken language, it is often not easy to decide whether people speak sentences or not. It is therefore often necessary to say that they *produce utterances.*
Generally, however, *utterance* is used to refer to a relatively short portion of speech, perhaps the amount of speech someone produces between major pauses.

speech this is a non-count noun which refers to the spoken use of language as oppposed to written forms:

> Speech differs from writing in a number of important ways.

a speech apart from its generally understood oratorical meaning (oral address to an audience) this is used in a more technical sense to refer to everything said at one go by one speaker in a dialogue:

> Amanda: A fire escape landing's a poor excuse for a porch. What are
> you looking at?
> Tom: The moon.
> Amanda: Is there a moon this evening?
> Tom: It's rising over Garfinkel's delicatessen.

There are four speeches here, though Amanda's first speech consists of two sentences, and Tom's first speech contains only two words. In the linguistic analysis of conversation, speeches are sometimes called *turns*. One would say that in the above dialogue there are four *turns*. This derives from the idea that in dialogue speakers take turns, speaking and listening alternately. Two turns together are sometimes called *an exchange*.

conversation a non-count noun referring to the general phenomenon of unplanned casual talk:

> People tend to think, quite wrongly, that conversation has no structure.

a conversation a casual friendly exchange between two or more people.

dialogue a technique in writing which involves directly imitating, rather than reporting, people's speech:

> Realistic dialogue is an important feature of Harold Pinter's plays.
> Pinter's dialogue is far more natural than Shaw's.

a dialogue most frequently a short passage of dialogue invented for language teaching, found in language textbooks. Also used to describe a kind of essay in dialogue form, modelled on Plato's dialogues.

vocabulary though a count noun, this is a collective term and cannot refer to single words or be used in the plural. It means something like "all the words in a text", "all the words you know":

> Hemingway uses a very limited vocabulary.

(i.e. he uses few words).

> English has a very large vocabulary, French a small one.

It is also sometimes used as a non-count noun:

> There is disagreement about the usefulness of learning vocabulary. Some language teaching experts have argued that practice in using the structures of the language is more important.

Here *vocabulary* means something like "lists of words".

a word   No problems. If in doubt about using *vocabulary*, consider if *words* will be better.

diction   a very tricky word. It is non-count, and refers collectively to the kind of words used in a given text or series of texts:

> To English poets of the eighteenth century, diction was all-important.

> If you discuss Emily Dickinson's diction, you are discussing the kind of words she chooses, and to some extent the words she does *not* choose. You are considering whether there is something especially meaningful about her choice of particular types of word rather than other types of word. Above all you are considering whether the words she uses are formal or informal.

wording   very similar to *diction*, in that it is non-count and refers collectively to the words used. It is NOT a synonym for *word*. It is often used in connection with official documents:

> Lawyers pay close attention to the exact wording of a contract.

slang   also a non-count noun, collectively referring to words which are not accepted in standard written usage, though they are popular with some particular group of people:

> "Groovy" and "fab" are examples of slang from the Sixties.

Naturally there cannot be any plural of *slang*.

jargon   another non-count noun, so no plural, no indefinite article. It collectively refers to the more or less technical terms used by a group of people with the same interests or profession:

> If you want to develop a good writing style, you should avoid using jargon.

a four-letter word   the same thing as *a swear-word, an obscenity, an oath* (slightly old-fashioned), *bad language*. Using four-letter words is known as *swearing, cursing, cussing* (colloquial), or simply *using bad language*. After swearing, people sometimes say jokingly, "Pardon my French!"

an alphabet   this is a count noun, but it is also a collective. English has only ONE alphabet, which it shares with most other European languages. Greek and Russian have their own alphabets:

> There are 26 letters in the English alphabet.

a sound   individual sounds cannot be adequately represented by *a, b, c, etc.*, since the letters of the alphabet stand for different sounds in different contexts. To represent sounds unambiguously you must use a special phonetic alphabet, and you refer to the sounds as *phonemes*.

a syllable   a word may have one syllable (in which case it is *a monosyllable* or *monosyllabic*) or more than one syllable (*a polysyllable*, or *pollysyllabic*). In some kinds of verse there is a fixed number of syllables in each line, but in most English verse the length of the line depends on the number of *stressed syllables*. English metre is composed of feet, each complete foot containing at least one stressed syllable and one unstressed syllable (see Appendix A).

2.6   Comparison

Comparing things is one way we can find out more about them. Sometimes the easiest way to say what something is is to say what it is not. This is similar to the way linguists talk about meaning: the sense of a word can be defined by the way it differs from the sense of every other word in the language (with the exception, perhaps, of a few synonyms).

However, when people compare things they usually do so for a purpose: they want to know which camera to buy, which film to see, and so on. In linguistics the point of comparison is to increase understanding of the items compared and of any system they form part of. The same applies in literary studies, but here evaluation and personal judgement is also often involved, whereas in linguistics the comparison is usually objective. In both linguistics and literature one may hope that comparison of items will lead to the establishment of a theory which will include and account for all the items compared.

Two things can be compared in a single sentence, in a paragraph, or in a whole essay.

> Fred is physically stronger than Miranda, but Miranda is better-educated and has a stronger personality. Fred's only hobby is collecting butterflies, but Miranda has a wide range of interests.

> Miranda on the other hand is better educated and has a stronger personality. She has a much wider range of interests and we get the impression that she is much more confident in her dealings with the world. Above all, Miranda has a vision of what she wants to get out of life.

In the first example both characters are mentioned, whereas the second example makes no explicit mention of Fred. However, in the second example the connective *on the other hand* suggests that a preceding paragraph dealt with Fred. The preceding paragraph might have been this:

> Fred is a product of modern urban civilization, narrow in outlook, resentful of those whom he sees as better off than himself, yet contemptuous of anything he does not understand. He is self-pitying, but he is not prepared to make any real effort to improve himself.

If the main purpose of your writing is to compare two items, it is often best to focus on one for a certain length of time (e.g. one or more paragraphs) before turning to the other.

An alternative method is to divide your subject into several aspects and

2. Some Basic Techniques   47

compare both items together in respect of one aspect at a time. That is, if you are comparing two stories you might compare the plot of each story in one paragraph, and then the characterization and style in subsequent paragraphs.

It is well worth remembering that you do not necessarily have to give equal space to each of the items you are comparing. It may be reasonable to concentrate on one and the ways in which it differs from the other. This in fact is the way in which comparison is commonly used. That is to say, a critic usually compares two works because he is trying to establish the particular qualities of *one* of them. Or in comparing plans, if we prefer one plan to others, we may only need to point out the advantages it has which the others lack.

2.6.1   Economy in comparisons

The chief problem in comparison is to avoid excessive repetition. Maximum economy is what you want to aim for. Remember that once you have made it clear that you intend to compare two items and have said what they are, the reader will probably assume that what you say about one is in contrast to what could be said about the other:

> Fred and Miranda are both about the same age and both living in the same country at the same time. But there the resemblance between them ends. Fred is lower middle class and has no parents. Fred is either a psychopath or highly abnormal.

We do not now need to be told that Miranda *has* parents, is *not* a psychopath and *is normal*. On the other hand we may need to be told about her class background which cannot be precisely deduced from the fact that it is not lower middle class.

Here is a parody of the kind of writing students tend to produce:

> ✗ John and David are quite different. John is tall but David is short. John is very athletic whereas David is not at all athletic. David likes reading, whereas John does not like reading. On the other hand, John likes playing football, but David does not like playing football. I get on better with David, whose interests are similar to mine, than with John, whose interests are not the same as mine …, etc.

This is grammatically correct, but redundant and very boring. All that is needed is something like this:

> ✔ John and David are quite different. John is tall and athletic and likes playing football. David prefers reading. I get on better with David, whose interests are similar to mine.

Or consider this comparison between two poems:

> The diction differs in the two poems. In the first the words are more difficult <u>than those which are used in the second one</u>.

Completing the comparison, as the underlined words here do, is unnecessary. It may also be quite difficult to do grammatically and often causes students to make mistakes.

2.6.2   Economy in comparative sentences

Use the most economical construction. For example, when you compare the same thing in a different time or place, it is often possible to omit everything in the second half except the adverbial phrase:

> There are more Rolls Royces in Hong Kong than (there are) in London.
> More people came to the lecture on Wednesday than (came to the lecture) on Friday.
> Their relationship is not as close as (their relationship is) (it is) in the previous scene.

These are much better without the words in brackets.

Similarly, everything that follows a second possessive can be omitted:

> Miranda's background is quite different from Fred's (background).
> Miranda's attitude to love and sex is much more open than Fred's (attitude to love and sex).

2.6.2a   *That of ...*

The last examples could be rewritten using *that of Fred*, but it would sound stilted (awkward, unnatural). In general it is best to avoid *that of*, *that which*, *those which* if you can. It may even be preferable to repeat the noun:

> Use of a second language as medium of instruction has many defects compared with *use of* the mother tongue.

The sentence is clear and straightforward like this; using *that of* would be confusing because there are several preceding noun phrases.

2.6.3 Brief comparisons

You may in writing about one thing want to make just a brief reference to something else as a point of comparison:

> *In comparison with* Shakespeare, Marlowe is somewhat monotonous.
>
> Compared with *A Room with a View, Ninteen Eighty-Four* is a very pessimistic novel.

Note that *When comparing with* is not normal English, but you can introduce a comparison explicitly with "When *we compare* A with B, we find that ...".

Another way to make this kind of brief reference to a point of comparison is to use *like / unlike*, which links two comparable nouns (or pronouns) within the same sentence:

> Unlike Tom, Amanda is extremely excited by the idea of a visitor.
>
> Like Tom, Laura finds her mother's behaviour embarrassing, but unlike Tom she does not openly criticize Amanda.

In the first of these, "Amanda" is linked to "Tom"; in the second, "Laura" is linked to "Tom". Note that the noun or pronoun following *like* cannot have the same reference as the sentence subject noun or pronoun (for this problem, the non-standard use of *Like* in unnecessary introductory phrases, see 3.3.1c).

Also it is best to position the two linked nouns as close together as possible, to prevent confusion:

> ✗ Unlike Amanda, we find that Laura is frightened by the idea of a visitor.

This makes it sound as if *we* are unlike Amanda. Assuming that is not what the writer meant, the sentence would be better written as:

✔ We find that Laura, unlike Amanda, is frightened by the idea of a visitor.

Similarity can be stressed in two sentences linked with *just as* (see 2.3.2a).

2.6.4   Marking contrast in comparisons

Two things can be different without there being a significant contrast between them:

> The two poems have the same topic, *but* treat it very differently. The first poem uses a traditional rhyme scheme and is strongly rhythmical. The second has very little rhyme and sounds much more like prose.

Contrast is marked (*but*) in the first sentence because the first half approximately says they are the same while the second half approximately says they are different; therefore there is a change of direction. Between the second and third sentences there is *no* change of direction, because though they say something different they both *illustrate the same idea*: that the two poems treat their topic differently. So it is best not to use another *but* between the second and third sentences.

Notice also that when approximately antithetical terms are used, one positively and the other negatively, their meaning is approximately the same and there is no contrast between them:

> The second poem is less figurative *and* more direct.

(In this context *figurative* and *direct* are approximate opposites)

Another way to explain this point is in terms of what we expect:

> The second poem is in free verse *and* does not use rhyme at all.

If it is in free verse, we expect it not to use rhyme. Compare the following where we would expect a poem in traditional form to use rhyme:

> The second poem is traditional in form *but* does not use rhyme.

A test for *and* or *but*, is that if you can substitute *rather than* you need *and*:

> He presents Shakespeare as an ordinary human being *and* not as the greatest dramatist the world has known.

(= He presents Shakespeare as an ordinary human being *rather than* as …).

This test will only work when the second sentence is negative. If it is positive, then remember *but* is used only if the meaning is contrary to our expectations:

He presents Shakespeare as an ordinary human being *but* also a genius.

This rule for *and* or *but* based on meaning does not apply however when the negative part of the sentence is placed in front of the positive part, because *but* is then required regardless of meaning:

He presents Shakespeare *not* as the greatest dramatist the world has known, *but* as an ordinary human being.

This can all be reduced to the formula:

Not A, but B.
A, and / but B (*and* or *but* depending on the meaning:
and = agreeing with expectations
but = contrary to expectations) (see 4.6.1a).

2.6.5 Saying how things differ

Generally *to be different* and *to differ* are synonymous. Problems sometimes occur in saying *how* two things are different:

The two poems differ *in that* the second has far more imagery.

Notice that here we could approximately substitute *because* for *in that*. There is therefore no need for adding *the way*. In the following, however, we do need *the way*:

Wordsworth differs from the eighteenth century poets *in the way* (that) he relates to nature.

Here we could not substitute *because*. If we did, it would imply that the eighteenth century poets did not relate to nature. We assume that the eighteenth century poets did also relate to nature, but *in a different way.* Compare this with the following:

> Wordsworth differs from the eighteenth century poets *in that* he uses more ordinary language.

Here we could not use *in the way (that),* because it would imply that the eighteenth century poets also used more ordinary language.

See also 4.6.3e.

2.6.6   Saying things are the same

The point to remember is that *the same as* is invariable. That is to say, you never change *the* to the indefinite article, and you (almost) never change *as* to *that*:

> Her interests are *the same as* mine.
>
> Our interests are *the same.*
>
> She has *the same* interests *as* I do.
>
> She goes to *the same* lectures *as* I do.
>
> *The same* situation is described in the second story.

If two things are not exactly the same, they may be *similar*:

> Her interests *are similar to* mine.
>
> Her interests *resemble* mine. (NB no preposition)
>
> There is *a similarity between* her interests and mine.
>
> *A similar* situation occurs in the second story.

Note that the indefinite article is used with *similar*, just as the definite article is used with *same*.

If you wish to say *how* things are similar, you can use the *in that* construction that we used for saying how things are different:

> Her interests are similar to mine *in that* we both like literature, but we are interested in different periods.

You could substitute the limiting expression *in so far as* for *in that* (see 4.6.3e).

2.6.7 Simile and metaphor

Simile and metaphor can partly be thought of as forms of comparison:

> O my luve's like a red, red rose …
>
> He was staggering about like a drunkard.

It is best to use *like* for comparison of a noun with a noun, and use *as* for comparison of adjectives and adverbs:

> (as) pretty as a picture
>
> (as) fast as lightning

In descriptive phrases like these it is possible to omit the first *as*. But when a real comparison is being made, the *as* is not usually omitted:

> · He is not *as* tall as I expected.

In similes there is a tendency to use adjective phrases, usually without the first *as*, where one might expect adverbs (see 7.5.6):

> ✔ Quick as a flash, he darted through the door.
>
> ✔ He stood there quiet as a mouse.

Notice that when the comparison is with a sentence you need *as if*:

> ✔ He sounded as if he was very angry.
>
> ✔ He walked as if he was drunk.

You will also meet *like* with sentences but this is colloquial and non-standard (as in the quotation from *The Collector*, 2.4.1):

> He sounded like he was angry.

2.6.8 Describing similes and metaphors

A writer's use of simile can be described as follows:

> The poet *compares* his love *with* / *to* a rose.
>
> The poet *likens* his love *to* a rose.

With metaphor it is perhaps more accurate to use a different kind of verb:

> The poet *describes* the fox *as* a "russet spark".

One could probably substitute here *speaks of* or *refers to* for *describes*.

But note that you must not mix up *to compare A with* / *to B* and *to describe A as B*. It is wrong to write: "He compares their situation as if they were in prison." This could be either "He compares their situation to a prison" or "He describes their situation as being like a prison".

2.7   Answering the question

One of the most important academic skills is giving relevant answers to questions. This seems so obvious, and students generally are so anxious to do the right thing, that it is surprising how often they give irrelevant answers. It is worth considering the reasons.

Sometimes of course the student gives an irrelevant answer because she doesn't know the right answer and has to guess — maybe because she missed some crucial lecture or was not listening. In that case, too bad. But often the enemy is not ignorance but knowledge: she has put a lot of effort into learning something and is determined to prove that she knows it — regardless of the question. Consider this question and the answer:

> Q: Discuss the use of metaphor in this sonnet by Shakespeare.
>
> (The sonnet is printed in the exam-paper.)
>
> A: A sonnet consists of fourteen lines and has a strict rhyme-scheme. Shakespeare's sonnets are different from Petrarchan sonnets. The Shakespearean sonnet rhymes abab ... etc.

I hope it is obvious what is wrong with starting the answer this way. Even if the writer goes on eventually to speak of the metaphors, it is still unpardonable to waste everyone's time (most of all her own) on irrelevant information.

I think we can take the example further. What exactly is the purpose of knowing what a sonnet is, how many lines it has and so on? For some students this question seems absurd: these things are what you get taught in a poetry course, so of course you have to learn them. But you ought to know *why* you are taught things.

Why then do students of English literature learn what a sonnet is? If you had lived in Europe in Shakespeare's time you would have needed to know in order to be able to write a sonnet. At that time, if you couldn't write a sonnet, you didn't have much of an education. However it is most unlikely nowadays that you need to write sonnets. What you do need, if you study English literature, is to be able to recognize a sonnet, because that recognition will help you to know that you are dealing with a certain kind of poem with certain characteristic kinds of subject matter and so on.

Recognizing the sonnet form is just *one step* towards understanding the particular sonnet you are looking at. To judge any object at all, you need to know why it is there and what it is intended to be.

Consider this part of an assignment on a recorded interview (students were provided with the tape and told first to listen to and transcribe it):

> Give a quantitative account of the amount of talk produced by the interviewer and the interviewees — by counting the questions asked, answers given, length of utterances, types of phrases and sentences, etc. Would you say this pattern is true of all conversational interactions? If not, identify some of the factors that may make a radio interview different from other types of conversational contexts.

Think what this involves and implies. Obviously the answer to the question in the second sentence is negative: the pattern is *not* going to be true of all conversational interactions. How do you know? Because if it was, there would be no point in the last part of the assignment, i.e. you would not be able to "identify some of the factors … etc". Almost as obviously (I think), you are being asked to compare things: to compare the speaking of the interviewer and the interviewees, and to compare the interview with ordinary conversations. You are being asked to say which person talks more, and in what way they talk more — does one of them ask more questions, use a greater number of complex sentences, or speak more politely or more of the time? Now I think common-sense would tell you that in an interview the interviewer will ask questions and the interviewee(s) will answer and also speak more of the time. But you are being asked to support common-sense with *evidence* from the actual recording.

I suppose for the first part of the question it would be enough just to provide evidence that the interviewer speaks less. But I think it would also be sensible to provide some sort of explanation of the facts: to show, if possible, how the interviewer uses questions to guide the conversation, and to encourage the interviewee to give information which may be of interest to the listeners. You might even want to turn this explanation to advantage by judging the success or failure of the interview.

You may think that the question does not clearly state that you should do all this. But sometimes you have to supplement a question with your own common-sense. You have to think why the question is being asked. What aspects of your understanding of the course or the material you have studied is the question trying to examine?

In any case, the best technique for answering a question which is based on some kind of text is to make your explanation arise from the given material.

Here is part of someone's answer:

> A radio interview is provided for a large audience. Thus the dialogue tends to be more formal and more grammatical, similar to a speech. However, daily conversation is different. It usually has only one hearer, who knows the speaker. Therefore the conversation is less formal and grammatical.

The answer continues like this, making many other perfectly correct points about radio interviews and carefully saying the opposite about casual conversation. The writer is therefore making each point twice over, which is unnecessary (see 2.6.1). But more importantly, she is not relating the points to the evidence she has to hand, i.e. the transcript of the interview.

There is absolutely nothing to show she did not find all the information in a book and simply copy it out. Such an answer should produce a pass, but not a really good grade.

Answering questions relevantly is part of a broader problem relating to academic study as a whole. Almost any subject provides you with systems of analysis with a number of more or less clearly defined technical terms. These systems and terms have to be mastered, certainly. But you must be able to apply them to specific instances. What is more, they are generally not ends in themselves, but rather tools to enable you to do something or understand something better. The most important thing of all is to know *what* they enable you to do, *why* you might want to use them. This is the kind of question you need to be always asking yourself — and your lecturers. You should be patient if the answers you get are not immediately clear, because such questions are generally very difficult to answer — particularly for experts who tend to take what they know for granted. But you — and your lecturers — should persist in wanting to know. It is true that some deeply philosophical thinkers deny that there is any ultimate meaning or purpose to anything and claim that a terminology (or jargon) can only be its own justification. I think you should not accept this idea — at any rate not until you are very advanced in your studies. Otherwise the danger is that you regard study as nothing but a means of acquiring a set of meaningless terms which you use to show off, in the same way as some people flaunt the designer labels on their clothing. I am not sure if this is better or worse than the simpler view that the purpose of study is merely to pass examinations — a view which is at least honest.

3
ORGANIZATION AND STYLE

I shall try in this chapter to deal first with some of the most general problems in students' writing. These are some of the broad features which distinguish what students produce from acceptable standard English texts with appropriate organization and style.

3.1 Organization

The most general fault in student writing is poor organization. Poor organization is revealed through some obvious signs: writing which rambles along without getting anywhere; writing which is disconnected, with various ideas suddenly appearing for no clear reason; and writing which is repetitive, with the same ideas recurring in different places. The aim of organization is to prevent these weaknesses. Good organization should provide a clear sense of purpose, link ideas in a meaningful and predictable way, and move from one point to another in an orderly fashion so that when a point has been made there is no need to repeat it. This is easier said than done. However, there are a few principles that can be helpful.

3.1.1 Openings

The simplest and most general principle is that a good opening can make everything much easier both for your reader and for you yourself. And in general one of the best ways to begin is with an opening sentence or opening paragraph which summarizes what you want to say in the essay. If you can manage this, you should find that everything else in your essay follows quite easily:

> Although *Hamlet* has many of the characteristics of the popular
> revenge plays from which it is derived, it is also much more.
> Shakespeare has taken a popular genre and given it a philosophical
> slant which questions the assumptions on which it is based and in
> doing so raises lasting questions about the human condition.

After such an opening, we know that the writer is going to tell us (1) why
Hamlet is like the popular revenge plays and (2) why it is unlike them. We
are prepared for the next two paragraphs to begin something like this:

Paragraph 2

> ✔ Like other revenge plays, *Hamlet* begins with a situation in which the
> protagonist has suffered a great wrong which needs to be avenged,
> and ends with a pile of corpses on the stage....

(various features of *Hamlet* which are like the other revenge plays)

Paragraph 3

> ✔ However, unlike the protagonist of a conventional revenge play, Hamlet
> fails to kill Claudius when the opportunity arises, and his eventual
> vengeance is more the result of chance than of planning....

(various features of *Hamlet* which are unlike the other revenge
plays)

Notice that this rough plan would be equally effective as an answer to the
question which might be expressed in any of the following forms:

(a) To what extent is *Hamlet* simply a play about revenge written to please
     a somewhat bloodthirsty Elizabethan audience?
(b) It has been said that *Hamlet* is more than just a play about revenge. Do
     you agree?
(c) Discuss the view that *Hamlet* is a typical Elizabethan revenge play.
(d) "The originality of *Hamlet* lies not in its theme of revenge, which
     Shakespeare probably inherited from an earlier play of the same name,
     but in the use Shakespeare makes of that theme." Discuss this view.

Two practical points are worth making about openings. First, that students
tend to start indirectly and only express their view, or their answer, at the
end of the essay. This method of arousing readers' interest by keeping them
in suspense is crucial to the art of story-telling, but is much less appropriate

in academic writing. If you find this is what you have done, take the ideas from your last paragraph and use them to remake your opening paragraph. Secondly, you may find that, as you write, your ideas develop or even change. If this is the case, you will probably need to go back and rewrite the opening paragraph so that it does summarize what you have actually said, rather than what you originally thought you were going to say — but didn't.

The essential point is that your essay should start as directly as possible. It should indicate immediately your general answer to the question or your overall opinion on the topic. This is not the only way to write an essay. However, if you get into the habit of writing like this it will also serve you well in exams, when time is limited and you certainly do not want to waste it on irrelevant introductions which will gain you no marks. It will also be a valuable aid to writing almost any kind of report, which means that later you can easily transfer the writing skills you learn at university to other fields.

3.1.1a How NOT to start

It is not advisable to start with a general introduction to the topic — unless you are specifically asked to do so. For example, if the question is "Discuss the view that *Hamlet* is a typical Elizabethan Revenge Tragedy," do NOT start like this:

> ✗ *Hamlet* is one of Shakespeare's mature tragedies, probably written around 1601–1602, about the same time as *Twelfth Night* and a little earlier than *Macbeth*....
>
> (followed by everything else you know about Shakespeare, Elizabethan theatre, etc.)

That would however be a reasonable start if the question had been: "Discuss *Hamlet* in relation to other plays which Shakespeare wrote about the same time."

It is not advisable, either, to start by defining all the key terms in the question or in your answer:

> ✗ Revenge Tragedy was a popular Elizabethan genre comprising plays like Kyd's *The Spanish Tragedy*, in which a large number of people are

killed during the course of the action in revenge for some wrong done
the protagonist. Elizabethan refers to the period during which England
was ruled by Queen Elizabeth … etc.

Again, this might be appropriate if the question had been "What do you
understand by the term 'Elizabethan Revenge Tragedy'?"

There are in fact two problems with definitions. The first, and most important, is that they do not express any opinion about the question. The second
is that they do not provide you with a good basis for developing your ideas.
After a definition you tend to feel everything important has been said. (The
exception is when the question asks for a definition: in such cases the
definition is likely to be controversial and you will spend the rest of your
essay supporting your definition and giving reasons for rejecting alternative
definitions.)

Of course it is sensible to consider the question carefully before you start to
answer it, and for your own benefit you must decide what its terms mean.
But don't put this process into your writing. If we look back at the original
question "Discuss the view that *Hamlet* is a typical Elizabethan Revenge
Tragedy," we will guess that it probably wants us to devote most of our
answer to *Hamlet*, though it also requires us to show that we know what an
Elizabethan Revenge Tragedy is. (Of course, you need to use common
sense in deciding what the question is asking. The interpretation of a
question may vary somewhat according to the title or nature of the course it
is related to; for example, if the question were part of a course called "The
Elizabethan Revenge Tragedy," rather than a course on Shakespeare, we
might reverse the emphasis in our answer.)

In fact we can deduce a little more about the question. It requires no
specialized knowledge of literature to know that Shakespeare is considered
a great dramatist. Is it likely that a great dramatist would write a "typical"
play of any kind whatsoever, rather than a play which has qualities which
are not found in other people's? On the other hand, if *Hamlet* does not have
something in common with those other plays, what would be the point of
the question? So the expected answer is that Shakespeare's play is in some
respects similar to other revenge plays, but is in other respects quite different and much greater. Now, I am not saying that you have to give the
expected answer. But you do need to see what it is, because if you argue

against it you will need to be especially careful to produce good arguments and good support for them.

Another reason for analysing the question carefully is that you will have to break up your answer into various subdivisions. I shall deal with this in the next section.

3.1.2   Subdividing the topic

The second important principle of organization is that your topic must be subdivided and your ideas on the subject collected under a series of headings, each of which can be turned into a paragraph. These headings do not have to be made explicit, nor do you necessarily have to decide before you start what all the headings will be. But some time before you hand your essay in you want to make sure that each paragraph of your answer deals mainly with ONE idea or ONE aspect of the question. It should be possible for the reader (including you, yourself, as you read through what you have written) to say what idea or aspect of the question each paragraph deals with.

Sometimes the question itself will have more than one part and this will provide an initial basis for dividing your answer into separate paragraphs. The question about *Hamlet*, for example, implied that you would give reasons why *Hamlet* was like other revenge plays, and reasons why it was different. Here is a clear basis for division into two or more paragraphs. Most probably you will need one paragraph to show why it is like other revenge plays. You will probably need more than one paragraph to show why it is different. Why more than one? Because the question is almost certainly inviting you to focus on *Hamlet* and say why it is a great and unique work … etc.

Whether or not you are dealing with a question that can be automatically subdivided like this, you will have to find a way of subdividing it, and to indicate how you are going to do this can be the second aim of your opening paragraph (the first, remember, was to give a brief statement of your answer to the question or opinion on the topic):

> Although *Hamlet* has many of the characteristics of the popular
> revenge plays from which it is derived, it is also much more than a

revenge play. Shakespeare has taken a popular genre and given it a philosophical slant which questions the assumptions on which it is based and in doing so raises lasting questions about the human condition. The play differs from conventional Elizabethan revenge plays in its plot, its characterization and its style. Above all, it has a universal theme which is as relevant today as it was when the play was written.

This opening suggests fairly clearly an organization along the following lines:

Paragraph 2   Reasons why *Hamlet* is like other revenge plays.
Paragraph 3   Reasons why the plot of *Hamlet* differs from other revenge plays.
Paragraph 4   Reasons why the characterization of *Hamlet* differs.
Paragraph 5   Reasons why the style is different.
Paragraph 6   The theme of *Hamlet* and reasons for its universal appeal, modernity, etc., as opposed to the other revenge plays.

This of course is just an example. It may not be appropriate to divide your analysis according to plot, characterization and style, or you may feel that my suggested opening is too mechanical. But still, these or other such traditional ways of analysing literature can be useful in suggesting ways to subdivide your topic. It would be the same if your essay were on a non-literary topic: you must either take some traditional scheme or you must invent one of your own, otherwise you will find yourself trying to write about everything at once and inevitably repeating yourself and making it very hard for the reader to know what you are really trying to say.

3.1.3   Repetition

One of the purposes of planning is to avoid repetition. If you deal with an idea in one paragraph, you do not want to deal again with the same idea in a later paragraph. Planning enables you to move forward all the time, from one idea to the next. This will give your writing a sense of purpose and suggest that you are thinking carefully. A poor essay often seems to be going round in circles and getting nowhere.

Repetition of course in not always a fault. In debates and speeches it is a useful form of emphasis: listeners may grasp your ideas better if you repeat them several times. Also in literary style, especially in poetry, repetition may have various kinds of value. But in academic writing it should be avoided.

3.1.4 Conclusions

Probably the best thing to do about concluding paragraphs is to forget about them. Or rather, if you can subdivide your topic as we did above, keeping the most general and most important statements about it for the last paragraph, you will not need any further summary. You will end with the last argument needed to support the view put forward in general terms in your opening paragraph; you will end with a sense of returning to the point from which you set out in your opening paragraph, having arrived where you wanted to go; you will end on a note of climax. If you can also manage in the last paragraph to build into your writing a feeling of excitement or a feeling of balance (as I tried to do just now by starting three sentences the same way, with "You will end …"), that will be best of all. But it is not essential. Any last paragraph which contains the last and most important argument in support of your view on the topic will be a good ending. You will have stopped because there is no need to say more.

3.1.4a Silly connectives

But let us consider for a moment how students usually end their essays. The last paragraph often starts with one of the following:

✗ In conclusion, …

✗ All in all, …

✗ In a nutshell, …

These are correct English (*Conclusively* is NOT correct) but they are not necessarily appropriate (see 3.3.2e and 4.6.3), and in any case they are unnecessary if they mean nothing more than "This is my last paragraph": the reader can see anyway that it is the last paragraph. They are generally followed by a straightforward repetition of something the writer said before — which we therefore already know. This adds nothing to the meaning or effect of the essay, except in so far as it irritates the reader by wasting his time.

3.1.4b   Unexplained ideas

An alternative and equally undesirable method, which students sometimes use, is to fill the last paragraph with some completely new idea which has nothing to do with what went before, or which suggests a completely new direction for the argument. This will leave the reader wondering why this idea was not raised before and uncertain how it relates to the writer's other views, in particular to the views suggested in the opening paragraph. Above all, it gives the impression that the writer has failed to think through his or her position and decide what really is the most important point to make about the topic.

3.1.4c   Essays and judgement

The nature of this last problem — new ideas in a closing paragraph — may be clearer if we think a little about the purpose of writing academic essays. Ideally, of course, an essay sets out the writer's new, original ideas, and it is worth reading because no one has thought of these ideas before. Every student ought sometimes to experience the excitement of producing an idea which he or she thinks is new and original. But it is unreasonable to assume that all written assignments will do this. Nor does it particularly matter. What does matter is that the student should integrate the ideas in the essay and assign degrees of importance to them. If you introduce new ideas in the last paragraph, it may suggest that you have changed your mind about what is most important. The reader is uncertain whether or not these new ideas are meant to supersede the main idea in the first paragraph.

3.1.4d   Essays and values

Another point about endings is this. A really good writer is likely not only to produce a unified, well-supported view relevant to the topic, but also in the last paragraph to suggest that her ideas relate to some system of values. This may sound intimidating, but what I mean is something quite simple. To take the previous example on *Hamlet*, it is reasonable to build into the answer the idea that, whatever the relationship between *Hamlet* and other Elizabethan plays, Shakespeare's play is great and unique. This is not strictly required by the question, but it provides a very good way of ending on a positive, enthusiastic note. Enthusiasm is a quality not often mentioned in connection with academic work, but it is basic, and so is the ability to communicate it.

3.1.4e   Useless solutions

Another popular way of ending, one which is justified in some circumstances but not in others, is to recommend some form of action that should be taken. Where this is justified is in questions that specifically ask you to report in writing on a situation and make recommendations for action. Such questions often simulate work situations and are a valuable means of training and testing your command of the kind of language needed in many kinds of job. But this kind of thing is not so common in academic study, where you are mainly asked to describe and analyse and to express opinion. If, for example, you are analysing the problem of student suicides it is not appropriate or helpful to end by saying "The government should do something about this," or "Therefore parents should be more careful about the way they treat their children."

It is not an aim of academic writing to produce "solutions" of this kind, which in fact are not solutions at all, since they can be produced by anyone without any thinking. Of course the government should try to find solutions for social problems. Of course parents should treat their children nicely, of course the world would be a better place if we were all more kind to each other, of course war is not a good way of solving problems. We all know these things, but the fact remains that the world is imperfect. It is more valuable to pinpoint some of the reasons for the world's imperfections than to suggest unreal, simplistic solutions. Your implicit aim in academic writing should be to increase understanding — your own as well as your reader's — not to lecture your readers as if they were in a kindergarten.

You can relate all this, if you wish, to the fact that literary studies agree with linguistics (and other academic subjects) in stressing the importance of describing things as they are rather than as you think they ought to be. Contemporary linguists are more interested, for example, in descriptive grammar than in prescriptive grammar. Similarly, although the study of literature is partly subjective because it involves personal judgement, there is also a strong element of objectivity in so far as the student is required to pay close attention to the literary text and support opinions by reference to it.

3.1.5   Opening phrases: topic introductions

Students often wrongly feel that they must start a sentence or paragraph with some special device to indicate what the topic is. The fact that this is generally not necessary may be partly due to a basic difference between English and Chinese syntax or sentence organization: in English there is a general assumption that the subject of your sentence announces what you are going to talk about, while the verb and complement express what you have to say about it. We can express this as a brief rule:

Sentence subject = Topic.

Thus in the following, we know that the topic is "The plot of *Hamlet*":

> The plot of *Hamlet* does not conform to the conventions of the Revenge Tragedy because the ultimate revenge is not the result of Hamlet's careful planning but of a series of accidental circumstances.

The student however may still feel uncomfortable about moving from one subdivision of the topic to another, without some such introduction as "Now I am going to talk about the plot of *Hamlet*" or "As for the characters, they are...." There is in fact no need for such introductory phrases if you have prepared the reader by expressing or hinting at your intentions in advance, as we did above in our suggested opening paragraph on *Hamlet*. The reader expects a paragraph on the plot, another on the characters and another on the style. All that is needed is to link the paragraphs which deal with these aspects:

Paragraph 2   *Hamlet* is like other revenge plays because ...
Paragraph 3   *However, the plot* of *Hamlet* differs from most revenge plays because ...
Paragraph 4   The *characters also* are somewhat different from those we meet in a conventional revenge play ...
Paragraph 5   *Another way* in which the play is unconventional is in its *style*.

If your plan is clear from the start, you can simply get on with talking about each aspect of the play in turn. There is no need to announce each one again. It may however be necessary or at least useful to remind the reader how what you are going to say relates to what you have said already: in the example, we have made each paragraph start with a sentence which contains the key word: plot, characters, style, but we have not needed to employ the clumsy device of "Now I am going to talk about the plot ..., etc". We have also marked the change in direction from the first paragraph (Paragraph 1: *Hamlet* IS like other revenge plays ... Paragraph 2: *Hamlet* is NOT like other revenge plays ...) by the use of *However*. And we have marked subsequent paragraphs as continuing in the same direction by our use of *also* and *Another*. These words mark the relations which I shall refer to as *contrast* (*however*) and *addition* (*also, another*). (See 4.6.1 for contrast connectives and 4.6.2 for addition connectives.)

Note, though, that if you really do need to announce the topic, you can do so in the following ways:

- ✔ As for the characters, we find that they are not at all conventional.
- ✔ Let us now consider the characters.
- ✔ In terms of its characters, the play is not at all conventional.

These forms are correct, but sentences beginning "*For* the characters, *they are* ..." are not acceptable forms of standard English. (see 3.3.1c)

I repeat, such sentence introductions are generally not necessary. However, in a very long, complex paper, you might want to mark very clearly the switch to a new aspect of the topic. You could use something like the following:

- ✔ Having dealt with the plot, I shall now turn to the characters.
- ✔ Turning now to the characters, we find that they are also quite unconventional.

3.1.6   Opening phrases: contrast

Adverbial phrases can be used at the beginning of a sentence for a number of purposes. One useful one is to set up a contrast which helps to control the development of your argument. For example, in 2.2.2 I said that it was generally unnecessary when discussing a story to start sentences with *In the story* ..., *In the novel* ... etc., but that this could be useful when you are comparing, say, a novel and a film:

✔ *In the film*, the protagonists marry and live happily ever after.

✔ *But in the novel*, the protagonists part company at the end and we are not told if they will ever meet again.

Some other phrases that can perform this kind of function are:

✔ At first sight. ... But on closer examination, we find ...

✔ At the beginning of the story. ... But by the end, ...

✔ From a superficial point of view, it seems that. ... But actually ...

✔ In theory. ... But in practice ...

✔ In some respects. ... But in other respects ...

Notice, however, that these initial adverbial phrases are not essential. Much the same effect can be produced by an introductory sentence which prepares the reader for the statements which follow it:

✔ There is one important difference between the novel and the film. *The film* ends with a marriage, *whereas the novel* ends on a question mark.

3.2 Style

Though most of the writing you do is probably formal and academic, it is useful to recognize other kinds of style. The way language is used varies according to the situation and the user's purpose. This variation of style between formal and informal is often referred to as *register*. A public speech will usually be made in a formal register, whereas ordinary conversation is usually carried on in an informal register. In writing, things are to some extent the other way round, because it is the style which conveys to the reader what the situation is. As readers we probably imagine a certain kind of voice speaking to us — this effect of writing is sometimes referred to as *tone*. The style and organization of the writing also work together to tell us what kind of writing it is, or what *genre* it belongs to — whether it is prose or poetry, and if poetry, whether it is lyric poetry or dramatic monologue or sonnet, and so on.

The main aim of academic writing is to express ideas in as clear and logical a way as possible. Doing so involves organizing your ideas carefully so that you proceed in clearly related steps to a conclusion which supports the idea you expressed at the outset, as I have tried to explain above in 3.1 I shall have more to say on clarity of style below in 3.3, where my remarks will be mainly *prescriptive*. First however I want to consider *descriptively* some of the ways style varies in other, non-academic types of writing.

Non-academic writing is often different in both style and organization. This is partly because of some difference of purpose. In academic writing, much of the pleasure and sense of achievement comes from being able to make good connections and strong but suitably qualified statements (see below, Chapter 4). Inevitably this leads you to feel that you write best when you produce complex sentences in which ideas are connected in a variety of ways. But in non-academic writing these ways of connecting ideas, which are typical of formal written style, may be inappropriate.

3.2.1 Formal and informal

Speech tends to be more informal than writing. Any attempt to represent speech in writing, or to bring qualities of spoken English into writing, involves a relatively informal style.

Informality in writing is sometimes a question of spelling. Abbreviations or special spellings which represent the way people speak tend to be informal. However, abbreviations like *isn't, hasn't, doesn't*, and even *he's, it's, we're* are now so widely used in writing that the degree of informality is very slight. Also, of course, what they represent is standard English not dialect.

(Note that while *I'd* represents both *I had* and *I would*, you cannot abbreviate any form of *was / were*: that is, *it's* means *it is*, not *it was*. Note also that the *subject + be / have* abbreviation is not possible when it stands alone, i.e. you cannot write or say "Yes, I'm" instead of "Yes, I am".)

Other abbreviations are strongly informal, and tend to be used to represent non-standard English (though not necessarily a regional or social dialect); examples are:

> *gonna* (= going to), *gotta* (= got to), *wanna* (= want to)
>
> *gimme* (= give me), *doin' etc* (= doing etc)
>
> *ain't* (dialect, = isn't, aren't, hasn't, haven't)

I got to go, I gotta go (= I have to go / I've got to go)

Teachers of English in Britain tend to deplore such forms. Around the 1960s there was an outcry because the Milk Marketing Board tried to persuade people to buy more milk with a poster which said: "Drinka pinta milka day" (Drink a pint of milk a day). This was just intended to be funny and eye-catching, but the teachers thought it was going to teach children bad spelling habits. A more sensible approach is to say that such forms, like slang, are inappropriate in formal writing. Flexibility, or the ability to match language to the needs of the situation, is an essential part of the educated language user's command of his mother tongue. Slang, for example, may be used very successfully in literature or good journalism for humorous or contrastive effect.

3.2.1a Informal standard English

Speaking informally, speakers of standard English may produce many verb-less sentences, like the following:

> Nice day.
>
> Lovely to see you.
>
> Not much good.

They may also omit subject pronouns and auxiliaries, as in:

> Hope you enjoy it.
>
> Looking forward to seeing you.

This is often done in friendly letters. It is also common to omit subject pronouns and auxiliaries in friendly, informal questions:

> Doing anything tonight?

Another common feature of friendly informal spoken English is the use of tag questions, particularly the form which removes the auxiliary and pronoun from in front of the verb and places them at the end:

> Enjoying yourself, are you?
>
> Had a good time, did you?

All these are what one might call examples of informal standard English. They are perhaps on the borderline between standard and dialect.

A similar pattern can be used for statements in friendly, gossipy story-telling style:

> Walking along minding my own business, *I was*, when up comes this big fellow and says if I don't stop seeing his sister he'll do something horrible to me.

(Another feature of the style here is the use of the present tense in telling a story.)

Tag questions and statements are standard English, but certain uses of them are associated with dialect: examples can be found in speeches of cockney characters in *Pygmalion*. They can be used in standard English to sound ironic or even threatening:

> Child: I want a bicycle for my birthday.
> Parent: Oh, you do, do you!

It is also worth remembering that speakers of standard English may use dialect forms for the sake of humour. It is not surprising, for example, to hear an academic, speaking in a formal situation like a lecture or a radio or TV interview, attempt to liven up his talk with something like: "It just ain't right!"

Not all forms of incomplete sentence are dialect or even strongly informal. There are many social speech acts (i.e. things you do like thanking people, congratulating people) which are normally performed by verb-less sentences:

> *Congratulations* on passing your exams.
> *Thanks* for all your help.
> *Sorry* I'm so late.

These are the normal forms, but completely formal versions (usually written) can be produced by using a verb:

> I am writing to congratulate you on passing your exams.
> I would like to thank you for all your help.
> I must apologize for being so late.

3.2.2 Style in narrative

There is a tendency in narrative to use shorter sentences and not to use any connectives, especially, for example, when a writer wants to imitate spoken style, mimic fast action or random thoughts, or create vividness and immediacy.

3.2.2a Spoken style

First-person narrative often imitates spoken style, because one of the advantages of first-person narrative is that the narrator appears to be talking to the reader. In speech people tend to say things more disconnectedly and to say things one at a time. This contrasts with academic writing where the emphasis is on planning and on making good connections, often relating several ideas in the same sentence.

3.2.2b Random thoughts

Our normal consciousness tends not to be strictly organized and much of the time thoughts occur to us through random association. This at least is the assumption made by modern novelists. Partly the reason why thoughts are not organized the way we organize an essay is that we are often involved in a number of things at the same time. That is to say, what you are doing at a given moment — say, working on a particular assignment — is part of a number of things you do at the university, including perhaps extra-curricular activities; and at the same time you are a member of a family, with certain family relationships to maintain and duties to perform, and there may be things in the past or in the future that you worry about or hope for. Thoughts or impulses connected with any aspect of your personality may at any moment become uppermost in your mind, as is obvious to you at moments when you become conscious of day-dreaming. This is all, of course, like any other way of describing thoughts, highly metaphorical. Whether or not the human mind really works like this, most modern writers assume something like it. The novelist who imitates what is known as the "stream of consciousness" is aiming to produce an effect of random thinking, somewhat like day-dreaming, and at the same time to build up an image of a complex personality composed of various, sometimes conflicting, impulses.

3.2.3 Description and action

Any kind of descriptive writing generally aims to make the reader "see" what is described, and tends to register objects, people and events one by one, as we might see them if we were onlookers or a movie camera, moving from one to another, and seeing *what* they are rather than *why* they are (generally you cannot literally see, or photograph, the reason for something). And a writer wanting to portray action also omits lengthy explanations and reasons for things. Fast action leaves no time for reasoning, and fast reading (more likely to occur when sentences are short and simple) is more likely to give the reader a sense of action.

Any of these aims can be disrupted by inappropriate style, even, for example, excessive use of coordinating expressions like *so + adjective ... that*; *both A ... and B ...*; *not only A ... but also B ...* which give an impression of careful planning and require the reader to grasp ideas or events in relation to each other rather than in simple succession.

On the other hand, long sentences may be useful for creating suspense and a sense of climax — provided the word order is carefully controlled to keep the important information till the end.

3.2.4 Dialogue

Generally dialogue in plays and novels is intended to resemble actual speech. It is not real speech, however, partly because it has certain additional purposes to perform in relation to the overall theme and structure of the work which contains it, partly because it is necessarily less tied to an explanatory context since its audience is the reader (or actor, director and theatre audience in the case of plays) not just the fictional participant in the dialogue. In conversation, speakers and hearers to some extent share the same situation and background. So too, presumably, do the characters in a play, but the problem is that it is not the shared situation and background of the audience, except in so far as the audience are able to project themselves imaginatively into it. Another point is that real speech is generally less perfect. Transcriptions of real speech often surprise people because they reveal so many hesitations and errors. Nevertheless, it is useful to compare dialogue with real speech and note ways in which both differ grammatically and organizationally from, say, an essay. Writers who are felt to be especially good at producing realistic dialogue generally make each character's speeches very short and not too explicit, since this is the way real conversations proceed.

If you are writing your own dialogue or reporting speech, there are certain conventions that must be followed. In drama you can simply write the name of the speaker in front of each speech. But in fiction, and reporting you generally have to indicate the speaker by using a phrase like *The Minister said*. If you use this at the beginning, it can be followed by either a comma or a colon:

> The Minister said last night: "We expect to make rapid progress in the coming months."
>
> The Minister said last night, "We expect to make rapid progress in the coming months."

If you put this phrase at the end, you must NOT end the quoted speech with a full stop; only a comma, a question mark or an exclamation mark can be used:

> "We expect to make rapid progress in the coming months," the Minister said.

When the phrase is at the end, you can, if you wish, invert subject and verb: *... said the Minister*. It is not normal to do this when the phrase is at the beginning, though you will find it as a typical feature in some journalistic writing, notably in *Time*:

> Said the new champion, "I was never more surprised in my life!"

3.2.5   Writing as mimicry

All the above comments on style suggest that writers seek to mimic certain aspects of what they are writing about: a situation, a kind of speaker, a kind of movement, and so on. Such mimicry may depend on some supposed analogy — as with onomatopoeic language, in which speech sounds mimic natural sounds — or it may depend on imitating specific varieties of English. There are many ways in which writing can mimic. These ways can often be studied in poetry and humorous writing, or in texts like advertisements, where form and content are very free but tone is especially important.

3.2.6 Archaic style

Although language is always changing, forms that go out of fashion often do not completely disappear but remain enshrined in literature and prover-bial sayings. They remain available for use, mainly in very formal style, or in parody. Sometimes they remain especially literary in tone and can be found in any careful writing. But the picture is complicated by the fact that literature is always trying to update itself; that is to say, writers frequently try to imitate spoken forms, for the reasons given above, and want to avoid sounding too artificial and literary.

I can only give a few examples of archaic or old-fashioned style here.

Constructions or expressions that tend to be literary in tone are the use of *for* meaning *because*, the use of *albeit* meaning *although*, the use of the inverted form *Should you* meaning *If you should*, and the use of *but* meaning *only* as is "We have *but* one child". These are somewhat more likely to be found in public speeches or written texts than in ordinary speech.

Old-fashioned forms found in Shakespeare, or any other classical author studied in schools, are sometimes adopted in humorous speech, as a kind of parody. Some examples might be the use of *thou* and the verb forms that go with it: "What dost think"? (= What do you think?); obsolete oaths such as *Forsooth! Sblood!* etc. Such forms are not likely to be found in formal writing.

3.3 Forming your own academic style

The word *style* has quite a number of different meanings. One of these meanings refers to the personal features that distinguish one writer's work from another's:

Ernest Hemingway's style is quite different from D. H. Lawrence's.

We can describe such differences in style, but we do not know how a writer arrives at his or her particular way of writing. Certainly there are no rules you can learn which will tell you how to do it. Finding a personal style is an important aim if you wish to write creatively, as important as, say, trying to tell an exciting story or trying to develop a significant theme. But it is presumably something which you have to do by yourself.

So far in this chapter, however, I have been using the word *style* in a much more general sense, to refer to any of the differences which distinguish different varieties of language. Here I shall continue to use it this way, and I shall assume that what is most important for you is to write clear formal academic prose. For this purpose there are some general rules of style which can be helpful (though like all prescriptive rules they are somewhat subjective and they do not apply in all contexts).

What you should aim at in your writing, then, is directness, simplicity and clarity. It is worth insisting on this, because so many people imagine good writing to be a question of indirectness, complexity and confusion. Or rather, they think that they can demonstrate their superiority if they produce a text which no one else can understand.

3.3.1   Directness

Whenever you can, make firm, direct statements (I am repeating here what I said in 1.3). I suggested before that it is preferable to write

> ✔ This story is about the problems of growing old.

rather than

> ✗ In my opinion, but I may be wrong, I think perhaps this story may be about something to do with old people, to a certain extent.

3.3.1a   Excessively personal style

I also recommended that you avoid using *I* and *me*. You can do this by focussing directly on the topic, as in the recommended example above. You can also do it by using *we*, *us* — especially when you want to discuss the effect of a work on the reader:

✔ We are surprised by the sudden twist at the end of the story.

✔ What strikes us immediately is that the author provides no answer to some obvious questions.

3.3.1b Unnecessary passives

A common stylistic fault is overuse of the passive (See 2.4.1 and 5.4)

It is best, for example, not to use the passive when you are making statements about your own views, or your method. The following is confusing:

✗ It is considered that this story is about the problems of growing old.

By whom is it considered? Presumably by the writer herself, in which case she should be brave and say what she thinks directly, i.e. "This story is about the problems of growing old."

Students sometimes think they have to produce a kind of parody of the scientific style, filled with passives, in order to make their writing sound serious:

✗ It is considered that this story is about the problems of growing old. In this paper three aspects of the story will be dealt with. First the plot will be discussed. Then the characters will be examined. Finally the style will be analysed and an attempt will be made to show how the author skillfully leads the reader to read between the lines and make his own judgement.

There is really no advantage for the writer in hiding behind all those passives. It would be better like this:

✔ This story is about the problems of growing old. I shall examine three aspects of the story. First I shall discuss the plot. Then I shall consider the characters. Finally, I shall analyse the style and try to show how the author skillfully leads the reader to read between the lines and make his own judgement.

This may seem to conflict with what I said about not referring to yourself. But the point is that if you really *do* want to refer to yourself, or your intentions, you should use *I*. On the other hand, in a short paper it is not necessary to describe what you intend to do so explicitly. You could rewrite the opening paragraph again as follows:

> ✔ This story is about the problems of growing old. The old man's state of mind is revealed through his growing irritation with his family and his former colleagues at the office. The causes of this irritation are embedded in the conflicting interests of the characters. Although the author appears not to take sides, her use of recurring images suggests that the protagonist has lived in a dream all his life.

This version says something very similar to the previous two. It implies that the writer is going to examine the story from the point of view of plot (what happens in the story), characters (their conflicting interests) and style (recurring images). But it says this more interestingly and more informatively. Notice that the passives here are not hidden versions of *I think*, *I will show*, but refer to the effect *the story* has on the reader.

When you *are* justified in using the passive is when you are referring to a view which cannot be ascribed to any particular source:

> ✔ *It is often said* that the great works of literature are those which have universal appeal.

The passive is reasonable because this is a widely held view, and you do not know exactly where it comes from. Notice, however, that if you were answering a question in the form: "Discuss the view that great works of literature are those which have universal appeal," it would be confusing to write in your answer: "It is said that great works of literature ..., etc." In this case the view is expressed in the question, so you *do* know where it comes from.

The same comment applies to quotations introduced by *As said by*. Since you know who said it, what is the point of the passive? It is always better to write *As Shakespeare said* than *As said by Shakespeare*.

3.3.1c   Unnecessary introductions

One form of stylistically faulty sentence seems to be the result of a false idea that a topic needs introducing. (see 3.1.5)

✗ For Jim, the gentleman caller, who works in Tom's office, he does not think Amanda is foolish.

(*he* refers to Jim)

✗ In John Fowles' novel, *The Collector*, it describes the kidnapping of a young girl.

(*it* refers to John Fowles' novel)

✗ Like Tom, he is also running away from reality.

(*he* refers to Tom)

The opening phrase and the later subject pronoun have the same reference, and the sentences should be simplified by turning the opening phrase into a straightforward sentence subject:

✔ Jim, the gentleman caller, who works in Tom's office, does not think Amanda is foolish.

✔ John Fowles' novel, *The Collector*, describes the kidnapping of a young girl.

✔ Tom is also running away from reality.

3.3.2 Desirable simplicity

The reason for insisting that simplicity is generally desirable is that many people think the opposite: they imagine that if they can make their style very complicated, the reader will assume that their ideas are deep and significant. The idea that complexity of language is profundity produces bad, unclear writing. Complexity, in fact, is often a result of laziness: the writer is simply not thinking carefully enough about what she wants to say.

This does not mean that short sentences are always better than long ones. There are times when long sentences may be better, and variety of sentence structure is also desirable. But there are some common faults which result from trying too hard to impress the reader, and not trying hard enough to make your meaning clear.

3.3.2a Pompous pairs of words

In certain rhetorical styles, particularly in public speeches, it is quite common to use pairs of words, because they sound forceful and even thoughtful. But in writing, a good general principle is not to use two words where one will do. So do not get into the habit of automatically using pairs of words. In the following I have underlined the pairs!

> ✗ No matter how <u>useful or substantial</u> the <u>techniques and methods</u> used by the writer, it is the <u>feeling and emotion</u> underlying the <u>ideas and themes</u> which provide the <u>reader or audience</u> with their <u>deepest and most lasting pleasure and enjoyment</u>.

This is the kind of writing that makes the reader suspect that you have nothing to say and are therefore forced to try and fill the page with unnecessary words. It could probably be rewritten as

> ✔ Whatever techniques the writer uses, the reader's main enjoyment comes from the emotions underlying the ideas.

Of course it is not always wrong to use pairs of words. Two words are needed if they express two quite different, though related, ideas, which are both important to what you are trying to say. Or you may need two words when you are trying to define some quality for which there seems to be no single precise word.

3.3.2b   Redundancy

To say something is redundant means that it is unnecessary. Redundant expressions are those which merely repeat what has already been said. One cause of redundancy is failure to understand the true meaning of a word:

> ✗ The situation was <u>very appalling</u>.
>
> ("appalling" already means extremely bad, so you cannot qualify it with *very*.)

> ✗ In order to evaluate the work we need some <u>assessment criterion</u>.
>
> ("criterion" already means a standard by which something can be assessed, so the word *assessment* is redundant.)

> ✗ <u>Nowadays</u> there are <u>contemporary</u> English writers whose mother tongue is not English.
>
> (if they are writing nowadays, they must be contemporary.)

Another cause of redundancy is the fact that words often imply something which is not obviously part of their meaning. Consider for example the adjective *obvious*:

✔ The effect of Bluntschli's words on Raina is obvious.

Obvious means something which can easily be *seen* by *someone*. It is therefore quite unnecessary to add anything after *obvious*. Phrases like the following are unnecessary

✗ obvious to be seen,

✗ obvious to the reader etc

Similarly, words which typically refer to *human* behaviour do not need the addition of some human participant:

This story is interesting (to the reader).

This plan will be harmful (to people).

Education is important (to human beings).

In such a play, where the death of the protagonist is partly comic, catharsis is impossible (to occcur).

The situation is under control. Further measures are unnecessary (to be taken).

She was prepared even to commit murder in pursuit of (attaining) her goal.

It is always a good exercise to go through your writing and remove redundant expressions, because it forces you to think carefully about the meaning of words.

3.3.2c   Unpleasing nominalizations

Most writers on English style recommend the use of verbs wherever possible rather than nouns, on the grounds that verbs are more energetic, vivid and direct. This does not altogether apply to academic writing, where correctly naming things is very important. But it is certainly true that formal writing can get very dense and hard to read (many readers would also say "ugly") if there are two many verbal nouns, or nominalizations. By "nominalizations" I mean words like *formation* and *provision*, which are nouns formed from verbs like *to form* and *to provide*. For example, I might want to say something like this:

> These notes are intended to help you write the kind of English you need in your written assignments on English language and literature.

I might also express this as

> The objective of these notes is the provision of assistance in the production of the kind of English required for the performance of tasks assigned in courses devoted to the study of English language and literature.

There are, I think, people who might feel the second version sounds more academic and therefore superior, and it is certainly not hard to find examples of academic writing which resemble the second version. But the first version says exactly the same thing, and says it more briefly and more sensibly. The string of nominalizations — "the provision of assistance in the production of …" — is particularly bad.

3.3.2d   Clichés, idioms, jargon

Clichés are ready-made expressions that spring to mind easily because they are used so often. The problem is that one then uses them without stopping to think whether they really fit the situation. People who speak or write in clichés give the impression that they do not think about what they are saying. The words they use are not really their own, so how can these words express their thoughts?

It seems that clichés can even pass from one language to another. An example is *a hot topic*. For a while every student essay on a topical question used to start:

> ✗ Recently, the problem of X has become a hot topic.

This is irritating both because of the cliché, and because such an opening is entirely superfluous when you have been assigned the topic to write on. The topic was almost certainly assigned precisely because it is controversial and widely discussed in the media.

Be on your guard against clichés and also beware of so-called idioms. An idiom is really just any expression which does not entirely obey the normal rules of the language. It is a combination of words which cannot be treated as if they were individual words. For example, the idiomatic expression *a sad kettle of fish*, meaning a bad state of affairs, has nothing to do with kettles or fish, and is only remotely connected to sadness. You cannot make it plural or change the article or make any of the other normal grammatical modifications; that is to say, you cannot talk about *two sad kettles of fish*, *the sad kettle of fish*, or *a sad fish-kettle*. This, however, is not the problem. The problem for students is that they are encouraged to learn lists of idioms and fill their writing with them without regard for their meaning and tone.

You can only gain an advantage from using idioms if you can use them very aptly, or humorously. Used wrongly they create an unintentionally comic or absurd effect. Many of the expressions students learn as idioms are so overused, and inappropriately used, that they are clichés. Common examples are *to try one's very best* which simply means *to try*, and *with flying colours*.

Jargon is specialized vocabulary belonging to a particular subject. To some extent it may be necessary to use the jargon of your field in order to sound professional. But the danger is that you create whole sentences out of jargon and put them in your writing because they sound good, not because they express something you want to say.

3.3.2e Meaningless connectives and introductory phrases

I shall discuss connectives in Chapter 4, but it may be worth making the point here that like the other examples I have been discussing, connectives are often used unnecessarily or without proper attention to their meaning. This is the case with some of the phrases students like to use for introducing a final paragraph (see 3.1.4a):

> ✗ In a nutshell we can say that the building of the new airport is essential to Hong Kong's economy because it will help to develop the economy and without it Hong Kong would be at a disadvantage compared to other Asian cities like Singapore. The reason for this is … etc.

In a nutshell is supposed to signal that you are about to express something very succinctly — i.e. briefly and cleverly!

All in all should only be used when you have considered two or more proposals or views of a situation and find it very hard to decide which is best, but eventually, and somewhat reluctantly perhaps, give your support to one of them. It is very seldom used correctly by students.

3.3.3   Clarity

The chief aid to clarity is good organization. Your writing is also more likely to be clear if you can keep it direct and simple. It can also be helped by focus. What I mean by focus is arranging each sentence so that it is easy to see what point you are making. This is partly a question of how you distribute your ideas between main clauses and subordinate clauses. It is also partly a question of word order and choice of structure. For example, there are some special structures which help to give prominence to the point you are making:

- ✔ People question whether the new airport should be built because of its cost.
- ✔ It is the cost of the new airport which makes people question whether it should be built.
- ✔ What makes people question whether the new airport should be built is its cost.

Here the second and third sentences give more prominence to the idea of cost because they take for granted the idea that people question whether the new airport should be built.

Another factor which determines focus is the natural word order and meaning of the English sentence — which I mentioned in 3.1.5 above. It is a kind of standard assumption that the sentence subject is its topic (generally this is something we know about already) and the *verb* + *complement* contains the point which is being made (this is the *new* information). Consider, for example, the following:

Fred kidnaps an art student called Miranda.

We are assumed to know who Fred is, but not to know what he does. The point of this sentence is to tell us what he does. The writer continues:

Eventually Miranda dies.

We already know who Miranda is, but we do not know what happens to her. The point of this sentence is to tell us what happens to her. The grammatical subject of the sentence is Miranda, which links it to the preceding sentence in which Miranda was introduced.

> After her death, Fred shows little remorse. At the end of the novel he is looking for another girl to kidnap.

The first sentence is linked to the preceding one (which told us that Miranda dies) by its opening phrase. The second sentence is linked by the pronoun, *he*, which substitutes for *Fred*.

Of course every text has to begin somewhere. The known topic of the first sentence may refer back to a title, or the writer may simply ask us, as it were, to accept that it is the topic he wishes to tell us about.

The complete text of our example above might look like this:

> *The Collector* by John Fowles
>
> The narrator of the first and last parts of John Fowles' novel, *The Collector*, is a lonely young man called Fred. Fred kidnaps an art student called Miranda. Eventually Miranda dies. After her death, Fred shows little remorse. At the end of the novel he is looking for another girl to kidnap.

The first sentence refers to the title, and takes it for granted that we know a novel is likely to have a narrator. Notice how each subsequent sentence links to the one before through its subject and then adds some new information. The general rule is that the informative point of a sentence is carried by the later part of the sentence — either the whole *verb + complement* unit, or just the complement or some part of it. There are frequent exceptions to this rule. But if you want to make what you write very clear, one method is to order the ideas in each sentence in this way.

3.4   Use of questions

There seem to be some differences between the way questions are used in writing in English and Chinese. It may be helpful to distinguish between two kinds of questions in English writing: rhetorical questions, which are a means of emphasis, and structuring questions, which are a means of clarifying the points that you are making.

3.4.1   Rhetorical questions

The main point about rhetorical questions is that you must not answer them yourself. If you do, you lose the effect of emphasis, and create an anticlimax instead. Consider the following, where the rhetorical questions add emphasis to the view that women are not treated fairly:

> ✔ Is it fair that women should be paid only half as much as men for doing the same work? Is it fair that only a tiny percentage of top managerial positions should be held by women? Of course women still have something to fight for.

The answer to the questions is so obviously no, that it is quite unnecessary to give it. Both could easily be rewritten as statements beginning *It is unfair that ...* but by expressing this idea in question form you oblige the reader to supply the answer and thereby to accept your view. If you give the answer yourself, it seems to suggest that the reader is not intelligent enough to find it, which is insulting.

Rhetorical questions are very similar to irony. Anyone who wanted to answer yes to the questions above would be committing himself to an obviously absurd belief, almost equivalent to saying that it is fair that women should be treated unfairly. Rhetorical questions are often made somewhat exaggerated or even absurd, so that there can be no mistaking what answer is expected.

Sometimes a rhetorical question is entirely ironic and is not expected to be answered by a denial:

> ✔ Does the government think we are fools? Does it think we will be satisfied with this obviously inadequate answer to our legitimate concerns?

The point here lies in the suggestion that the government is treating the public like fools by giving them an inadequate answer.

One quite important point about rhetorical questions is that, although equivalent to a statement, they do not fit into an argument in quite the same way as a statement would. For example, they cannot be followed by *therefore*. Compare the following:

- ✔ Women are still paid only half as much as men for doing the same work. Therefore women still have something to fight for.

- ✗ Is it fair that women are still paid only half as much as men for doing the same work? <u>Therefore</u> women still have something to fight for.

There are some forms of question that seem to have a built-in rhetorical force (that is, they assume a certain answer):

- ✔ *How can it be* fair for women to be paid only half as much as men for doing the same work?

  (It definitely cannot be fair.)

- ✔ *Why should* women work for only half the pay that men get for doing the same work?

  (They definitely shouldn't.)

Similarly, a sentence including *surely* has the force of a rhetorical question:

- ✔ Surely it is not fair that women are paid only half as much as men for doing the same work.

  (The writer thinks you must agree that it is not fair.)

You will sometimes find a question mark at the end of statements with *surely*.

Note that *surely* does not mean simply *It is certain that*. The reader cannot disagree with a statement which begins *It is certain that …*, except by contradicting the speaker quite rudely; theoretically the reader is able to disagree with a statement including *surely*.

3.4.2 Structuring questions

What I call structuring questions are questions used as a means of clarifying the direction and purpose of an argument. In this case the writer asks the question and then answers it immediately. The effect of this kind of question is not particularly emphatic:

✔ Why does Hemingway leave these questions unanswered at the end of
his story? The reason must be that they are not the important questions.

Note that this is a genuine question. If the answer were obvious you would
not ask it. Instead of the question and answer, you could achieve exactly the
same effect with a simple statement expressed in a single sentence:

✔ The reason why Hemingway leaves these questions unanswered at the
end of his story must be that they are not the important questions.

The only reason for preferring the question and answer form is that it is a
little simpler and makes your idea more obvious.

It is possible, in fact, to see every statement that you make in a piece of
writing as the answer to some unexpressed question. It has even been
suggested that a possible way to check the relevance of each of your
sentences is to try expressing the questions which they answer. For example, we might expect the above passage to continue:

(Why are they not the important questions?) Hemingway wants us to
concentrate on the relation between the protagonists. (Why does he
want us to do this?) His story is about the conflict between two people
who are discovering that they each want something quite different.
(What is it they want?) He wants X, whereas she wants Y. (Is there any
solution to the conflict?) At the end of the story the conflict remains
unresolved etc.

Clearly it would be tedious for the reader if you included all the possible
questions in your writing, but to do so occasionally can be helpful in
explaining to the reader (and to yourself) what you are trying to do and how
each new sentence is relevant because it answers a question which could
arise from the sentence before.

3.5   Creative writing

I would need another book to deal adequately with style and technique in
creative writing, but it may be worth pointing out some of the faults
students commonly make when they write stories or dialogue.

(a) Long speeches in dialogue. Students commonly give each character too much to say, the speeches are composed of unrealistically complete sentences, and are over-explicit.

(b) Overuse of connectives. The effect of both narrative and dialogue can be spoiled by giving reasons for everything and connecting the ideas logically — as you should connect them, of course, in an essay.

(c) Overuse of adjectives and adverbs. It is more effective to show how your characters behave and leave the reader to deduce what they are like, than to give your own detailed explanation of their appearance and reasons for acting as they do. A scene is often more vivid if described briefly with few adjectives.

(d) Overuse of narrative linking words. Words like *then* and *suddenly* are often used unnecessarily.

(e) Problems with viewpoint. A story is often weakened by the failure to adopt any consistent viewpoint. For example, when describing an exciting incident from the point of view of the protagonist, the writer suddenly introduces a passive: *a shot was heard*. This implies that it was heard, not by the protagonist, but by someone else. But who? The reader's sense of sharing danger with the protagonist is immediately lost.

(f) Clichéd expressions of emotion. If all the tears that have run down the faces of characters in students' writing were collected together, there could be a repetition of Noah's Flood.

4

SENTENCES AND CLAUSES

I shall deal here with some of the problems students have with basic English sentence structure. I shall also look at ways of qualifying or emphasizing statements, since these are important for the construction of precise meaning. And I shall discuss some of the problems with using connectives, since failure to relate sentences meaningfully is a major obstacle to expressing clear and reasonable arguments.

4.1 Basic English sentence structure

Remember the basic sentence structure is:

Subject	Verb	Complement
Fred	kidnaps	an art student called Miranda. (noun phrase)
Fred	says	that he loves Miranda.(clause)
Fred	behaves	very strangely. (adverbial phrase)

In formal English, every sentence should contain ONE verb. If there are subordinate clauses, every main clause and every subordinate clause should contain ONE verb.

Verb-less sentences are quite common, however, in informal kinds of English, e.g. lecture notes, recipes, advertising, conversation, etc., and in writing which mimics thought or action — usually fiction.

If a verb appears without any subject in a sentence, it is likely to be an imperative:

If I should die, *think* only this of me ... (Rupert Brooke, "The Soldier")

This is a useful point to bear in mind when reading poetry: poets quite often use imperatives addressed to the reader, to themselves, or to some other imagined person (sometimes not a person but a thing or an idea, e.g. the Moon, Death — as in John Donne's sonnet beginning "Death, *be* not proud. ..." In such cases we say the thing has been *personified*).

You may also meet verbs without subjects in various kinds of informal style (see 3.2.1).

4.1.1   Incorrect sentences with too many verbs

Common student mistakes involve sentences with more than one verb. There seem to be various causes:

4.1.1a   Sentence as subject

One of the commonest causes is trying to make a sentence (e.g. Higgins speaks rudely to Liza) into the subject of another sentence, resulting in something like this:

> ✗ Higgins *speaks* rudely to Liza *shows* that he considers her inferior.

The correct way to do this is to turn the first sentence (the "subject" sentence) into a clause:

> ✔ (The fact) *that Higgins speaks rudely to Liza* shows that he considers her inferior.

Note that you must have at least "That" — "The fact that" is not absolutely necessary, but it makes it clearer.

It is also possible to correct the problem by making the first verb into a gerund, but this can be awkward because if there is a subject it has to be turned into a possessive noun or pronoun:

> ✔ *Higgins's speaking* rudely to Liza shows that he considers her inferior.

This is a question of ear: if the sentence sounds awkward this way, use the other way. In this case you can say *Higgins's* or *Higgins'* but even native speakers are uncertain about which it should be and may prefer to avoid both.

An alternative way of dealing with the problem is to use two sentences instead of just one to express the idea. This will probably require you to find an appropriate substitute noun (see 8.2.4) as subject of the second sentence:

> ✔ Higgins speaks very rudely to Liza. *This behaviour* shows that he considers her inferior.

Students sometimes try to solve the problem of the sentence-subject by making a relative clause, but this only seems to make the problem worse:

> ✗ Students who cannot cope with a foreign language does not mean that they are not university material.

Again, there are at least two ways to correct this:

> ✔ The fact that students cannot cope with a foreign language does not mean that they are not university material.

> ✔ Not being able to cope with a foreign language does not mean that students are not university material.

Notice how in the second version the awkward possessive noun has been avoided by rearranging the sentence slightly. Otherwise it would have to be "Students' not being able to cope …"

4.1.1b   *There is + second verb*

Another common mistake is to start a sentence with *there is* and then go on to a complete sentence with a main verb:

> ✗ *There are* many factors *must be considered* before we reach a decision on this question.

This can be corrected either by removing *There are* (students tend to overuse *there are* and you should put a warning sign beside it in your mind), or by making the second part of the sentence a relative clause:

> ✔ There are many factors *which* must be considered before we reach a decision on this question.

This mistake may be connected with the mistaken idea that the sentence subject, *Many factors*, needs some kind of introduction (see 3.1.4, 3.3.1c), or it may come about through the influence of sentences like "There are a number of problems (which) students have with pronouns." In this case the second verb is part of a relative clause, but this may not be obvious because *which* can be omitted when it stands in place of a noun object. Thus the original sentence would be correct if the second verb were active instead of passive:

> There are a number of factors (which) we must consider before we reach a decision on this question.

When *which* is omitted the second part of the sentence is still recognizably a relative clause because *factors* is object, not subject, of consider.

4.1.1c   Failed participle or relative clause

Another incorrect, two-verb sentence may be the result of either an incorrect participle or an incorrectly formed relative clause:

> ✗ Amanda <u>keeps</u> remembering all the things <u>happened</u> in her youth.

Although *happened* looks like a simple past tense, it may be intended by the writer as a past participle. There is, however, no past participle of intransitive verbs, like *happen*. (see 5.3 and 5.6)

This can be corrected by making a relative clause:

> ✔ Amanda keeps remembering all the things *which* happened in her youth.

It may also be that the writer thinks *which* can be omitted, as it can when it stands for the object of the verb in the clause: "Amanda keeps remembering all the things (which) she did in her youth."

4.1.2   Incorrect sentences with no verb

Another common mistake is sentences which have no main verb.

4.1.2a Confusion in long sentences

The most likely reason for verb-less sentences is probably that you lose your way in a long, complex sentence:

> ✗ Students *who* have to study in English *and* may be good in science *but* do badly *because* their English is not good enough.

> ✗ *Since* he is a professor, *who* is presumably an educated man *who* should have good manners, *but* he speaks very rudely to Liza.

The remedy is to remove either a relative pronoun (e.g. *who*) or a conjunction (e.g. *and*). There are many ways to correct these sentences, but each one will produce a slightly different meaning. The most obvious way would be as follows:

> ✔ Students who have to study in English may be good in science *but* do badly *because* their English is not good enough.

> ✔ *Since* he is a professor, *who* is presumably an educated man, *he* should have good manners, *but* he speaks very rudely to Liza.

4.1.2b Non-verbs

Verb-less sentences can also be the result of thinking a word is a verb when it isn't:

> ✗ The diamond *worth* a fortune but he didn't insure it.

There are a number of words like *worth* which look like verbs but are not, until you add the verb *to be* (see 5.7 for a list of some others). In your mind you should put a warning sign beside such words.

4.1.2c Subordinate clause sentences

Sometimes students use a subordinate clause as if it was a sentence:

> ✗ Although the English of Shakespeare's plays is quite difficult.

> ✗ Since poetry usually contains many metaphors.

This kind of thing is permissible in some kinds of informal English — particularly advertising. But it is not acceptable in formal written papers.

Another popular form of this is:

✗ As every reader will recognize that Professor Higgins is a very rude man.

This consists of two subordinate clauses, and probably results from the confusion of two structures, both correct on their own:

✔ Every reader will recognize *that* Professor Higgins is a very rude man.

✔ *As* every reader will recognize, Professor Higgins is a very rude man.

4.1.3   Commas and sentences

Sentences should be separated by a full-stop, colon or semi-colon, or joined with *and*, *but* or *or*, unless one of them is made into a subordinate clause by *who*, *because*, etc. Sentences should not be joined by commas. Consequently the following are wrong:

✗ Tom is bored by his job, it doesn't satisfy his desire for adventure.

✗ Figurative language is typical of poetry, almost all poetry contains figurative language.

Note also that connectives like *however, moreover* and *therefore* should not like *and, but,* and *or* connect sentences after a comma; a full-stop or at least a semi-colon is needed:

✗ In the end Tom leaves his mother and sister, however this does not mean he does not love them.

✔ In the end Tom leaves his mother and sister. However, this does not mean he does not love them.

Joining sentences just with commas is a fault in writing which seeks to analyse ideas or convey an argument, because it suggests a lack of thinking and planning. You will however find a good many exceptions to the rule in fiction, especially where the writer is trying to mimic fast movement or random thinking (3.2.2 and 3.2.3).

It is also possible in formal English that you want to list sentences, in which case you follow the rules for listing (4.3), using *and* only between the last pair:

Just before the exam we work in the library all day, sit up reading our notes all night, eat always in a hurry, and generally lead a very unhealthy life.

4.1.4 Infinitives in coordinated structures

Great care must be taken with verbs in long sentences where more than one verb depends on another verb or auxiliary:

- ✗ Lucy <u>wants to be</u> herself and <u>do</u> what she likes.
- ✗ Charlotte thinks Lucy <u>should behave</u> like a lady and <u>not speak</u> to people she has not been introduced to.

Problems arise because "Lucy wants to" and "Lucy should" are not repeated in the second part of the sentence, yet the second verb still needs to be in the infinitive form.

4.1.5 Impossible *that*

I put this problem here because I cannot find a proper place or name for it. Some students have a tendency to join all their ideas together with *that*. This cannot be done, and it provides no clue about the connection intended by the writer:

- ✗ In those days society was very unequal <u>that</u> women were born inferior to men.
- ✗ Life is absurd <u>that</u> all ambition ends in nothing.

Generally such sentences can be made grammatical by changing *that* to *and*. Probably, however, the writer intends some tighter connection, something for example like the *so … that …* connection (see 4.2.6). But that will not do in the examples above, because there is no literal cause-and-result relation. The second part can however be seen as evidence supporting the truth of the first part, so one could join them with *because*. However, that still may not quite capture the intended meaning. Probably the best solution here is *in that*:

- ✔ Life is absurd in that all ambition ends in nothing.

Whether that is correct or not depends on whether you see the second part (ambition ending in nothing) as an instance of, or explanation of, the first (life's being absurd). For more on *in that*, see below 4.6.3e.

But students who are addicted to *that* use it in such a variety of contexts that there are many different ways of correcting it. It may be that what they intend is a noun clause, as in "It is absurd that we should have to take so many exams".

All I can say is that you need to be careful not to use *that* without any justification.

4.2   Structure in clauses

I shall deal here only with one or two obvious and frequently recurring problems.

4.2.1   Subordinate clauses

When you have a subordinate clause introduced by *although*, *since*, etc., you should not use a second connective at the beginning of the main clause:

> ✗ Although Tom is rebellious, <u>but</u> he loves his mother.
>
> ✔ Although Tom is rebellious, he loves his mother.
>
> ✔ Tom is rebellious, but he loves his mother.
>
> ✗ Since Amanda is worried about her daughter's future, <u>therefore</u> she wants Tom to find her a boyfriend.
>
> ✔ Since Amanda is worried about her daughter's future, she wants Tom to find her a boyfriend.

An exception is conditionals: after an *if* clause, you will sometimes find a main clause beginning *then*, particularly when the writer is trying to express a complicated argument in a long sentence:

> If you do an average of six hours work a day, and if you do all your assignments regularly and make sure you revise your work carefully before handing it in, *then* you can expect to get a good degree.

4.2.2 Repeated elements in clauses

In coordinate clauses (sentences joined by *and*, *but*, etc.) repeated elements can be omitted in the second part:

> Tom wants adventure and (Tom) doesn't like his work.
>
> Tom wants to leave home and (Tom wants to) have a more adventurous life.

Subordinate clauses however, like sentences, must have subject and verb; neither can be omitted. Students have particular trouble with the following two kinds of clause.

4.2.2a *While* clauses

A clause beginning with *while* generally needs a verb:

> ✗ One student studies biology in English, while the other in Chinese.

Here the mistake is that the verb has been omitted. It can be corrected by restoring the verb:

> ✔ One student studies biology in English, while the other studies it in Chinese.

Another way to correct the sentence would be to exchange the subordinate clause for coordination, which does allow you not to repeat the verb:

> One student studies biology in English, and the other in Chinese.

Another mistake is to omit the subject of the clause:

> ✗ Miranda, while still plans to escape, tries to convince Fred that she is content to stay with him.

This ought to be "while *she* still plans to escape...."

A possible reason for the mistake with *while* clauses is the fact that you *can* omit the subject when instead of the verb you use a participle or adjective phrase:

Miranda, *while still planning to escape*, tries to convince Fred that she is content to stay with him. (present participle: *planning*)

Miranda, *while obviously unhappy*, is not at first ill-treated.

This is only possible of course when the subject is the same in both parts — when it is Miranda who is unhappy and Miranda who is not at first ill-treated.

4.2.2b *Though* clauses

The common mistake with *though* clauses is to omit the subject:

✗ Miranda pretends to be nice to Fred, though only wants to escape.

This should be: "… though *she* only wants to escape".

Again, it would be possible to omit the repeated subject in a coordinated sentence:

✔ Miranda pretends to be nice to Fred, but only wants to escape.

And it is also possible to omit the subject if it is the same in both parts and if there is no finite verb:

Miranda, *though detained against her will*, is not at first badly treated.

Miranda, *though reluctant to make promises*, wants Fred to think she will go on seeing him if he lets her go.

4.2.3 *Even*

A clause cannot be introduced by *even* on its own. The following is wrong:

✗ Miranda could not love Fred, even he was handsome.

What is required here is *even if*.

✔ Miranda could not love Fred, even if he was handsome.

In other sentences it may be *even though*, or *however much*. For example,

✗ She cannot love him, even he gives her everything she asks for.

should be

- ✔ She can't love him, *however much* he gives her.
- ✔ *Even though* he gives her everything she asks for, she cannot love him.

4.2.4 *No matter*

A clause cannot be introduced by *no matter* on its own:

- ✗ Lucy decides to marry George, <u>no matter</u> her family approve or not.

This should be:

- ✔ Lucy decides to marry George, whether her family approve or not.

No matter must always be used together with a question word: *no matter who*, *no matter what*, *no matter how much*, etc:

- ✔ No matter what she says, Miranda would never marry Fred.
- ✔ Raina really loves Bluntschli, no matter how much she pretends to despise him.

4.2.5 *That / whether* and indirect questions

Indirect statements are introduced by *that* and indirect questions are introduced by a question word, *if*, or *whether*. Do NOT combine them (e.g. He asks her <u>that whether</u> she will go to the party):

> It is surprising *that* the protagonist acts in this way.
>
> We ask ourselves *why* the protagonist acts in this way.
>
> We may wonder *whether* the author really intended to say this.

Another troublesome point is that there is no subject–verb inversion in indirect questions (unlike direct questions), and therefore also no need for the operator *do / does*:

- ✗ We ask ourselves why <u>does</u> the protagonist act in this way.

However you may find in informal style (see 3.2.1) and lively narrative (see 3.2.2) a kind of semi-indirect question:

> What am I going to do, she wonders.

In formal English this would be either a direct question or an indirect question:

> "What *am I* going to do?" she wonders.
>
> She wonders what *she is* going to do.

Notice that in the informal, semi-indirect form there is some doubt about the punctuation. Writers sometimes use a question-mark, though I think more often they don't.

4.2.6   *So + adjective ... that ...,* and *too + adjective ... to ...*

So + adjective introduces a clause that describes a result:

> Laura is *so* scared of meeting people *that* she refuses to answer the doorbell.

This construction must not be confused with the *too + adjective* construction, which has a similar meaning:

> Laura is *too* scared *to* answer the doorbell.

There is a difference between the two constructions in that the result following *too + adjective* is always negative in sense (i.e., in this case, Laura will *not* answer the doorbell). You could not, therefore, make a *too* version of

> Miranda is so desperate that she tries to kill Fred with an axe.

because it would not make much sense to say she is *too desperate not* to try to kill him.

In cases where both constructions are possible there may be a slight difference in meaning. In the sentences above about Laura, the *so* construction tends to put the emphasis on explaining her character, while the *too* sentence tends to emphasize the action:

> Laura has a strange, withdrawn character and is very highly-strung. The thought of seeing Jim makes her so scared that she refuses to answer the doorbell when it rings.

The doorbell rings. But Laura is too scared to answer it.

(For *so* see 4.5.7 and 7.2.5a)

4.2.7 *As (so) long as,* and *provided that*

These are forms of conditional, like *if.* There is a tendency to interpret *as long as* as introducing a condition that the speaker wants to see fulfilled:

As long as you finish your homework, I will let you watch television.

(I want you to finish your homework.)

As long as you don't disturb me, I don't care what you do.

(I want you not to disturb me.)

The tendency is even stronger with *provided that,* which can be substituted in both the above examples.

The following therefore is not normally acceptable:

✗ As long as you don't finish your homework, I won't let you watch television.

It seems unlikely that the speaker wants the hearer NOT to finish his homework. What it should be is one of these:

If you don't finish your homework first, I won't let you watch television.

Until you finish your homework, I won't let you watch television.

This implication that the condition is something you want can be emphasized by adding *just*:

Just as/so long as you are happy, I don't care what you do.

(all I want is that you should be happy)

It doesn't matter whether you use *as long* or *so long.*

You may sometimes find my rule about *as long as* is broken:

You won't pass, as long as you go on making that mistake.

But I think here the effect is slightly ironical, just as you can say something like "I promise you're going to fail", when really what you are saying is a threat, not a promise.

4.2.8   *Apart from, other than*

It is best not to use *apart from* or *other than* as synonyms of *in addition to*. Both are normally used with some kind of negative sense and can usually be paraphrased using *only*:

> Apart from the last two lines, this poem does not rhyme.

(= only the last two lines rhyme; the rest do not)

> Apart from the first two lines, the metre is regular.

(= only the first two lines are *not* regular)

It seems that *apart from* places some kind of limitation on something you are saying and contradicts the idea in the main clause. It can introduce a gerund:

> Apart from *locking* Miranda up, Fred does not harm her in any way.

When the sense is positive, use *in addition to*:

> In addition to collecting butterflies, Fred becomes a collector of girls.

Even more care should be taken with *other than*, which students (and perhaps journalists) tend to overuse. It is best used with a negative sense, and when both parts of the sentence are parallel (i.e. both centred on a noun phrase or both centred on a verb phrase):

> Other than *Jim*, there was *no one* she knew at the party.

(the only person she knew at the party was Jim)

> Other than *write a letter* to Jim, she *did nothing* all morning.

(the only thing she did all morning was write a letter to Jim)

The bare infinitive, without *to*, seems more common than gerund after *other than*.

Students tend to use *other than* when there is no negative sense:

✗ Other than write a letter to Jim, she finished two assignments and did the washing-up.

This would be much better as "In addition to writing to Jim", ... or as "Besides writing to Jim, ..."

(Despite this advice, you will sometimes find *other than* used with the same sense as *in addition to*, especially in journalism.)

4.2.9 *As well as*

It is best not to use *as well as* instead of *and*, although it can sometimes be helpful to do so in a long sentence:

I believe my proposal will increase our productivity and our sales by something like a hundred per cent, *as well as* creating around a hundred new jobs.

The meaning here is something like *at the same time as*, and in simple lists of items this does not make sense:

✗ Students study mathematics, phsyics, chemistry, biology, English and history as well as geography.

Such a sentence is grammatical, but it would really only be sensible if you were responding to someone who thought students studied *only* geography. Notice too that *and* is still needed to link the last two items in the list before *as well as*. (see 4.3)

In fact *as well as* tends to create an ordered relationship between two items, the one which follows *as well as* being regarded as the known topic (see 3.3.3) even when it comes last:

The successful candidate will have a *high level of intelligence*. But he/she will require a friendly personality as well as *intellectual ability*.

Clearly *intellectual ability* is more or less the same thing as *a high level of intelligence* in the first sentence, and the emphasis in the second sentence is on *a friendly personality*. You could not change the order of *a friendly personality* and *intellectual ability* in this sentence. You could however move the whole *as well as* phrase to the beginning:

But as well as intellectual ability, he/she will require a friendly personality.

4.3   Joining lists of words and phrases

The rule is simple and, I think, well-known: items in a list are normally separated by commas, except the last two which are joined by *and*, usually with no comma:

The meeting was attended by undergraduates, graduate students *and* members of staff.

Problems can arise, however, when the items in the list are not all of the same status:

✗ Their form, content and emotion expressed are different.

This is incorrect because the last phrase should be "*the* emotion expressed". Consequently the word "Their" can only apply to the first two nouns, not to "emotion". So the sentence ought to be:

✔ Their form *and* content, *and* the emotion expressed, are different.

This may seem pedantic, but it is important to get into the habit of checking items in a list to make sure they match.

✗ In Miranda's account, long passages about her past life, social and aesthetic values occur.

Here the *and* is being used to join two adjectives, "social and aesthetic". Another *and* is needed therefore to join the two noun phrases:

✔ In Miranda's account, long passages about her past life *and* social and aesthetic values ...

You need to take particular care when you join verbs or adjectives that need to be followed by different prepositions:

The audience will be interested *in* and excited *by* this ending.

The second preposition can only be omitted if it is the same as the first. It would be incorrèct therefore to write "interested and excited by this ending".

The same kind of problem often occurs when comparatives are joined:

> ✗ There are several differences between ordinary conversation and a radio interview. In a conversation the sentences are much shorter and <u>incomplete</u>. In an interview the sentences are better organized and <u>informative</u>.

What you have to decide is whether the comparative should apply to the second adjective or not. If it does apply you will get:

> ✔ In a conversation the sentences are much shorter and *less* complete. In an interview the sentences are better organized and *more* informative.

If it does not apply you will get:

> ✔ In a conversation the sentences are much shorter and *are* in-complete. In an interview the sentences are better organized and *are* informative.

Of course, if you join two adjectives which both form their comparative by the addition of *more / less*, you can omit this in front of the second:

> The second poem is more lyrical and (more) personal.

The same applies when the same comparative adverb form is used:

> Her ideas are better organized and (better) presented.

Note that when you use *as well as* in a list of more than two items, *and* will be required also:

> She is clever, rich and beautiful.
>
> She is clever *and* rich, as well as beautiful.
>
> She is clever, rich *and* beautiful, as well as being the best cook I know.

It is also impossible to use *as well as* in joining two negatives:

> ✗ This word normally refers to something which cannot move <u>as well as</u> speak and is therefore inanimate.

> ✔ This word normally refers to something which cannot move *or* speak, and is therefore inanimate.

A useful point to remember is that almost any list containing a modifier + noun combination is potentially ambiguous:

> The writer's work is shaped by his awareness of women's status, social problems and power.

What is the writer aware of? Is it women's status, women's social problems and women's power? Or is it women's status, all kinds of social problems, and power in general? Ambiguities of this kind can be removed by repeating or adding elements:

> ✔ The writer's work is shaped by his awareness of women's status, their social problems and their attitude to power.

4.4 **Word order and clarity**

Some problems with sentence structure can produce a wrong meaning, or cause ambiguity and loss of clarity. They can also produce problems of cohesion and relevance (by *cohesion* I mean the way sentences are related to each other meaningfully in a text, often through pronouns, see Chapter 8; by *relevance* I mean the way in which any sentence in a text, except the first, is relevant to the sentences which precede it).

4.4.1 **Confusing ambiguity**

In the heading to this section I have qualified *ambiguity* because ambiguity may also be a valuable, and perhaps inevitable, quality of literary writing. But in academic writing ambiguity is generally confusing and undesirable.

4.4.1a **Ambiguous relative clauses**

Relative clauses can be a cause of confusing ambiguity, when the relative pronoun (*who*, *which*, etc.) gets separated from the noun which it modifies:

> I still haven't read the book which you lent me.

> I still haven't read the book about Einstein and the theory of relativity which you lent me.
>
> ✗ I am still looking for a book about how to look after a pet dog which she lent me.

Only the last of these is confusing, because what she lent you could be either the book or the pet dog. The remedy may be to change the order:

> ✔ I am still looking for a book which she lent me about how to look after a pet dog.

If the relative clause is placed immediately after the first noun, there can be no confusion.

4.4.1b Ambiguous negatives

Negatives can also cause meaning problems. Generally the scope of a negative main verb includes adverbial phrases and dependent clauses — that is, the negative applies to them also:

> ✗ Fred uses adjective forms when he should use an adverb. This tells the reader that he is not an educated person who comes from the lower class.

Here the writer is unintentionally saying that Fred does NOT come from the lower class. What she meant to write can be expressed by either of the following:

> ✔ Fred is an uneducated person who comes from the lower class.
> ✔ Fred is not an educated person and comes from the lower class.

Notice how the negative does not carry over if it is incorporated in the adjective with a prefix (*uneducated*), or if the second part is a full sentence joined with *and*.

A similar example is

> ✗ She asked him not to go out and look after his sister.

This means she asked him NOT to look after his sister, whereas the writer meant to say:

✔ She asked him not to go out, but to stay home and look after his sister.

Sentences which betray the writer's intended meaning are unacceptable, but a sentence can be quite correct even though genuinely ambiguous; that is, there may be two equally possible meanings:

I didn't ask you to do it in order to save you trouble.

Is the speaker saying he wanted to save the hearer trouble or he didn't want to save the hearer trouble? The negative can apply to either the asking or to the reason for asking. If there were a comma after *it* we would tend to think he wanted to save the hearer trouble, but this is not conclusive. Note, however, that the second meaning can be made completely clear by writing:

It wasn't in order to save you trouble that I asked you to do it.

This takes for granted that I asked you to do it, and focuses on the reason. (It wasn't in order to save you trouble).

4.4.1c   Ambiguous adverbial phrases

Adverbs and adverbial phrases can also cause ambiguity:

He asked them to leave quietly.

Is he speaking quietly or does he want them to leave quietly? We may tend to assume the latter, because in cases of ambiguity it is slightly more normal to apply the adverb's meaning to the nearest verb. On the other hand, if we change *quietly* to *politely*, the meaning will be less clear:

He asked them to leave politely.

Ambiguity can usually be avoided by changing the word order. The following make it clear that *he* is being polite:

He politely asked them to leave.
He asked them politely to leave.

Here is an example where the writer clearly conveyed an unintended meaning:

✗ A dead man cannot talk clearly.

What she meant was "Clearly a dead man cannot talk", or "A dead man clearly cannot talk". The confusion is caused by the fact that two uses of *clearly* are distinguished by its position in the sentence. At the beginning of the sentence or before the verb it functions like a connective and expresses something about the writer's attitude to the sentence, like *obviously* and *of course*. After the verb it usually functions as a normal adjective and describes the manner of doing something.

4.4.1d   Ambiguous coordination

Coordinated phrases can often be ambiguous, even when they are grammatically correct (see 4.3 for ungrammatical coordination):

> Only impoverished old people and students will be admitted.

Do the students have to be impoverished or will any students be admitted?

Whether or not ambiguity of this kind is a flaw in your writing is a matter of judgement. It depends greatly of course on the kind of text you aim to produce: no degree of ambiguity can be tolerated in a legal document for instance. The main point however is that it is always valuable to read through your own writing critically, to remove the chance that the reader will misunderstand something.

4.4.2   Implied subject of participles and other phrases

There is a formal rule about participles occurring at the beginning of a sentence which native speakers often break. It is unlikely that breaking it causes much confusion, but for many people it is a clear sign of bad writing, so it is a good idea to observe it. The rule is this: when a sentence starts with a participle phrase, the unexpressed subject of the participle is understood to be the subject of the verb in the main clause (see 5.6.1):

> *Leaping* down the stairs and *charging* out into the street, Jim just reached the bus-stop in time to see the bus disappearing round the corner.

We understand it is Jim who leapt down the stairs and charged out into the street. (This rule does not apply so clearly when the participle appears later in the sentence: "This plane has an extended range, *enabling* it to fly to

London non-stop". Here the implied subject of *enabling* would be something like "The fact that it has an extended range".)

Sentences starting with other kinds of subject-less dependent phrase are often understood in the same way:

> In order to keep Miranda hidden, Fred buys a house in a remote area.

We understand that it is Fred who wants to keep Miranda hidden. The following therefore are all stylistically weak (though the first two are quite possible for a native speaker to write):

> ✗ Leaping down the stairs and charging out into the street, the bus disappeared round the corner as Jim reached the bus-stop.
>
> ✗ In order to keep Miranda hidden, she is not allowed to go outside.
>
> ✗ As a student, many problems affect us.

The third of these examples also has an agreement problem. The best way to rewrite it would be:

> ✔ As students, we have to face many problems.

Another point about participle phrases is that they tend to imply causality:

> Not being a smoker, I find it hard to understand why so many people cannot give up smoking.

The implication is that I find it hard to understand *because* I am not a smoker (see also 5.6.2). Many readers (myself included) find it irritating therefore to come across sentences like this:

> Living in Hong Kong, he is thirty-two years old.

What connection, you ask yourself, is there between living in Hong Kong and being thirty-two years old? This kind of writing occurs in the programme notes you get at a concert or theatrical performance and in journalism, when the writer is desperately trying to vary sentence structure in a piece which has to be brief and factual. But that is not an adequate excuse for writing something which sounds like nonsense.

4.5   Emphasis and qualifying

By *emphasis* I mean making a statement stronger, more assertive, and by *qualifying* I mean softening it or making it weaker. In general you try to express your views as strongly as you think you can. But you avoid the expression of a view which would be too strong to prove or support. This process of adjusting statements to fit circumstances plays an important part in all writing, and is especially important in academic writing and good journalism.

Often you will find that a writer uses a combination of emphasis and qualifying. For example, immediately before the British election in 1992, a journalist was asked on the radio what he thought the opinion polls proved. He replied: "The polls point to the certainty of a hung parliament (a hung parliament = one in which no party has a majority). That is, I think, as firm as one can decently be at this moment." Here he explicitly states that he is following the strategy I outlined in the last paragraph: qualifying the expression of his view (*point to = suggest*), while making it as strong as possible (*the certainty*). What he says is more or less equivalent to "It is *probably certain* that there will be a hung parliament". Events proved him wrong, because the government obtained a clear majority in the election. But if we met the journalist now he could still maintain that he was not wrong, since he was not giving his own opinion on the election, but describing what the opinion polls suggested, or "pointed to".

Given the need for accurate information and balanced judgement in public affairs and business, the ability to provide a statement with the right degree of emphasis or to qualify it appropriately is extremely important.

4.5.1   Ways of qualifying

There are many obvious and well-known ways of qualifying statements — for example, by using adverbial expressions like *to a certain extent*, *in many ways*, etc., but it may be worth noting that modals like *may be*, *could be*, are also very useful, as are special verbs like *seems to be*, *tends to be*, *suggests that* (as opposed to *shows that*), etc. (See 5.9.1 for relative strength of verbs of saying.)

> The economic success of Hong Kong is *to a certain extent* due to lack of government interference.
>
> The economic success of Hong Kong is *partly* due to lack of government interference.
>
> It *may be* due to other factors as well.
>
> It *appears to be* due to two main factors.
>
> The success of Hong Kong *suggests that* a society prospers when the government does not interfere.

Subject nouns or pronouns can be qualified (compare *Some people think …* with *Everyone thinks …*) and even tenses can affect the truth value of a statement by limiting its scope:

> Accidents *are* caused by carelessness.
>
> (= always, usually)
>
> Accidents *have been* caused by being too careful.
>
> (= sometimes)

The present tense tends to imply universality. Any implication of universality can also be blocked by qualifying the subject noun:

> *The cause* of accidents is carelessness.
>
> *One of the causes* of accidents is carelessness.

Note that the noun following *one of the …* must be plural, though the following verb agreement will be singular.

4.5.1a   Over-qualifying

You should not qualify all your statements just because you like the sound of expressions like *to a certain extent*. Consider the absurdity of the following:

> ✗ To a certain extent water freezes at 0˚C.

You should also beware of qualifying words which express some absolute meaning:

> ✗ It is rather impossible.

Although you may hear this kind of thing in conversation, in writing it suggests a failure to think logically: something either is or is not impossible; there can be nothing in between. (Of course all kinds of illogical statements can be made deliberately for the sake of a humorous effect).

Sometimes it is confusing to use two ways of qualifying in the same sentence, unless you are doing so for the sake of accuracy:

> ✗ *Some* students *often* think that they will get good exam results by writing down everything they know, but this is not the case.

Here either *some* or *often* would be sufficient. Such a sentence however might be appropriate in reporting the results of a statistical survey:

> *Most* students *sometimes* have problems with this course but *few* students have problems *all the time.*

4.5.1b Parenthetical qualifying

A slightly informal way of qualifying a statement is to include a parenthetical qualification, often introduced with *at least*, or *at any rate*:

> Students, or at least most of them, are by nature lazy and look for short cuts.
>
> I do not think we should adopt this policy, at any rate not for the time being.

4.5.2 Ways of emphasizing

There are also many ways of emphasizing statements. Notice that, as I pointed out above in 4.5, a qualified statement can also be emphasized:

> *There can be no doubt* that the *main* cause of Hong Kong's economic success is lack of government interference.
>
> (It is not the only cause but according to the writer there can be no doubt that it is the main cause.)
>
> The *main* cause of Hong Kong's economic success is *definitely* the lack of government interference.

Here the statement is qualified by *main* (not the only cause) and emphasized by *There can be no doubt that* or *definitely*. Other emphatic expressions are *undoubtedly, without a doubt, there is / can be no doubt that, it is certain / undeniable that, no one can deny that*, etc. But beware of *No doubt* which is not used in this way, *certainly*, which often has a different use, and *surely* which is usually quite different in meaning. (see 4.5.3 and 4.5.4)

4.5.3   Ways of introducing a concession: *no doubt, certainly*

It is very hard to pin down the meaning of *no doubt* because it has a rather personal, ironic tone. But a common use is to introduce a counter-argument or concession to other people's ideas:

> *No doubt* some will say that Hong Kong's economic success is due to lack of government interference. *But* this does not mean Hong Kong should neglect all forms of social welfare.

Another possible use is in making assumptions about other people or about a situation, in very much the same way as the modal *must* can be used:

> I forgive her for her bad temper. No doubt she was tired.

(= She must have been tired)

Other expressions that can be used to introduce concessions are *obviously, certainly, of course, true, it is true that*:

> Certainly violent crime is on the increase. But it is doubtful whether enforcing the death penalty would affect the situation.

This concessive meaning of *certainly* and *of course* is probably related to the fact that both can be used in granting permission:

> A: May I sit down?
> B: Certainly / of course.

Notice that *certainly* is more likely to be simply emphatic if it is placed closer to the verb:

> Violent crime is on the increase. Enforcing the death penalty would certainly help to change this.

4.5.4   *Surely*

This cannot normally be used as a synonym for *It is certain that*, because it has a personal tone and introduces a kind of rhetorical question, strongly persuasive in tone, asking the hearer to agree:

> Surely it can't be right to make the sandwich class bear the greatest burden of taxes.

Notice, however, that if it is not placed first in the sentence the meaning does become much closer to *It is certain that*:

> It is surely wrong to make the sandwich class bear the greatest burden of taxes.

Here *surely* seems to waver between the meaning of *definitely* and the meaning of "please agree with me!"

4.5.5   *By all means*

This expression does not belong here at all, but I include it because of a problem with its meaning. It normally does NOT mean something like *using every possible means*. Its normal use is in giving permission, or politely agreeing to someone's request:

> A: May I sit down?
> B: By all means.
>
>   (= Certainly, please do!)

It can therefore be used emphatically in an argument to stress willingness in making a concession:

> By all means let us question our politicians about their policies. But let us leave their private lives out of it.

The negative version is more straightforwardly emphatic, and can qualify both sentences and adjectives:

> By no means *should you* give up, just because you have failed once.
> He is by no means *poor*.
>
>   (= he is probably quite rich)

(Notice that when it comes first in the sentence, subject–verb inversion is required.)

If you want the more literal sense of *by all means* it is best to use an emphatic phrase like *by every possible means*, or *by every means at one's disposal*:

> We shall try to promote the new product by every possible means.

4.5.6   *Even, only (merely)*, etc.

Even can be used to emphasize an idea which is stronger, more surprising, than a preceding one:

> Miranda tries to please Fred, to put him at ease. She *even* offers herself to him, or, as he sees it, tries to seduce him.

But beware of *even*! It cannot be used alone to introduce a clause. (see 4.2.3)

Only or its synonyms (*merely*, *simply*) can be used in a similar way to emphasize that an idea is NOT surprising:

> We cannot criticize Miranda for trying to seduce Fred. She is *merely* trying to save her life.

Note that if *only* comes first in the sentence, there will be subject–verb inversion in the main clause:

> Only when he went to bed that night *did he* realize what a lucky escape he had had.

(See 4.5.10)

4.5.7   *So* and *such*

So is emphatic, but more used in conversation than in writing; students tend to introduce it wrongly into formal writing. Used on its own before an adjective or adverb it has an exclamatory, emotional tone which is why it has to be avoided in formal writing:

> She is so beautiful!

This could not be used, for example, in analysing a literary character:

> Raina, the heroine, is beautiful. But she is spoiled.

It is possible, however, to use *so* objectively when there is either a following *that* clause (4.2.6) or some clearly implied sense of result:

> I was *so* late *that* I didn't think it was worth coming to class.
>
> I didn't think it was worth coming to class *because* I was *so* late.

If the result needs to be linked to a noun phrase (rather than adjective or adverb), you can use *such (a) … that …*:

> Higgins is *such a self-centred man that* one cannot imagine him ever getting married.
>
> Bluntschli has *such self-control that* one cannot imagine him panicking.

Note the need for *a* when *such* is used with a count-noun.

4.5.8 Negatives and understatement

The following seem to be fairly emphatic, even though it is not always clear whether they strengthen or soften a statement:

> *It is far from certain that* the use of English as a medium of instruction will improve the English standard of our students.
>
> *It is by no means certain that* the use of English as a medium of instruction will improve the English standard of our students.
>
> *It is highly unlikely that* the use of English as a medium of instruction will improve the English standard of our students.
>
> *It is hardly likely that* the use of English as a medium of instruction will improve the English standard of our students.

All the above mean approximately the same as the direct statement, which would be:

> The use of English as a medium of instruction *will not* improve the English standard of our students.

Both the first and second examples are quite likely to be used ironically, i.e. when the speaker thinks it is obvious that the equivalent statement is true but is pretending not to be sure; the third example sounds quite emphatic, but it stops short of actually saying "... will NOT improve ... etc."; the last example is a conventional *understatement.*

Hardly is often used to signal understatement:

> Forcing students to study in a language they do not understand is *hardly* likely to improve their general level of education.

Another expression which signals understatement is *to say the least* (another form of this is *at the very least*, which must not be confused with *at least*):

> Forcing students to study in a language they do not understand is, *to say the least*, an odd way to go about trying to improve their educational standard.

To say that understatement is a means of emphasis may sound paradoxical. One can perhaps regard understatement as a form of irony. The writer seems to be saying to the reader: "This is how my opponents would like me to express myself — with moderation; but it is not really the way I think."

4.5.9   Emphasis in coordinating structures

Coordinating sentences rather than expressing the ideas in separate sentences is often a way of organizing emphasis.

4.5.9a   *Not only ... but also*; *both ... and*

When two ideas are linked with *not only ... but also ...* there is usually some degree of emphasis on the second. This accords with a general principle of climax (putting the most important thing last):

> The use of English as a medium of instruction not only fails to improve students' standard of English but also creates serious problems in their education as a whole.

It is clear here that the second idea is bigger, more general and more important. The same kind of linking can be performed by *both ... and (also) ...*:

> The use of English as a medium of instruction both fails to improve students' standard of English and also creates serious problems in their education as a whole.

An alternative way of ordering these ideas would be to start with the bigger, more obvious problem and move to the smaller but more surprising one:

> The use of English as a medium of instruction may be both harmful to the students' overall intellectual development and also ineffective in achieving the professed aim of improving their standard of English.

This arrangement can be made even clearer by using *even*, which underlines the unexpectedness:

> The use of English as a medium of instruction *not only* harms students' overall intellectual development; it *even* fails to achieve its professed aim of improving their standard of English.

4.5.9b *Rather than, instead of, far from, let alone,* and *still less*

Similar implications of unexpectedness are conveyed by some other difficult structures:

> *Rather than* improving students' standard of English, the use of English as medium of instruction *may* (even) cause standards in both languages to drop.

Here something which ought to help actually does the opposite. One could substitute *instead of* without any change in meaning. Emphasis could be added by substituting *far from*.

> *Far from* improving students' standard of English, the use of English as medium of instruction *may* (even) cause standards in both languages to drop.

Let alone is somewhat similar in meaning to *far from*, but is extremely difficult to use correctly:

> Memorizing model essays will not help you to pass exams, *let alone* teach you to think for yourself.

The context must be negative, and what follows *let alone* must be something which is even less likely than whatever was mentioned in the first part of the sentence. It is possible to think of *let alone* as a kind of negative version of *even*.

The same effect can be achieved by using *still less*, which differs from *let alone* however in that it introduces a new sentence:

> Memorizing model essays will not help you to pass exams. *Still less* will it teach you to think for yourself.

4.5.10   Negative adverbials: *not only, scarcely, seldom*, etc.

When *not only* is placed at the beginning of a sentence, subject and verb must be inverted:

> Not only *does* the use of English as a medium of instruction *fail* to improve students' standard of English, (but) it also creates serious problems in their education as a whole.

(In the case of the simple present and past tenses, the inversion is achieved in the same way as in questions, by adding *does, did,* etc.)

A number of other expressions, all with negative meanings, can be used at the beginning of a sentence and cause subject–verb inversion:

> *Seldom have I* seen a more exciting film!
> *Never in my life have I* loved anyone like you!
> *Still less will it* teach you to think for yourself.
> *By no means should you* give up.

Subject–verb inversion also occurs in complex sentences with an initial negative adverbial and a *when* or *if* clause. There are two patterns:

> *Scarcely had he* reached home *when* it began to pour with rain.
> *Only when* the trouble was over *did he* offer to help.

Expressions which follow the first pattern (inverted main clause immediately following) are *no sooner, hardly*. These can also be used without inversion if they are not placed first in the sentence:

> He had scarcely reached home when it began to pour with rain.

Expression which follow the second pattern (uninverted subordinate clause first, inverted main clause second) are *Only if*, *Not unless*.

(Some of these expressions are not exactly negative but they are at least restrictive in sense, e.g. *only*, *seldom*. For more on *no sooner ...*, *hardly ...*, etc. see 8.3.1d, 8.3.1e)

All of these constructions are emphatic or even exclamatory. In the sentences beginning with adverbial clauses one could in fact say that they are dramatic in tone, because of the way they create a climax by postponing the point of the sentence. Compare the position of the main verb in the following:

> He did not offer to help until the trouble was over.
> Not until the trouble was over did he offer to help.

The second is definitely more emphatic.

4.5.11   Emphatic elaboration: *on the contrary*

Emphasis can be achieved by first stating an idea negatively, and then introducing a positive version with *on the contrary*:

> Using English as medium of instruction may not improve students' English. On the contrary, it may cause the standard of English to decline.

Note that the common use of *on the contrary* is not to indicate contrast. If you want to indicate contrast it is probably better to use *In contrast*.

Other connectives which can be similarly emphatic are *In fact*, *Actually* and *Indeed*. (see 4.6.3a)

4.5.12   Negative and emphatic elements keep to the left

It is very unusual (except in student writing!) to find sentences like:

> Everyone cannot escape from death.
> I always do not go there.

These are not grammatically wrong, and they could occur with some special meaning, but the normal form would be:

> *No one* can escape from death.
>
> I *never* go there.

There seems to be a tendency in English to put the negative or emphatic element on the left. Compare the following, which also sounds quite strange:

> ✗ *What* the other diners do is *only* eat.

It is more natural to transfer the sense of *only* = *nothing else* = *all* to the beginning of the sentence:

> *All* the other diners do is eat.

Note that the bare infinitive is used here, not the gerund, i.e. *eat*, not *eating*.

4.6   Connectives

By "connectives" I mean words like *moreover, however, for example*, which make the relation between sentences explicit. They can be both a help and a hindrance in expressing your meaning. It is important to get them right if you use them, but it is even more important to get the connection between ideas right, and for this you do not necessarily have to use connectives. For example, after a generalization the reader expects to find reasons, examples or explanation. It is therefore often clear that you are giving an example, even if you do not introduce it with *for example*.

The main point always is to know what you are trying to say, what point you are trying to make and to be clear about the direction of your argument.

It can, however, be helpful, and is sometimes necessary, to label sentences with connectives. For convenience, I shall divide connectives into three kinds: contrast connectives, addition connectives, and elaboration connectives.

4.6.1   Contrast connectives

The main contrast connectives are *but, however, on the other hand, nevertheless, yet, although, in contrast.*

An important function of contrast connectives is to mark a change in direction of your argument.

> It is said that women already have equal work opportunities. *But* the percentage of women in top management positions is still very low.
>
> At first sight the poem appears so simple that we might wonder how there could be any argument about its meaning. *But* on closer examination we find that it contains an important ambiguity.
>
> Students complain about getting low grades for written assignments. *Yet* they fail to take some obvious steps which would ensure better grades.

In the first example it was essential to use *but*, otherwise the writer would seem to be contradicting herself. In relation to the question of whether or not women are fairly treated, the two sentences present opposite views. In the second example, *but* is not absolutely necessary since the change of direction is foreshadowed by *At first sight*, which leads us to expect something different will appear "on closer examination". In the third example, note that no comma is needed after *Yet*.

There does not seem to be much problem about using contrast connectives. They are easily understood, and in most cases it does not much matter which one you use. However, students do tend to overuse them.

There are times when a contrast connective is essential. Try reading the last sentence of my last paragraph without the *However* which begins it. It will sound like nonsense, because I would be saying "There is not much problem" and then "There is a problem". It is necessary, therefore, to use a contrast connective. But if I changed that last sentence to something like "There is only a slight tendency for students to overuse them", this agrees with the idea that there is not much problem and no contrast connective would be needed.

A contrast is not always there when you think it is, and there are also cases where two ideas can be either contrasted or not contrasted. Consider the following:

> Shakespeare's plays are written in verse *and / but* Shaw's plays are written in prose.

Here either *and* or *but* can be used.

When you compare two things like this, you may simply want to make statements about each of them. Not being concerned with contrast, you join them with *and*. Contrast generally only comes into the picture when you are evaluating things:

> Shakespeare is the greater dramatist *but* Shaw is easier. I suggest we do a play by Shaw.

4.6.1a   Unnecessary *but*

No contrast exists when you join two ideas one of which is simply a negative version of the other:

> Lucy is involved with two men, Cecil, who thinks he is doing her a favour by proposing to her and George who really loves her. In the end Lucy marries George, not Cecil.

You do not use but here, because the two ideas are complementary rather than contrasted; marrying George implies *not* marrying Cecil.

(There is an exception to this when you change the word order: "Lucy marries not Cecil but George" and "It is not Cecil Lucy marries but George". It seems that *but* is required when the two nouns are linked and the negative is placed first.) (see 2.6.4)

4.6.1b   *(Al)though*

This is generally an alternative to *but*, only it has the advantage of allowing you to subordinate one of the contrasting ideas; that is to say, you can make one of the ideas less important than the other:

> Although Shaw's plays are written in prose, the dialogue is quite different from ordinary speech.

Here the fact that the plays are written in prose is relatively unimportant. If it were an important point, you would state it first and then introduce the second idea with *but*:

> Shaw's plays are written in prose. But the dialogue is quite different from ordinary speech.

What you should not do is combine both methods:

> ✗ Shaw's plays are written in prose. <u>Although Shaw's plays are written in prose</u>, the dialogue is quite different from ordinary speech.

This is much too repetitive. The underlined clause can be replaced by one word: *But*, *Nevertheless*, or *However*.

4.6.1c *In spite of, despite*

These are identical, but it is important to note that *despite* has no prepositions attached to it. Both can only be followed by a noun phrase, so to use them as connectives you have to find a suitable noun or use *this*:

> The Japanese are in fact very obvious. In spite of this the girl does not notice them.
>
> Despite the fact that the Japanese are very obvious, the girl does not notice them.

4.6.1d *On the contrary*

In its most common use, *on the contrary* links two complementary rather than contrasting ideas, the first one being put negatively:

> The Japanese are not invisible, of course. On the contrary, they are so visible that the narrator's attention is drawn to them repeatedly.

As I explained above in 4.5.11, *on the contrary* is most often used like this, not for contrast but for emphasis. It really belongs therefore in 4.6.3 as an elaboration connective. In cases where two ideas are genuinely contrasted, it is better to use *In contrast*.

4.6.1e Too many *buts*

Probably the most important point about contrast connectives is that an argument can become very confusing if it contains too many of them, since it suggests that the argument keeps changing direction. This is really a question of organization, but here are some examples of what sometimes happens.

Generally you use a contrast connective to introduce your refutation of a counter-argument — a view expressed by other people that you introduce deliberately in order to refute it. But sometimes the view that you want to quote and refute already contains a contrast connective. Suppose for example you want to quote and then refute this view:

> It is said that women already have equal work opportunities. But the percentage of women in top management positions is still very low.

First, what exactly is the view? The argument is about women's rights. The first sentence quotes the view that women now have equality, and the second sentence refutes it. The other writer's view, therefore, is that women do NOT yet have equality.

You now want to argue that in spite of the above, women DO have equality. You want to refute the refutation. It is awkward to write:

> It is said that women already have equal work opportunities. But the percentage of women in top management positions is still very low. But this is hardly surprising, because in many organizations it is only recently that women have joined the work force.

This is very confusing, because we will tend to assume that the first sentence beginning with *but* is your refutation of the counter-argument, not part of the counter-argument itself. Then with the next sentence you seem to be reversing your view, because it also starts with *but*.

It would be better to rearrange the quoted view, using *although*:

> It is said that, although women now have equal work opportunities, the percentage of women in top management positions is still very low. But this is hardly surprising, because ...

Here we have combined the two sentences of the counter-argument into one. It is clear, therefore, that both are what other people say, not what you say. And your refutation is clearly contained in the sentence starting with *but*.

All this is probably quite complicated to follow, so I will provide more examples. First a clumsy text on euthanasia, in which I shall mark each sentence as for or against euthanasia:

> ✗ It is argued that terminally ill patients with no chance of recovery should be allowed euthanasia (for). But this places too much responsibility on the doctor, who has to decide when a patient has no chance of recovery (against). But anyway doctors make such life-and-death decisions all the time, because funds and hospital beds are in limited supply and they have to decide which patients can be treated (for).

Here the two sentences beginning with *But* give the impression that the writer is swaying this way and that quite aimlessly. Assuming that the writer is in favour of euthanasia, the paragraph might be reorganized as follows:

> Terminally ill patients with no chance of recovery should be allowed euthanasia. The argument that this places too much responsibility on the doctor, who has to decide when a patient has no chance of recovery, is not convincing because doctors make such life-and-death decisions all the time. Funds and hospital beds are in limited supply and they often have to decide which patients can be treated.

One thing you will notice if you compare these two paragraphs on euthanasia, is that connectives may be completely unnecessary. In the second and better version, even *because* has been eliminated. The last sentence is quite clearly a reason for or explanation of the preceding one, in other words, an elaboration. There is no need to label it as such because an elaboration is exactly what we expect at that point in the text.

Here is another example:

> ✗ It is important that students should be able to express their opinions. But certain student publications on campus are abusing their freedom of speech and publishing articles that are either obscene or unreasonably critical of the university authorities. However they should not be censored.

This could be rewritten as

> ✔ It is important that students should be able to express their opinions. It is true that certain student publications on campus are abusing their freedom of speech and publishing articles that are either obscene or unreasonably critical of the university authorities. But censorship is not the best answer to this problem....

Of course, the writer of the above must now go on to explain what the best answer to the problem is.

Notice that, just as *but* marks a refutation, a counter-argument is often marked with *It is true that*, or some expression with a similar meaning. This is because in introducing someone else's argument you are partly making a concession to an opposing view, before showing that it is not convincing or not relevant. (You may have noticed how in oral discussion people often begin by agreeing with something you have said, when really they are about to attack your view.)

The main point is that in this kind of writing it is a good idea to monitor your argument to make sure you are not changing direction too often. If you are, the remedy may be to combine some of the arguments in one sentence, or it may be to reorganize and group counter-arguments together.

4.6.2 Addition connectives

The typical addition connective is *moreover*. It can be used to introduce a new additional point in an argument. But it must be a point which supports the same general idea — to use my previous metaphor, it must *point in the same direction*. And it must also be a different point, not just an elaboration of the preceding one.

Moreover is very popular with students, who tend to use it all the time, forgetting that *also* and *other / another* can be used to perform the same function:

> The two poems *also* differ in tone.
>
> *Another* difference between the two poems is the tone.

Besides overuse, there is a problem when *moreover* is used incorrectly.

This occurs (1) when there is no parallel previous point to which you are adding another point, and (2) when the point you claim to be adding is not a new one but an elaboration of the preceding one:

> ✗ Shakespeare lived and wrote in the latter part of the sixteenth century. Moreover his plays are written in blank verse.

Here the two sentences linked by *Moreover* simply state two facts; they cannot be seen as parallel points in some kind of argument, as they can in the following:

> Modern actors cannot perform Shakespeare well without special training. Shakespeare lived and wrote in the latter part of the sixteenth century and his language is very different from ours. Moreover his plays are written in blank verse and people nowadays are not accustomed to speaking verse.

Here two reasons are given for saying that modern actors need special training to perform Shakespeare, so it is correct to link the second one with *Moreover.*

Using the same text we can illustrate the second problem like this:

> ✗ Modern actors cannot perform Shakespeare well without special training. Shakespeare lived and wrote in the latter part of the sixteenth century and his English is very different from ours. Moreover it is difficult for modern actors to understand.

Here there is only one point, stated in the second sentence and elaborated in the third. The fact that Shakespeare's English is difficult for actors is *due to* the fact that it is different from ours. *Moreover* should be omitted.

Generally it is not appropriate to open a new paragraph with *Moreover,* because a new paragraph usually involves a slight shift of topic and cannot clearly be seen as adding a new point to the same argument. It is generally better to open a new paragraph with something like "*Another* aspect of the question is ..." or "We must *also* consider ..." Alternatively, you can list the sub-divisions of your topic in your opening paragraph (see 3.1.1), in which case a paragraph on each one will be expected in advance.

Another tip which may be helpful is not to use *moreover* (if you do want to use it) as the first word in the sentence. You should try placing it after the subject, and even after the verb, to see which sounds better. Here is an example in a longer text:

> Many changes are taking place in Chinese society. Modern Chinese children do not respect their elders as they used to. They do not see themselves as obliged to follow their parents' wishes in everything. Discipline problems are arising in schools, and young people increasingly want to question the customs and beliefs that are handed down to them by the older generation. Chinese parents, moreover, do not automatically expect that their children will live with them and look after them for the rest of their lives.

Here the idea that Chinese society is changing is first supported by examples of changing attitudes among children and young people. It is then further supported by the example of parents — a slight modification of the topic, but still part of the same idea: that Chinese society is changing. Notice how the organization is highlighted by placing *Chinese parents* before *moreover*: Modern *Chinese children* do this and this ... *Chinese parents* do this and this.... The first position in the sentence can often be used to provide this kind of linking contrast.

However, the same text could easily be organized without using *moreover* at all. We could begin

> Many changes are taking place in Chinese society. Both children and parents are changing. Modern Chinese children ... Chinese parents ...

There is no need now for *moreover* because you have announced in advance that you are going to supply two sets of examples, one for children and one for parents.

4.6.2a *Besides*

Another common problem is the misuse of *besides*. It can only correctly be used to add a further *reason* for something, and it is commoner in speech than in writing. It is NOT synonymous with *moreover*:

> The plan should be rejected because it is too costly and would require a huge staff to carry it out. Besides, there is no guarantee that it would work.

This is correct because *besides* introduces a second reason for rejecting the plan.

There is also often a suggestion that the reason introduced by *besides* is a kind of afterthought — something which you thought of later. In the example above you could in fact substitute *anyway* for *besides*, and the effect would be more or less the same.

Here is one of the many cases where you should not use *besides*:

> Miranda is better educated than Fred. She speaks a socially superior form of English and is far more confident.
>   Besides, she is a more interesting person and can talk about many subjects.

Besides is definitely a "warning sign" word. In normal academic writing it almost shouts to your reader that you have not done the work of organizing your ideas properly.

4.6.2b *In addition*

Sometimes it is possible to substitute *in addition* for *moreover*, but its scope is more limited and it cannot be used in cases where there is the kind of slight shift in topic that we saw with *moreover* in the paragraph about Chinese society changing:

> University is quite different from secondary school. In our first year at university we have to take many new subjects and adapt to a much more independent way of studying. In addition we have to take P. E., and are encouraged to participate in other sports and extracurricular activities.

Probably it is best to use it very literally to mean "This is something additional, something that is added to what I have just said."

4.6.3 Elaboration connectives

The remaining group of connectives can be seen approximately as elaborating or explaining preceding sentences, by introducing examples, reasons, explanations and so on. But these, as I said before, often do not need to be labelled with a connective because they are usually what we expect, following any kind of statement.

I shall deal with a few elaboration connectives that cause problems.

4.6.3a   *Indeed, in fact, actually, as a matter of fact*

All these are very often misused. It is useful to think of the first two, *indeed* and *in fact* as almost opposite in meaning:

> We may be surprised by the word "invisible" in the title. How can the Japanese be invisible? It is *in fact* a trick of the author's to draw our attention to an important point.
>
> We may suspect that the word "invisible" has something to do with the story's meaning. When we reach the end of the story, we find that the apparent invisibility of the Japanese is *indeed* the key to what the writer wants to say.

Note the difference: *in fact* introduces a slightly surprising conclusion, whereas *indeed* introduces confirmation of what was expected.

Indeed, especially when it comes first in the sentence, generally introduces an idea which is similar to but stronger than a preceding one, or simply a stronger statement of the same idea:

> Life is stressful in Hong Kong. Indeed, Hong Kong is probably one of the most stressful cities in the world.

If used wrongly, *indeed* can produce an absurd effect:

> ✗ She is a brilliant person. Indeed she is very clever.
>
> ✗ Hong Kong is the meeting-place of east and west. Indeed it is a very busy city.

In both examples the second sentence is an anti-climax. There would of course be an anti-climax even without the connective, but *indeed* makes it more obvious.

The connective use of *indeed* should not be confused with the use of *indeed* after an adjective, for emphasis: "She is very clever indeed." Notice also that in standard modern English this sounds a little strange if you omit *very*.

Actually can be used in writing in the same way as *in fact*. In speech it is used much less carefully, and may only be a way of introducing a new thought, signalling that the speaker is changing the subject slightly (in this use it is similar to *by the way*).

As a matter of fact is conversational in tone and can seldom be used in formal writing. It is similar in tone to *By the way*, which is used to introduce a change in topic. Both should only be used in writing which imitates the informality of conversation, and to do this you need a very good ear for the way people speak.

4.6.3b *On the contrary*

I have dealt with this above in 4.5.11, where I explained that it is commonly used for emphasis rather than as a contrast connective.

4.6.3c *Therefore*

If you introduce an idea with *therefore*, you are saying that its truth depends on an idea expressed in the preceding sentence:

> Chinese society is changing. Young people no longer like to live with their parents and look after them in old age. The care of the aged, therefore, presents a growing problem.

However, you should not use *therefore* to introduce an idea which self-evident, or necessarily true by itself:

> ✗ The problem with capital punishment is that justice sometimes makes mistakes and the wrong person is sometimes convicted. Therefore it is unjust to execute an innocent person.

This is complete nonsense because it is necessarily always unjust to execute an innocent person. This statement does not in any way depend on anything else that has been said before or will be said after. What the writer perhaps meant was something like this:

> The problem with capital punishment is that justice sometimes makes mistakes and the wrong person is sometimes convicted. Therefore an innocent person is sometimes executed.

Any sentence with *therefore* can be rewritten using *because*. Our first example in this section can be rewritten as:

> Chinese society is changing. The care of the aged presents a growing problem because young people no longer like to live with their parents and look after them in old age.

But you have to decide whether you want to present the reason first or the result first. It is generally wrong to use *therefore* and *because* in the same sentence, because it probably means you are saying the same thing twice:

> ✗ The Japanese are very visible but the girl does not notice them. There-fore she is unobservant because she does not notice the Japanese who are very obvious.

This would be better as either of the following:

> The Japanese are very visible but the girl does not notice them. There-fore she cannot be called observant.

> The girl is unobservant because she does not notice the Japanese, who are very visible.

Notice that *because* says that the proof follows, whereas *therefore* says that the proof precedes.

Sometimes when *therefore* and *because* are used together it has the effect of providing two reasons for the same result without saying how they are related:

> ✗ Capital punishment is very cruel. Therefore it should not be carried out because sometimes an innocent person is executed.

Should capital punishment not be carried out because it is cruel, or because an innocent person is sometimes executed? Probably the writer meant both, but it is wrong to combine the two ideas in this way. Here is one of many acceptable ways of combining them:

> ✔ Capital punishment should not be carried out, both because it is cruel and because an innocent person may sometimes be executed.

It is usually possible to replace *therefore* with some other expression like *because of this, this shows that* …, etc. which have the same meaning and function:

> The Japanese are very visible but the girl does not notice them. This shows that she is not very observant.

You should not use more than one of these methods of making the causal connection:

> ✗ <u>Therefore this shows that</u> the girl is not very observant.

This is like saying

> ✗ <u>This shows that this shows that</u> the girl is not very observant.

4.6.3d *For* and *because*

In one of its meanings, *for* means something like *because*:

> She hesitated at the door, *for* she was afraid of what she might find inside.

This use of *for* is slightly literary and old-fashioned, and is seldom found in modern spoken language. More importantly, it has the particular effect of allowing focus to remain on the first part of the sentence, with the following reason added almost as an afterthought. If the focus of your sentence is on the reason for something, you cannot use *for*:

> (Why did she go to London?) She went to London because she had to see her publisher.
> (What did she do next day?) She went to London, for/because she had to see her publisher.

In the second of these, the focus is on the fact that she went to London, not on her reason for going.

4.6.3e *In that*

This can be very useful for providing an instance of some judgement you make:

> Miranda is more interesting than Fred, in that her mind is full of ideas.

> Tom is lucky this term, in that he does not have any 8:30 lectures.

Here the following clause is something between an example and a reason. It is also limited, in the sense that it indicates a particular aspect of things in which the main clause is true but does not support the idea in the main clause absolutely: it remains possible that Miranda is not more interesting than Fred in some other respect, or possible that Tom is not lucky in some other respect.

If you want to make this sense of limitation very explicit, you can use *in so far as* (also sometimes written *insofar as*):

> In so far as I do not have any early lectures, I can say I am lucky this term. But I do have a somewhat heavier work load.

You may have noticed that a few lines earlier I used *in the sense that*. This should be used only when you are explaining the meaning of a term, as I was then. When I said "… it is limited *in the sense that* …" I was explaining what I meant by *limited*. Students tend to use it quite unnecessarily, when all they mean is *in that*. Students also confuse the connective use of *in that* with *in the way that*, which actually introduces a relative clause:

> Miranda's sense of social superiority can be seen *in the way that* she speaks to Fred.

Notice here that the words of *in the way* are to be taken quite literally, Miranda speaks to Fred *in a certain way*, and it is *in* this way of speaking that we can see her sense of superiority.

5

VERBS

I now want to turn to some quite detailed aspects of the language which you are both using and studying. I don't intend to give a comprehensive account of English grammar; for that you must consult reference books. But I do want to draw attention to areas where you may have a problem and wherever possible to try to make it easier to think about such problems by relating them to meaning. I hope at the same time that this will lead you to meditate on some of the broader aspects of language use.

I shall start with verbs because I think for most people this is where language learning begins to get complicated and where the match between language and reality is at its most complex.

If you lived among people who spoke a language that you did not know, you could probably obtain essential things by pointing. This would be made easier if you simply learnt the names. But to do anything more elaborate — to set up organized activities, to discuss future plans, to examine past experience — you need verbs; verbs allow you to make sentences indicating what you want to do or want other people to do, to discuss things in their absence, and to work with ideas that have no concrete existence at all.

There are several ways in which verbs are especially important in your academic work. One important function of verbs is to create relations between things, and finding the right verb is often the most difficult part of trying to express an idea (See Appendix C for a list of verbs that are useful for relating ideas).

Verbs also are important both in conveying communicative intentions (e.g. I *apologize* for my rudeness indicates your intention to apologize) and in describing them in linguistic analysis (e.g. The speaker of the sentence "I am sorry" is apologizing).

Verb tenses also convey important meanings. What is commonly called tense actually includes aspect (the difference between the English continuous and non-continuous tenses) and mood (the meaning of *may*, *should*, *would*, etc.). But it is common to lump all these features together under the name "tense", and that is what I shall do here.

A further interesting point about tense is that different text types are often conventionally associated with certain uses of tense: the past tense, for example, is typical of narrative, the simple present of process descriptions (for example, describing how a game is played, how an object is manufactured, or how an appliance should be used), sports commentaries and certain kinds of conversational story-telling.

5.1   Tenses

English verbs are labelled in terms of time — past, present, future. This part of their meaning is what we call tense. They are also labelled simple or continuous (e.g. simple present, present continuous) to indicate a difference which is technically known as aspect. But the contrast between English tenses can be more complicated than that suggests, and it is useful when you analyse a text closely to bear in mind that tense and aspect can combine with context to give special meanings.

Let me remind you again that I am only going to deal with tenses that are misused or uses of tense that are not well understood.

5.1.1   Simple present

Standard meaning   The present tense usually refers to repeated actions, habits, or generalizations. It will occur frequently in scientific and academic writing because such writing is frequently concerned with general laws and typical cases, which are not tied to one particular time or place:

> Water freezes at 0°C.
> Women drive better than men.

It is sometimes said that the simple present is used for statements that are scientifically true. It is, but in fact it makes no difference whether a generalization is actually true or not. The point is that the speaker claims it to be true. It even makes no difference if the speaker believes it or not — he may, for instance, be joking.

As you can see from the second example above, a sentence with the simple present can sometimes be quite provocative, unless qualified: the implication is that *all* women drive better than *all* men. It is for this reason that qualifying statements is an important aspect of academic writing. (4.5.1)

It partly follows from the standard meaning of the simple present that you do not use it in the standard formula for making an offer "Would you like …?" You do not say "Do you like …?", because you are asking the hearer to make a present choice, not inquiring about the hearer's general likes and dislikes.

5.1.1a *Always*

Students tend to overuse *always*, in stressing that an action is repeated. It is unnecessary to use *always* because the present tense alone will convey this meaning. In any case, in writing it is inadvisable to use *always* unless it is literally true; other words like *repeatedly* or *continually* are often more precise:

> The guests at the Pension Bertolini look down on the Emersons because they come from a lower social class.
>
> Higgins continually insults Liza and treats her like an object.
>
> Miranda repeatedly tells Fred she cannot love him while he holds her prisoner.

It would not be appropriate to use *always* in any of these. You actually judge the behaviour of characters in a literary text from a limited number of examples.

5.1.1b Special meanings

Notice that it is owing to this aspect of the meaning of the simple present that a question like "Does he drink?" has got to have a special meaning. Obviously no one can stay alive if they don't drink, so it would be absurd to ask this question with the literal meaning of "Does he take in fluids of any kind?" The question is therefore understood to mean "Does he drink alcohol?" (See *The Glass Menagerie*, scene 5)

5.1.1c Special uses

The simple present also has some special uses which are important when you are writing about literature. It is used for commenting on a writer's technique:

> Shaw *portrays* Higgins as overbearing and insensitive.

You would only use the past tense (*portrayed*) if you were concentrating on Shaw's life and personality: for instance in a biographical study that linked Shaw's characters to the author's own psychology:

> Shaw *portrayed* Higgins as overbearing and insensitive because he had similar tendencies himself.

The present tense is used also in literary analysis for recounting events in a story. In linguistics it is used when you are analysing a text and for referring to events in a narrative. If you want a reason for this, you can say that stories are timeless. Once they exist they can be told or read over and over again:

> The play *opens* with the family having dinner. Tom *is* irritated when Amanda *starts* to reminisce about the vanished world of her youth. But life *is* hard for Amanda and it *is* not surprising that she *prefers* to live in a world of illusion. She *married* an irresponsible man, who *abandoned* her, and Amanda *had* to raise the family on her own. Later, Tom, like his father, *will leave* them. Amanda *reveals* her insecurity when she *tells* Tom how afraid she *is* that he *will start* drinking, like his father.

Note that the present tense is used here as a *time base*. That is to say, it is used for events that take place within the main line of the narrative. Events which precede the story will be in past or present perfect (normal rules decide which) and future events will be in future tense.

If you study literature, it is worth practising the art of summarizing a story, because it is fundamental to any comments you want to make about any form of narrative. Your writing will seem unprofessional, and sometimes confusing, if you do not follow the convention of using the present tense.

The present tense is also used for stage directions:

> The curtain rises and reveals a typical middle-class sitting-room. Mrs Jones, the daily help, is dusting.

5.1.2   Past and present perfect

One problem is to know which to use. The essential rule is that the present perfect (*have* ... *-ed*) cannot be used in a sentence containing an expression of past time:

> I have been to London many times.
>
> I went to London last summer.

There is a corresponding difference in the following:

> Have you seen *Pretty Woman*?
>
> Did you see *Pretty Woman*?

There are many situations where both would be correct. But the first would be appropriate if you were with a friend at a video shop, trying to decide what video to borrow. The second would be appropriate if the local cinema had recently stopped showing the movie. With the present perfect you are interested in the other person's experience and the present effects of that experience: if she *has* seen *Pretty Woman*, you will borrow something else. But consider the following:

> Did you go to the concert?
>
> Have you seen the Impressionist Exhibition?

A concert is usually a one-off event, that is to say, it is not repeated. The present perfect therefore would not normally be appropriate (though it is possible to invent situations where it would be). An exhibition of paintings will normally continue for several months, and, assuming that it is still continuing at the time of speaking, the present perfect is appropriate.

Note that *once* counts as an expression of past time, and cannot be used with the present perfect:

> ✔ I once went to Bali for a holiday.

✗ I have once been to Bali for a holiday.

5.1.2a Present perfect for describing experience

The present perfect is used to describe experiences that have become part of your general life experience, the kind of things you might put down on a very comprehensive C.V.:

> I have been to China, Japan, Korea, Taiwan, Singapore, Malaysia and Thailand. I have never been to America.

This is the kind of information that might be relevant if you were being considered for a job with a company which wants to expand its sales in Asia.

The following, however, is different:

> I have been to London *before.*

You would usually only say this *when you are in London.* The definite implication is that this is not your first visit and that is the meaning you convey by saying it.

It would also be appropriate if you were planning a holiday with a friend and you wanted to give reasons for not going to London: "We've been to London before. Let's go somewhere new."

5.1.2b *Since*

The present perfect is generally required with *since* (referring to time):

> We have been waiting *since* ten o'clock.

If this were set in a past tense narrative, the past perfect would be used:

> At half-past eleven the bus finally arrived. We *had* been waiting since ten o'clock.

Neither present nor past is possible in a *since* sentence, though speakers of other European languages frequently get it wrong and say "We are / were waiting since ten o'clock."

5.1.2c   *Yet* **and** *still*

Present perfect rather than past tense is normally used with *yet* and *still*. You might meet something like the following, but they are non-standard:

✗ Did you see that movie yet?

   (= Have you seen …)

✗ No, I still didn't see it.

   (= I still haven't seen it.)

However, *yet* and *still* can both occur with the past tense in narrative, in which case they will tend to involve the reader/hearer in the character's experience:

He was not out of trouble *yet.* He *still* did not know if he had shaken off his pursuers.

5.1.2d   *The first time*

Notice that the present perfect is used in this kind of sentence:

This is the first time I have ever been to England.

In a past tense narrative this would become:

It was the first time I had ever been to England.

5.1.2e   *Become*

This, like other verbs describing gradual change (e.g. *change, develop, turn into*), is often met in the present continuous or present perfect rather than the simple present because it often describes a tendency in a specific situation. That is to say, the simple present is not appropriate unless you are making a generalization, with no reference to a particular time and place:

Armed robbery *is becoming* almost an everyday occurrence in Hong Kong.

Armed robbery *has become* almost an everyday occurrence in Hong Kong.

Both sentences refer to the present state of affairs in Hong Kong and are specific rather than general. Whether you choose the first or the second depends on your assessment of the situation: is the trend fully established (*has become*) or is it still developing (*is becoming*)?

Compare the above with the following, which are true generalizations:

> When law and order break down in a country, armed robbery *becomes* common.
>
> If you have to travel by air very frequently, it *becomes* boring.

This rule does not apply, however, when *become* is used in the present tense in retelling a story:

> Romeo thinks that Juliet is dead. He *becomes* desperate and kills himself.

5.1.2f   Special use of past tense

The past tense (or past continuous) is sometimes used a little oddly in inquiries, invitations and so on, when the speaker is politely trying to justify asking for the hearer's attention:

> I *wondered* if you were doing anything tonight, or would you like to have dinner with me?
>
> I *was wondering* if you could help me.
>
> I just *wanted* to ask if ...

5.1.3   Past perfect

Some students may still have problems with the past perfect (*had ... -ed*). Do NOT use it to emphasize that something happened a very, very long time ago. The past perfect is not concerned with *length* of time but with the relationship between two past events. It should be used when your time base is already past tense and you want to refer to something which *at that (past) time* was already in the past:

> We took a taxi to the theatre, but we were held up in a traffic jam. When we *arrived* there, the performance *had started*.
>
> (The performance started before you arrived; you were late and missed the beginning.)

We generally assume that what is mentioned first is what happened first. So if you used the past tense instead of the past perfect ("When we arrived, the performance *started*"), we would understand that the performance started after you arrived, so you were not late but just in time.

The past perfect is also used whenever you transfer a present perfect tense into the past, e.g. in reported speech:

> She said she had been to London before.

5.1.4   The conditional

Most students overuse the conditional (*would*). They seem to think it is more polite than other tenses. Since they wish to be polite, they constantly decorate their writing with conditionals.

Certainly the conditional plays a part in many politeness formulas:

> *Would you like* a drink? (see 5.1.1)
>
> *Would you* sit down please?
>
> (The second of these in fact is not particularly polite — it could even sound impatient.)

But in other circumstances the conditional should only be used when there is a definite reason, e.g. in certain *if* sentences, after *wish*, etc:

> Your written work *would be* better if you *checked* it before handing it in.
>
> (Note that you do not use *would* if the verb in the *if* clause is not in the past: Your work *will be* better if you *check* it before handing it in.)

In writing, you should not use the conditional when what you are saying is not hypothetical but a statement of your intentions, expression of your opinion, or statement of fact:

> I *shall discuss* this point in more detail later on.
>
> We *can find* many images of death in this poem.

In speech you might hear something like "I would like to discuss this point...." This is a form of request for permission, and although no answer is expected it is theoretically possible for the hearer to say "Yes, let's", or "No, I don't think it's relevant". It is not so appropriate in writing because the reader cannot answer.

In speech you will also hear *would* used as a softener in introductory phrases like *I would think that* ..., *I would imagine that*. ... But again, do not do this in writing.

Let me repeat, the conditional should only be used when what you are saying is hypothetical, as in the well-known writing task, "Describe how you *would spend* the money if you won the lottery", to which almost your whole answer will consist of sentences with *I would* ..., because they all depend on the imaginary situation in which you have won the lottery.

Students frequently produce sentences like the following, which are confusing because they imply a condition, that is, an *if* clause, but we cannot imagine what it is:

    ✗ I would discuss this point in more detail later on.

5.1.5   Tenses with *hope* and *wish*

Generally the future tense is used after *expect*, either the future or the present after *hope*, and the past after *wish*:

    I expect he *will* come.

    I hope he *comes* / *will* come.

    I wish you *were* here.

People find these verbs confusing partly because of their meanings. We mostly think that *hope* refers to something in the future, but in fact the only tense that normally cannot be used after it is the conditional:

    I hope she passes her exam.

    I hope she will pass her exam.

    I hope she passed her exam.

The point is that you can still express hopes about something which has already happened, so long as you do not yet know the result.

The most common mistake is to use the conditional after *hope:*

> ✗ I hope the government <u>would</u> do something about this.

Although it is just about possible to invent a context for such sentences, we can probably say that the only normal context for the conditional after *hope* is when the main verb is in past tense:

> He said he hoped the government would do something about it.

The chief difference between *hoping* and *wishing* is that your hopes relate to something factual: either she passed or she didn't, either he will come or he won't. *Wishing*, on the other hand, relates to something non-factual or counter-factual:

> I wish you were here.
>
> (You are *not* here.)
>
> I wish it wasn't raining.
>
> (It *is* raining.)
>
> I wish you wouldn't make so much noise.
>
> (You *are* making a lot of noise.)

The last of these is often a form of request.

5.2   Modals

5.2.1   *May* and *can*

Teachers used to insist that it was wrong to use *can* in the sense of giving permission. This is no longer so in contemporary English. "You may go now" and "You can go now" are more or less interchangeable.

There are in fact times when *may* is inappropriate, because it would be unfriendly to give the impression that you are granting permission (because it would imply that you have authority over the hearer):

> Come in! Sit down! You *can* put your books down on the table.

Here the speaker is simply suggesting a convenient solution. It is ironic that many students would use *may* here because they have been taught that it is more polite. It is in fact less so, because it establishes the relationship as one between a superior (the speaker) and an inferior (the hearer). It would be even worse in the following situation: two friends are in a car, looking for a parking-space. The passenger sees a vacant place and says "You <u>may</u> park there". This sounds very patronizing.

5.2.2   *Must*: reasonable assumptions

Students are sometimes not familiar with the use of *must* to express assumptions based on some form of evidence. For example, if you know someone has been working very hard, you say:

> You must be tired.

You cannot normally say to someone "You <u>are</u> tired" because you are not in a position to know whether that person is tired. Students tend incorrectly to use *should* in this context. In some cases the difference between *must* and *should* is only a question of certainty. If it takes twelve hours to fly to London and someone left fourteen hours ago, you say:

> He must be in London by now.

If you feel doubtful about the reliability of the airline, you can say:

> He should be / ought to be in London by now.

This does not work however when you are making a polite guess about someone else's feelings. The reason seems to be that the other meaning of *should* (= *ought to*, obligation) interferes. So "You should be tired" will be taken to mean "You ought to be tired", implying that, surprisingly, you appear NOT to be tired!

Parents will probably be familiar with the situation where you have guests and the baby refuses to go to sleep. The mother may well say: "He should be sleepy — it's long past his ordinary bed-time".

Normal usage can be demonstrated like this:

> You *must* be tired. You *should* go to bed.

5.3 Transitive and intransitive

A major problem is the transitive / intransitive distinction. The important points about this are (1) that transitive verbs usually require an object, and (2) that intransitive verbs have no passive form:

✔ We received the letter.

✗ We received.

Did you receive our letter?

✔ Yes, we did, / Yes, we received it.

✗ Yes, we received.

✔ The accident occurred at 4:00 p.m.

✗ The accident <u>was occurred</u> at 4:00 p.m.

An object is normally required after the transitive verb *receive*. There can be no passive form of the intransitive verb *occur*.

A frequent problem is that students try to use passive forms of these intransitive verbs:

happen / occur, disappear, rise, faint, succeed, result, depend, prevail, refer, die, originate

The reverse problem also occurs, with verbs like *express, limit, confine, reveal, enjoy* which must either have an object or be in the passive:

✔ Orwell's view of the importance of language is expressed in *Nineteen Eighty-Four.*

✗ Orwell's view of the importance of Language <u>expresses</u> in *Nineteen Eighty-Four.*

✔ Orwell's criticism is not limited to any one political system.

✗ Orwell's criticism <u>does not limit to</u> any one political system.

In the case of *enjoy* the problem can also be solved by using *pronoun + self*:

✗ Lucy enjoys Italy because it is so different.

✔ Lucy enjoys herself in Italy because it is so different.

Note that since intransitive verbs have no passive, they have no past participle that can stand on its own, though they do have a present participle:

✔ Accidents <u>resulting</u> from carelessness are common.

✗ Accidents <u>resulted</u> from carelessness are common.

The past participle is wrong because an accident cannot <u>be resulted</u>.

However, a good many verbs (including *refer* in the list above) seem to occur both transitively and intransitively:

> She ran fast.
>
> She ran the campaign.
>
> She ran the marathon.

In such cases there is either a fairly clear meaning distinction (*run = manage*, *organize* is transitive) or there is a clear limit on the kinds of word which can follow the verb: in its intransitive sense *run* can be followed by *race* and its synonyms, just as *sing*, normally intransitive, can be followed by *song* and its synonyms.

Certain verbs are confusing because they have both transitive and intransitive forms with approximately the same meaning: e.g. *begin / end, open / shut, break / smash, drop, spill, fail / pass*, etc.

> He opens his shop at 9:00 a.m.
> The shops open at 9:00 a.m.
>
> Jim breaks the unicorn.
> The unicorn breaks.

This means that there may be a choice between using the verb intransitively and using a passive form of the transitive verb:

> The door was opened.
>
> The door slowly opened.

In a story, "the door slowly opened" will create more immediacy and suspense, because it describes what the narrator actually sees. He doesn't see the person who is opening the door — perhaps the door is opening by itself, perhaps it's a ghost, perhaps it's a thief?

On the other hand, if the house has been robbed and a detective is investigating, he might say "The door was opened from the inside" — clearly in this case the focus is on the fact that someone must have opened the door, though it is not possible to say who.

You can find similar differences between *broke* and *was broken*, *smashed* and *was smashed*. (It's an old joke that when a child breaks something he tends to say "It broke, Mummy", not "I broke it".)

In some cases transitive and intransitive are carried by two different but closely related verbs. These are always a cause of confusion, even in some cases for native speakers: *lay* (transitive), *lie* (intransitive); *raise* (transitive), *rise* (intransitive); *arouse* (transitive), *arise* (intransitive):

> Critics say the policy is inflationary and will cause the cost of living to *rise*. To combat this inflation, they say the government should *raise* interest rates.

Much of the confusion arises (intransitive) from the similarity of the two forms: for example, the past tense of *lie* is *lay*. You should lay (transitive) a dictionary or reference grammar on the table beside you when you write, and consult them over words like these.

Here are some other interesting things to look out for in relation to this question of transitivity.

5.3.1   Special uses, special meanings

As with all modifications to normal grammatical rules, if a normally transitive verb comes to be used intransitively, or vice versa, this is usually connected with some specialized meaning.

5.3.1a   Non-human subjects

Some normally transitive verbs may be used intransitively with a non-human subject in preference to a passive or with a specialized meaning:

> Your essay *reads* well.
>
> The new product *sold* like hot cakes.

These uses are a well-established part of standard English, but you may meet similar new meanings.

5.3.1b   No object

A normally transitive verb may come to be used without an object in the specialized language of a profession or interest group: e.g. in a discussion of rugby football, you might find: "He kicked brilliantly"; "Who is kicking for your team?" The verb *receive* is used similarly in tennis jargon: "If Becker is serving, his opponent is receiving."

An interesting case is the camera advertisement which proclaims: "The camera you can take with wherever you go." It seems likely that a pun is intended, but it doesn't work in standard English. Although *take* can be used intransitively in the sense of "take photographs", it cannot be used intransitively in the sense of "take something with you." Probably the advertiser wants to imply (1) You can take pictures with this camera wherever you go; (2) You can take this camera with you wherever you go. But only the first of these is strictly grammatical; for the second meaning it would have to be "The camera you can take with you wherever you go."

5.3.1c   New technical meaning

The same may happen when a word develops a new meaning in the language of some profession or interest group: e.g. in athletics: "She kicked at the start of the last lap" (meaning, she began to run faster, started her final spurt).

There is a strong tendency for new intransitive or intransitive uses to be formed in the specialized language of professional groups or craftsmen (and journalists?). If you are alert in your reading you may find unusual uses.

5.4   The passive voice: good and bad uses

In 3.3.1 I suggested that the passive can be stylistically inappropriate or confusing. There are however many occasions when the passive is appropriate and useful.

5.4.1 Use of the passive when information is unavailable or unnecessary

The passive can be useful when the active voice would require the writer to give information which is not known or which is totally unnecessary:

> The accident *occurred* at 4:00 p.m. Both drivers *were badly hurt* and *have been taken* to hospital.

The intransitive *occur* is convenient because nothing need be said about the cause of the accident, which is probably not known. Similarly, it would be awkward to say who or what *hurt* the drivers, so the passive is preferable. And although *someone* must have taken them to hospital we are not interested to know who it was.

5.4.2 The passive in journalism: authority and objectivity

Consider the following, from a news report:

> The zoo at Laichikok has been described as one of the worst in the world.

The passive is convenient here for the journalist because it avoids giving the impression of a personal opinion. The journalist is reporting "what has been said", not giving his or her opinion.

The passive is also convenient for the journalist because it implies that more than one person has described the zoo in this way; there is probably an additional implication that someone who has some expert knowledge of zoos has said it. The sentence is likely to impress us for both reasons. It is by no means certain, however, that either implication is correct. Still, even if only one member of the general public has said it, the writer might argue that it is still literally true (the zoo *has* been described this way) and may also be a correct assessment. The writer may claim (not entirely reasonably) that the sentence does not actually tell us either that many people have said it or that those who have said it are experts. I say "not entirely reasonably", because the statement is clearly intended to sound authoritative.

Note that the use of present perfect is essential here. If it were simple past, *was described*, we would have to know something more: *by whom?*

when? where? Using the simple past would force the writer to give more information (which he either does not have, or feels to be irrelevant to his present purpose).

Clearly the use of the passive to make authoritative-sounding statements can be abused. When making such statements you should check that what you are saying is reasonable.

There are a number of popular opening phrases which are in an impersonal, passive form:

> It is generally considered that ...
>
> It is often said that ...
>
> It is agreed that ...

Jane Austen makes fun of this kind of language by opening her novel, *Pride and Prejudice*, with the sentence "It is a truth universally acknowledged that a single man in possession of a good fortune must be in want of a wife." She is of course very well aware that she is saying something which is NOT reasonable. She is making fun of the view she expresses, of the characters in her story who appear to think this way, and also perhaps of the way we can all be momentarily tricked by such impressive introductions into accepting a view which is clearly false.

5.4.3   The passive in reporting experimental results

The passive is often used in scientific reports, where the identity of the human agent is irrelevant, or in describing processes which occur without human intervention:

> The substance is then heated till it melts.
>
> The cards are printed on both sides.

In this kind of writing, intransitive verbs (*melts*) achieve the same effect as the passive of transitive verbs. This is probably one reason why new intransitive forms seem to appear quite regularly in technical language. (Cf. computerese: "You boot the computer or the computer boots.")

It may be worth noting that sentences like the second example above are ambiguous, because they can describe either a state or a process:

> The cards are printed on both sides. There is a picture on the front and a short poem on the back. (state)
>
> As they pass over the rollers, the cards are printed on both sides. (process)

5.4.4   Awkward or evasive uses of the passive

The impersonality of the passive can be useful and persuasive, but it can also be used to deceive the reader and you should be aware of this. As I suggested above, the passive can be used to make statements sound authoritative even when no proof is offered to support them:

> Our face cream has been shown to restore skin health and remove wrinkles.

Has it? How and by whom?

When you use the passive yourself, it is a good idea to make sure what you are saying is reasonable and qualify it if necessary (but only if necessary):

> It has been established that smoking causes cancer.

(Is there valid scientific evidence?)

> It is agreed that smoking causes cancer.

(Are you sure there aren't some people who do not agree?)

> It has *sometimes* been *suggested* that smoking causes cancer.

(Is it really that doubtful?)

The passive may also be used to conceal the writer's opinion or intention under an appearance of objectivity:

> Your work is found to be inadequate.
>
> No credit is given because your work was handed in late.

Is some sort of machine responsible for these decisions? Or is it simply the teacher who decides? If the latter, wouldn't it be more honest for him to say so? But of course nobody likes to take responsibility for unpleasant announcements.

I have dealt elsewhere with two student errors of style: the use of passive in introducing a quotation (As said by ... 2.4.1) and the excessive use of passive in stating intentions in a paper. (3.3.1)

There are also cases where a passive introductory phrase is used quite incorrectly to introduce a fact:

> ✗ It is considered that *The Collector* is composed of two first-person narratives.

The Collector is composed of two first-person narratives. It would be equally silly to say "I think that *The Collector* is composed of two first-person narratives." It is a fact about the novel which can be observed by anyone without any assistance from outside authority. You can simply state it, without the unnecessary and confusing introductory phrase.

5.4.5   Wrong tense with the passive

Students sometimes have problems deciding between simple and continuous forms of the passive. It does not always matter:

> Most of the films that are made / are being made nowadays are full of sex and violence.

Here both tenses mean pretty much the same. Since you are making a generalization, *are made* is correct. If you want to stress that the making of these films is continuing, *are being made* is also correct. But the following is odd:

> You should always stick to the topic which is being assigned.

Assigning a topic is not something that can last a significant amount of time. The teacher simply says: "The topic is X". You can say "the teacher *assigned* a topic", or "the teacher *has assigned* a topic", but it is very odd to say "the teacher is assigning a topic." In the passive, therefore, you would say either "the topic which is assigned", or "the topic which has been assigned":

> You should always stick to the topic which is assigned.

In this respect, it is worth noting that you can also use a participle here instead of the relative clause:

> You should always stick to the topic assigned.

You can also use *assigned* as an adjective, which gives:

> You should always stick to the assigned topic.

It makes no difference which of these three patterns you follow.

In reporting or retelling a story you need to be particularly careful with the continuous passive forms, since they will be quite inappropriate for any steps in the story. The following, however, may help to show how they can be used:

> If you hear that someone died in a car accident, you may well feel sorry for him. Would you feel differently if you heard that at the time of the accident he *was being chased* by the police after committing a robbery and shooting two people?

5.4.5a   Passive infinitive

Although there are occasions when a passive infinitive is necessary ("This problem needs *to be dealt with* urgently"), adjectives like *difficult, easy, important*, etc. are followed by an ordinary infinitive, not a passive one:

> This problem will not be easy *to solve*.
> This point is useful *to bear* in mind.

See 7.3.3.

5.4.6   Effect of the passive on word-order, relevance and cohesion

In our sentence about the zoo in 5.4.2, the passive puts "zoo" at the beginning of the sentence, and thus makes it the subject and topic of the sentence. It is interesting to see the effect the passive has in a slightly later sentence in the article:

> The zoo at Laichikok has been described as one of the worst in the world.
>
> ....
>
> *The zoo is owned* by businessman, Mr Spencer Lam, who has been repeatedly criticized by the RSPCA.

It is natural, once a topic has been established, to try to keep it in the subject position. This will ensure a smooth transition from sentence to sentence because it keeps the topic unchanged, while each sentence adds new information about that topic. In this case the topic in the later sentence is still the zoo, and the sentence tells us who owns it. Once Mr Lam is introduced we are told about something that has happened to him. Without the passive in the later sentence, we would have

> The zoo at Laichikok has been described as one of the worst in the world.
>
> ....
>
> The RSPCA have repeatedly criticized Mr Spencer Lam, who owns the zoo.

This forces us to switch our attention to a new topic, the RSPCA, and then to a second new topic, Mr Lam, before we know why the new topics have been introduced, or what connection they have with the preceding topic, the zoo. This version is much more awkward. Compare it with the original passive version, which establishes the connection first — "the zoo" — before giving us the new information about it.

(If the active version of the sentence were read aloud the final stress would have to be on "owns", not, as is more normal, on the last noun, "zoo". In speech, stress picks out the new, interesting part of the sentence. Since there is no way of writing stress, this function can only be parallelled in a written text by word order, or the use of the special constructions mentioned in 3.3.3)

To maintain a convenient word-order and improve cohesion is therefore another reason for sometimes using the passive, in addition to its value of impersonality and its authoritative tone.

5.5 Stative verbs

Some verbs cannot normally be used in the present continuous tense (unless they are used with a special meaning). Typically, these are verbs of thinking, feeling and sense perception:

exist, think, know, remember, love, like, prefer, appreciate, see, smell, hear, taste, etc.

> I *think* you are right.
>
> Shut your eyes and tell me what you *hear*. Now open your eyes and tell me what you *see*!

You may meet these verbs with present continuous (e.g. "I am thinking you are right") in certain non-standard forms of English used by non-native-speakers, or when a writer wishes to characterize this kind of speaker.

5.5.1 Non-stative meanings

Many of the verbs however have different non-stative meanings, which do allow the use of present continuous:

> Q: What is David doing? A: Sh! *He's thinking*!

Here you perhaps imagine David sitting quietly, with his chin resting on his hand, in the attitude of Rodin's famous statue, *The Thinker*.

And *see*, *hear*, *smell* and *taste* all have meanings which do not describe sense perception:

> Susan is seeing her doctor.

(Susan is visiting her doctor, but she may not in fact be looking at him.)

> The judge is hearing a case.

(He is conducting the trial.)

> The chef is tasting the soup.

(= trying it)

She bent down and smelled the roses.

(= an action of putting one's nose close to something and sniffing it
— you can still do this even if the roses have no scent)

5.5.2   *Can* with verbs of perception

With *see, hear, smell, taste* something like the continuous meaning is often
indicated by adding *can*:

I am looking out of my window. I *can see* the sea.

The use of *can* here makes the meaning clearly specific rather than general.
("I see the sea.")

5.5.3   Beginning and ending

The stative meaning of many of these verbs does not include any sense of
beginning or ending. A purely stative verb like *know*, therefore, cannot be
used in the second sentence of the following:

Yes, I know her. I *met* her at a party.

It would be impossible to say "I knew her at a party." But you might find
know used to mean *recognize*:

He *knew* her the moment he saw her. (= recognized her)

The relationship between *know* and *meet* (= *begin to know*) is parallelled
with some of the other verbs:

think that: realize / understand that (= begin to think that);
love: fall in love (= begin to love)

5.5.4   Imperative of stative verbs

The imperative of stative verbs produces some strange effects, since they
mostly refer to sense experience which is not under conscious control:

✗ Like icecream!

Love Helen!

> Think that I'm right!

It seems however that God and advertisements can tell you to do anything, and so can anyone in a bullying tone:

> Love your neighbour!
>
> Taste the freshness of real fruit!
>
> Like it or leave it!
>
> (= I don't care if you like it or not, it's all you're going to get!)

In general the familiar principle of meaning applies here, that when a straightforward meaning is blocked a special meaning is created:

> Think!
>
> (= use your brain, don't just say the first thing that comes into your head!)
>
> Believe me!
>
> (= I beg you to believe me, this is the truth!).

There are other factors involved in the use of the imperative. Orders can only be given by those with authority and what is ordered must be possible for the hearer to perform. Poets exploit this kind of fact:

> Oh do not die, for I shall hate
> All women so, when thou art gone,
> That thee I shall not celebrate,
> When I remember thou wast one.
>
> (John Donne, "A Feaver" in *Songs and Sonnets*)

We can interpret "do not die" as either the expression of a strong wish or a sign of extreme self-centredness in the lover who would command the woman not to die because of the effect her death would have on him.

5.6 Participles

Participles can provide an economical means of packing more information, particularly descriptive details, into a single sentence:

> Smiling bravely and holding her three-month-old baby, Mrs Maureen Connolly explained how she escaped when a man burst into her house and threatened her with a gun.

Problems may arise, however, because in some contexts participles have special implications which students are not aware of.

5.6.1   The implied subject of present participles

When a sentence starts with a participle phrase, the unexpressed subject of the participle is understood to be the subject of the main clause:

> Dashing into the room, Cynthia flung open the windows to let some air in.

We understand that it is Cynthia who dashed into the room. If you are not careful about this rule, you can easily produce an absurd meaning:

> ✗ Hurriedly throwing on her clothes, the storm hit her as she went outside.
> ✗ Slipping into her dress, he greeted her when she came to the door.

In the first of these, *the storm* throws on her clothes; in the second, *he* slips into her dress! (see 4.4.2)

5.6.2   Causal implications

When they appear in front of the main clause, such phrases often describe an action or event which occurs earlier or at the same time. They can also imply causality when the meaning of the verb suggests it:

> Not wanting to disturb her, he closed the door quietly and left.

The implication is that he closed the door quietly *because* he did not want to disturb her. You should be careful not to use the present participle as a substitute for a *when* clause without any causal implication, when the meaning of the verb tends to suggest causality:

> Being a university student, she was entitled to cheap tickets.
> ✗ Being a university student, she failed her exams twice.

The first is correct, but in the second it sounds as if all university students should be expected to fail their exams twice, whereas the writer actually meant "When she was a university student, she failed her exams twice". (see 4.4.2)

5.6.3 Past participles

Past participles at the beginning of a sentence should also have the same unexpressed subject as the main verb, though the effects are less disastrous if this rule is not followed:

> Situated at the foot of a mountain, the town is sheltered from northerly winds.
>
> Situated at the foot of a mountain, we came upon an attractive old city.

The second of these is acceptable, but not quite so clear. It would be more normal to write:

> We came upon an attractive old city, situated ...

5.6.4 Idiomatic exceptions

There are some idiomatic phrases to which this participle rule is not applied, or not always applied: *considering, depending on, relying on, judging from / by, compared with, based on*. For example, *considering* has really lost all sense of being a participle and means something very similar to *since, because*, or *as*:

> It seems very unreasonable for her to criticize the plan, considering she was the one who suggested it.

However, there is a contemporary tendency to overuse *based on*, so it is probably best to check and see whether your use of it is reasonable:

> He drew up a plan of action, based on his research.
>
> Based on his research, he drew up a plan of action.

The first of these is fine, and the second seems perfectly acceptable because we easily understand that the plan he drew up *was based on* his research. The following are less happy:

> Based on his research, it seems unlikely that we can expect much growth in the coming year.
>
> ✗ Based on his research, he went to London immediately to sell the product.

In the first of these *Judging from* would be more appropriate. The second would be better with *As a result of* or *Acting on*.

5.6.5   Participles of intransitive verbs

Another problem with participles is that intransitive verbs (see 5.3) have no past participle and the present participle is used instead:

> He said that accidents *occurring* in the home were the commonest cause of injury. The chief problem is accidents *caused* by carelessness.

Accidents can *be caused*, but they cannot be occurred. You can check this by trying it with a relative clause:

> accidents *which occur* in the home ...
>
> accidents *which are caused* by carelessness ...

5.6.6   Present participles with prepositions

As we saw in 5.6.2, a bare present participle can have a causal implication; there is no need for any preposition. Prepositions are only used in front of a present participle when a different sense is needed; *in* and *by* are both possible. There are two slightly different uses for *in*:

> In writing about literature, you should try to support all your points with evidence from the text.
>
> In saying that the story contains no real action, I do not mean that it is boring.

The first example could be paraphrased as "When you are writing about literature ...". It is a generalization. The second example also means something like "When / If I say that ...", but it could be the model for a whole range of sentences in which you want to explain your intention *in* doing something:

> In proposing that we should appoint a new director, I am not implying that the present director is incompetent.

Note that the speaker *has* made the proposal; his purpose now is to explain what the proposal does and does not imply.

By is used when you want to suggest a *method* of doing something:

> By approaching the question from this angle, we can avoid getting bogged down in irrelevant detail.

This could be paraphrased as "Approaching the question from this angle *enables* us to avoid...."

But before using either preposition with the present participle, make sure the preposition is really necessary; often the bare participle is enough.

5.7 Non-verbs

Adjectives cannot function as verbs. Many adjectives however can be added to the verb *to be* to make verbs:

be content with / to, be discontented with
be eager to, be anxious to, be keen to, be happy to
be likely to, be inclined to, be liable to, be apt to
be ready to
be aware of / that, be conscious of / that
be like, be similar to
be called, be known as, be famous for, be wanted for
be worth, be worthwhile
be busy
be afraid of

The common mistake is to omit the verb *to be*:

> ✗ He <u>aware</u> of the problems.
>
> (= He *is* aware of the problems.)

Sometimes students attempt to turn these words into verbs:

✗ It <u>worths</u> doing.

(= It *is* worth doing.)

It is important to distinguish *to like* (an ordinary verb) and *to be like* (*like +
to be = to resemble*):

He likes football. In this he is like his father, who also likes football.

5.8   A few problems of meaning

5.8.1   *Have*

The problem with *have* is that in its ordinary sense of *possess* it does not
have a present continuous:

She has a Mercedes–Benz.
Q: Why weren't you in class today?
A: I have a cold.

There are however a number of slightly idiomatic phrases where *have*
means something more like *take*:

I'm having lunch with Eve tomorrow.
Can you call back later? She's having a bath.

Probably the best way to recognize these is to see that there is a kind of
active element in their meaning, i.e. they imply not just passively owning
something (e.g. a Mercedes–Benz) but *doing* something, or suffering something (e.g. a cold).

Don't however confuse this rule of thumb with the grammatical active/pas-
sive distinction, because the second kind of *have* is also found in idiomatic
expressions with passive force like the following:

She is having her hair permed.
They are having central heating installed.

The rule of thumb seems to work fairly well for idiomatic expressions like:

She is having a Mercedes–Benz for her birthday.

> I am having a few friends over to dinner on Friday.

These mean respectively that someone is going to give her a Mercedes for her birthday and I have invited a few friends to dinner on Friday. Neither refers to anything like mere possession.

More problematic are these, which seem to be on the borderline between the two meanings of *have*:

> She is having second thoughts about it.
> She is having a lot of luck lately.

I think these just have to be regarded as idioms.

5.8.2 *Get*

The important point about *get* is that it means something like *obtain* and cannot be used as a synonym for *have*. A sentence like "he got a new car", tells us that he went out and bought one, not simply that he owns one. The confusion probably occurs because in colloquial English *has got* is commonly used instead of *has*, meaning *possess*. You may also find that in written versions of non-standard English speech (of relatively uneducated or non-native speakers) *has got* is abbreviated to *got*. Consequently there are two possible meanings for the following:

> He got a car.

In standard English this can only mean something like "He went and bought a car", but in some forms of non-standard English it can also mean simply "He has a car". Similarly in informal and non-standard speech "I've got to go" becomes "I got to go", sometimes written "I gotta go" to increase the impression of informality.

Needless to say, you should not use *got* for *has* or *got to* for *have to* in formal writing (*has got* is permissible, but still relatively informal).

5.8.3 *Doubt* and *wonder*

The problem with *doubt* is one of meaning. Its usual meaning is not that you are doubtful about something, but that you think something will not happen:

> I doubt if / whether he will come.

(= I think he will not come.)

Note that it is usually followed by *if* or *whether* (*that* is possible but rather literary and unusual). If your meaning is really that you are *uncertain* if he will come or not, you should say:

> I wonder if he will come.

5.8.4   *Persuade, find*

The meaning of certain verbs includes the idea of successful completion:

> She *persuaded* me to cancel my trip to London.

(= I cancelled my trip to London, because of what she said.)

> After looking for my glasses for half an hour, I *found* them on my desk.

It is not very normal to use such verbs in a continuous tense. If a student writes "She was finding her glasses", she probably means "She was *looking for* her glasses". If a student writes "She was persuading me to go" she probably means "She was *trying to persuade* me to go."

5.8.5   *Feel, seem, look, sound, prove,* etc.

This small group of verbs resemble *to be*, because they can be followed immediately by an adjective complement, or sometimes a noun phrase (see 7.3.8):

> It sounds good.
> She seems a wonderful person.
> It tastes wonderful.

A particular problem arises with *feel* because students forget that a following adjective must refer back to the subject. Here there is no problem:

> The readers feel surprised.

It is the readers, obviously, who are surprised. But consider this:

> The readers feel unrealistic.

It is the readers who are unrealistic, but this is not what the writer meant. The writer was criticizing a literary work, and what she intended to say was: "The readers feel *it is* unrealistic". In other words, "unrealistic" was meant to apply to the literary work, but instead the writer makes us wonder if the *readers* think they are turning into ghosts.

The important point then is to distinguish clearly between (1) *feel + adjective / noun* and (2) *feel + (that) + noun clause*

> He feels a fool.
>
> (*he himself* is a fool)
>
> He feels foolish.
>
> (*he himself* is foolish)
>
> He feels it is a tragedy.
>
> (something else is a tragedy)
>
> He feels it is tragic.
>
> (something else is tragic)

A slightly different case is *prove* which is normally transitive, but can be used intransitively with a slightly different meaning:

> His attempt proved a failure.
>
> We took umbrellas, but in the end they proved unnecessary.

The meaning is something like "turned out to be", and this really has nothing to do with providing proof or proving, so it is inappropriate to use a passive:

> ✗ His attempt <u>was proved</u> a failure.

5.8.6   *Apply*

The verb *apply* has some meanings that get confused. Part of the problem is that it can be both transitive and intransitive. In the transitive form you apply a word or term to a situation etc.:

> We should not apply the term "tragedy" just to any story which has an unhappy ending.
>
> The word "tragic" is often applied to any serious accident, but that is not its true meaning.

In its intransitive meaning *apply* is typically used in talking about regulations:

> The rule that no grade will be given unless all course work is completed *applies to* all students.

In this sense *apply* is often used of critical judgements or opinions:

> *Othello* is a tragedy because the hero commands our respect but is destroyed by a fatal flaw in his character. The same applies to *Macbeth*.

5.9   Writing about speaking

This deserves a section to itself because the business of reporting what people say, or reporting their views, plays such an important part in literary and linguistic analysis, as well as in other more everyday activities like news reporting:

> A spokesman for the White House *said* today that the President is about to announce his new policy.
>
> Romeo *tells* Juliet that he loves her.
>
> The critic, N. Z. Parker, *suggests* that the work is an allegory.

Verbs with approximately the same meaning as *say* are likely to be needed not only for reporting news, but also for summarizing what characters say in a story, for referring to what critics say about the story, and even for expressing what the story "says" to us as readers or what words "say" to us as speakers (i.e. comprehenders) of the language. The same words may be needed for describing people's ways of speaking and their intentions in speaking. In linguistic analysis, such words may be needed for naming speech acts.

5.9.1 Some problems with verbs of speaking

Unfortunately there are a large number of problems here, both in the meanings and implications of such verbs, and in the structures that go with them.

5.9.1a Implied meanings

Some verbs of speaking imply something special either about the manner of speaking or about the extent to which you accept what is said as true. Consider the following list:

tell someone, state, point out, assert, argue, suggest, claim, allege, imply, explain, indicate, reveal, disclose, mention, add, complain

Grammatically these can all be substituted for *says* in this sentence:

> The critic, F. R. Leavis, *says* that Jane Austen and George Eliot are major English novelists.

But there would be the following differences:

tells us, states   more or less neutral.

points out   he and you both think it is unquestionably true.

asserts, argues   Leavis presents arguments for his view.

suggests   *he* is not certain.

claims, alleges   *you* are not sure if he is right.

implies   he does not say it directly but you are reading between the lines.

explains   he knows something you don't.

reveals, discloses   it was a fact previously kept secret.

indicates   he gives signs from which we can deduce that he thinks this.

adds   you have already mentioned some other view of his.

mentions   he says it in the course of discussing something else and also you accept it as a fact.

complains   the idea is probably true but he doesn't like it.

There are a number of particular dangers to beware of:

(a) *tell* must normally be followed by an object, so "He tells <u>that</u> ..." should be something like "He tells *us* that...."
(b) *point out* and *mention* introduce statements you consider factual and should not be used to refer to matters of opinion. *Mention* also implies a certain casualness, and cannot be used in describing the main point of someone's speech.
(c) there are a number of words not included in the list which cannot be followed by a *that* clause (see 5.9.1b).
(d) *talk* and *speak* are not included here because they cannot be used at all in this way; they can only describe the fact and manner of someone's speaking, not what he said:

> She spoke fluently. She spoke for nearly an hour.

Other words that could be substituted above are:

show, prove, demonstrate, establish

These all mean that he gives support for his view and imply that you accept it. It is quite common to use them in the present perfect tense:

> F. R. Leavis *has shown* that Jane Austen and George Eliot are major English novelists.

You could also substitute any of the verbs which describe thinking:

think, believe, consider, assume, agree, accept, be convinced realize, understand, etc.

Under some circumstances, e.g. reporting a meeting — these would imply speaking:

> The chairman *agreed* that it was not profitable to discuss this issue at the present time.

5.9.1b   No *that* clause

A number of verbs describe ways of speaking and / or the intentions of the speaker, but could not be substituted above because they cannot introduce a *that* clause:

criticize, blame, reproach, praise, accuse, express, speak, utter

The first four have a special construction which can be used instead of a *that* clause:

> Amanda blames Tom *for not caring* enough about his sister.

There is a special construction also for *accuse*:

> Amanda *accuses Tom of being* selfish.

The others can only be followed by a noun or pronoun:

> Liza utters a strange sound.
> Higgins expresses his disgust at the way she speaks English.
> Fred does not express himself well.

It is possible to use some of these "no-*that*-clause" verbs in reporting people's views if you add some word like *view*:

> F. R. Leavis *expresses the view* that Jane Austen is a major English novelist.
> F. R. Leavis *criticizes the view* that Dickens is the most important English novelist.

Similarly, there are verbs of thinking, like *misunderstand, regard,* that cannot introduce *that* clauses:

> Amanda misunderstands. She thinks Jim is coming specially to see Laura.
> She thinks, wrongly, that Jim is coming specially to see Laura.
> She mistakenly supposes that / believes that / imagines that ...

Notice that there is no short-cut — you cannot use *misunderstands* in place of *thinks* to introduce a *that* clause. You can however say more about the circumstances in which the misunderstanding occurs:

> Amanda misunderstands *when* Tom tells her he has invited a friend to dinner.

There are also a few very descriptive verbs which occur often in fiction but which are not likely to be used in formal reports. These are used rather for describing the manner in which people speak:

shout, yell, cry, whisper, mutter, murmur, grumble, etc.

5.9.1c Verbs of ordering, requesting

Verbs of ordering / requesting, which involve getting the hearer to do something, vary in the constructions they can fit into:

tell, order, command, require, forbid, ask, request, invite, advise, suggest, propose, demand, insist

The standard construction is:

> Amanda asks Tom not to go out so much.

Unfortunately this construction is not available for the last four verbs:

> Amanda suggests *that Tom should not go* out so much.

Notice that these verbs cannot normally be followed immediately by a human object, so "She suggests <u>him</u> ..." is always wrong.

5.9.2   Quoting

Direct quotation of someone's words is not introduced with *that*. The best way is to use a comma or a colon:

> ✗ She said <u>that</u> "I don't know what you are talking about."
>
> (= She said, "I don't know what you are talking about.")

5.9.3   Referring to someone's speech act

Many verbs of speaking have convenient noun forms, which sometimes can introduce noun clauses:

> In reply to X's accusation / claim / complaint that ...

But note that there is not a convenient noun form of *say* (the noun *saying* has another meaning, more or less synonymous with *proverb*).

Tom is irritated by Amanda's words / speech.

Tom is irritated by what Amanda says.

5.9.4 Reporting on naming or referring

You may want to discuss the actual way in which one character describes another or speaks to another:

Higgins calls Liza "a baggage".

Higgins refers *to* Liza *as* "a baggage"

Higgins uses the word "baggage" to refer to Liza.

Higgins describes Liza *as* a "baggage".

Notice that *call* is *NOT* followed by *as*, and *refer* must be followed by both *to* and *as*.

More generally you can describe behaviour:

He treats her like a servant.

He treats her with contempt.

He treats her as an inferior.

He treats her as if she were not human.

His treatment of Liza is inhumane.

His behaviour towards Liza is inhumane.

Notice that there is a slight difference between *treats her like* (= as if she were ...) and *treats her as* (= she is a servant).

You can describe his way of thinking about her:

He considers her inferior.

He regards her as inferior.

He sees her as inferior.

He thinks *of* her as inferior.

Again, notice that *consider* is not followed by *as*, while *think* is usually followed by *of* and *as*.

<u>5.10</u>   Verbs and prepositions

The problem can be omitting prepositions when they are needed, but it can also be putting in prepositions when they are not needed.

<u>5.10.1</u>   Verbs which must be followed by a preposition

Here are some verbs which cause problems:

listen to, interfere with, discriminate against / between, object to, agree to / with, sympathize with, comment on

If the verb requires a preposition, the preposition cannot be omitted when the verb is used transitively:

> Even in advanced societies like America, women still complain that they are being discriminated *against*.
>
> · Women object *to* being treated as sex objects.

The preposition can only be omitted when the verb is used intransitively:

> The boss said I had to go and gave me no chance to object.

Students tend to forget about the preposition when the verb occurs in a question or relative clause:

> Which of the characters do you sympathize *with*?
>
> Why are women still discriminated *against*?
>
> What is the name of that piece of music (which) you were listening *to*?
>
> He developed some habits which his father objected *to*.

The relative clause can alternatively be written as "… that piece of music *to which* you were listening"; "… habits *to which* his father objected". In old-fashioned grammar books this latter form was preferred, since it was said that you should not put a preposition at the end of a sentence. Nowadays this rule is no longer followed. It generally sounds more natural to put the preposition at the end.

There are two meanings of *agree*:

He agreed *with* his colleagues.

(= had the same opinion)

He agreed *to* the proposal.

(= accepted)

5.10.2   Verbs (surprisingly) without prepositions

Some verbs surprise students by not having prepositions:

discuss, emphasize, lack, match, marry, mention, oppose, regret, resemble

Her hat resembled a Christmas tree.

She regretted not having asked him to help her.

These two expressions do not match.

Her handbag matches her shoes.

He lacks experience. His lack of experience is a handicap.

Sometimes there is confusion because a preposition is needed when the word is used in adjective or noun form, or because another expression with the same meaning has a preposition:

They *were opposed to* my plan.

The *emphasis* is *on* self-sufficiency

Her handbag *goes well with* her shoes.

He is *lacking in* experience.

5.10.3   *Make* and *let*

Both *make* and *let* are followed by an infinitive without *to*:

My boss made me work overtime.

My boss let me go home early.

Notice that *let* can normally only be used for something you have requested to do or want to do, or in cases where you are blaming the person who lets something happen: "He almost let me drown".

It sounds quite ironic therefore if you say:

> He let me do all his work.

It is surely unlikely that the speaker really wanted to do all of someone else's work. The irony could be emphasized like this:

> He very kindly let me do all his work.

It is possible to substitute *cause to* for *make* and *allow to* for *let* but note that these require *to*:

> The recession caused them *to* lose a lot of money.
> The holiday allowed me *to* catch up on my correspondence.

5.11   Infinitive or gerund?

The infinitive is commonly used after certain verbs like *want*, *decide*, *hope*, *plan*, *intend*, *try*, etc:

> We decided *to* do it.

The gerund (the *-ing* form) is used after prepositions or verbs which normally take a preposition and after *avoid*, *cannot help*, etc:

> She is interested in writing.
> I can't help envying her.

Confusion can arise partly because *to* usually goes with the infinitive, as in "We decided to do it", but in some cases it is a preposition attached to the verb, as with *look forward to*:

> We look forward to seeing you on Saturday.

A number of verbs (e.g. *like*) can take either infinitive or gerund, but the meaning is sometimes slightly different:

> She likes swimming.
> She likes to get up early and go for a walk.

The *-ing* form often seems to have a somewhat more general sense: there is nothing here to tell us if she actually goes swimming, even though we know she likes it. The *to* form is somewhat more specific: there is a strong implication that she actually does get up early and go for a walk.

Verbs of sense perception, particularly *hear* and *see*, can be followed either by an *-ing* form or by a bare infinitive without *to*. There is often a slight difference in meaning:

> At 4.00 a.m. I heard him come in. I heard him stumbling about drunkenly downstairs. Then I heard him climbing the stairs. I heard him trip over the dog and curse. Two hours later I heard his alarm go off.

The difference in meaning is approximately equivalent to the difference between simple and continuous tenses. The *-ing* form can only be used for something which lasts a certain length of time. When the emphasis is on something which happens relatively quickly or suddenly, the bare infinitive is more appropriate. Compare these:

> I saw her coming down the street towards me.
>
> I saw her come into the room.

6

Nouns

Traditionally, nouns are said to be the names of things. This idea actually creates some problems, because it is not so easy to know what a thing is: fire, a finger, the sky, a city, a stock exchange, a poem, music, a pig, a rainbow — what do all these have in common, apart from the fact that they are all nouns? And then again, there seem to be "things" that we do not have a name for. It's a frequently quoted linguistic example that Eskimoes have different names for kinds of snow and Arabic speakers have many words for camels, whereas to English-speakers all camels are just camels, and snow is just snow (except to winter sports enthusiasts perhaps). Though this is probably an exaggeration, some languages certainly have names for things that are not named in other languages. To some extent the way we actually view our environment and the way we divide it into a collection of separate "things" seems to be related to the nouns we have available for naming these "things".

However, I don't intend here either to discuss reality or to define grammatical terms. My aim is simply to draw your attention to some facts about English nouns.

6.1 Count and non-count

English nouns, unless they are proper nouns (i.e. names of people or places) are either count nouns or non-count nouns. The distinction is a difficult but important part of English grammar. It does seem in some ways to affect the way English speakers analyse their environment. To give just one example, *a wood* (count noun) is a group of trees, and probably every speaker of

English can summon up some kind of picture of a typical wood (think of Robert Frost's poem beginning "Whose woods these are I think I know"). But *wood* (non-count noun) is a material and you cannot picture it; you can only picture things that are made of wood, like tables, chairs, or planks.

The grammatical rules are simple (but easy to forget).

Count	**Non-count**
a table	*strength* (NB no article)
tables	no plural
the table(s)	*the strength of ten men* (NB no plural)
many table(s)	*much strength* (NB singular agreement)

None of this applies to proper nouns (names of people or places) which cannot normally be modified in any way, though you may occasionally find them treated as if they were ordinary nouns:

> There are two *Evas* in my class.
>
> (= There are two people called Eva in my class.)

> Is that *the* Eva Wong I know?
>
> (= Is that the person called Eva Wong that I know?)

> There is only *one* Paris.
>
> (= Paris is unique.)

> *A* Van Gogh.
>
> (= a painting by Van Gogh.)

> There is *a* Mr Smith to see you.
>
> (= I don't know him but he says he is called Smith.)

The important points are:

(a) a singular count noun cannot occur alone, without an article or some equivalent determiner (*this*, *our*, etc.):

> *A dog* is an animal.

(an exception is when you refer to the word only, not the thing it represents: "Dog" has three letters.)

(b) a non-count noun cannot occur with the indefinite article, nor does it occur with *the* when it is used in a general sense:

> Hard work and persistence are essential to success.

(c) different quantifiers are used with count and non-count nouns: *many / much, few / little, fewer / less, such a / such*:

> *many years, much time*
> *few hours, little time*
> *such an event, such courage*

The following are therefore not correct because they contravene the rule in (a):

> ✗ Dog is an animal.
> ✗ Advertisement can be seen everywhere.

Note however that in lecture notes, recipes, stage directions and other informal uses of English, it is acceptable to omit articles: "Tom crosses to *fire-escape*, stage left". In an essay referring to the play, the article should not be omitted unless the stage direction is directly quoted: "We are told in a stage direction that Tom goes to *the* fire-escape".

The following are also not correct, because they contravene the second part of the rule in (b):

> ✗ Wordsworth writes about the nature.
> ✗ She studies the history.

And the following contravenes the rule in (c), though it might be heard in informal speech:

> ✗ I have less friends than James.

(In fact there is an example of this incorrect form in the slogan "Use less plastic bags" which is quite widespread in Hong Kong at present.)

In relatively informal English the problem of different quantifiers can be avoided by using *a lot of* which can quantify non-count nouns as well as plural count nouns:

> We have *a lot of problems*, and these problems are likely to cause us *a lot of trouble*.

It is more formal to use *many* with count nouns: "We have many problems". It is not so easy to know how to quantify non-count nouns in a more formal style. If you use *much* it sounds literary and slightly old-fashioned. For the general style of reports and written papers, it is more usual to find *a good deal of, a considerable amount of* or some variant of these:

> These problems are likely to cause us a considerable amount of trouble.

In cases where you want to quantify a noun more vaguely, you can use *some* with both non-count and plural count nouns:

> There is some milk in the refrigerator.
>
> There are *some students* to see you.

6.1.1   Distinguishing count and non-count nouns

The real problem, however, is not learning the rules, but knowing which kind of noun is which. The rule of thumb for classifying nouns as count or non-count is that non-count nouns are abstract ideas (*strength, education*) and substances or materials (*coffee, silk, steel*).

Like most rules of thumb, this can be helpful but also confusing. After all, what could be more abstract than *an idea*? — and yet *idea* is a count noun.

Another suggested distinction is that non-count nouns cannot be directly pictured: if they are abstract they have no visible form, only events or scenes which might symbolize them (try picturing *courage*, or *love*, or even *childhood*); if they are substances any picture you make will be a picture of something else as well (i.e. for *wood*, a wooden table or a wooden plank, etc).

But again, how do you picture *an idea*? Or take the word *thought*: as a non-count noun it refers to the process of thinking; but it can also be a count noun, as in "A thought suddenly came into my mind". There are in fact many nouns which can be either count or non-count and the status of a noun

— as count or non-count — is not established by its meaning, though it does affect the meaning.

It may help to give some sort of meaning to the count / non-count distinction if we consider how some nouns which can be either count or non-count change their meaning accordingly:

coffee   a drink and the substance from which it is made, takes the shape of whatever container it is poured into.

a coffee   a cup of coffee.

football   a game, has rules and teams and techniques but no shape.

a football   the round object used in the game, frequently kicked.

fish   something you eat, no characteristic shape, depends on how it is cooked.

a fish   something which swims in water, various characteristic shapes.

We can perhaps assume, then, that to speak of "an idea" or "a thought" is to treat the workings of our minds as if they involve single, separate entities (i.e. *ideas*, *thoughts*) which enter and leave them. It is interesting that emotions are usually non-count and we typically treat them more as if they were some kind of indivisible liquid: "Love suddenly flooded his heart".

Trying to think about the count / non-count distinction may help you in distinguishing words which are often confused like:

poetry, drama   kinds of writing, kinds of literature

a poem, a play   particular examples of this kind of writing, usually printed on paper or performed

advertising   a profession or industry in which people work

an advertisement   a specific text in the newspaper, on TV, etc.

Notice however that there are some words students make mistakes with because they have never properly learnt their meaning: *an alphabet*, for instance, is a normal count noun. The problem is not with its status as a count noun, but with its meaning: it means the complete set of letters used for writing a language; it does NOT mean just one letter. So English, for example, has only *one* alphabet. Similarly, *vocabulary* (which can be count or non-count, but is seldom used in the plural) means the complete set of words in a language, or the set of words used in a particular text; it does not mean just one word.

6.1.2   Singular or plural?

It is not always easy to know whether to use a noun in the singular or the plural. And there are some nouns which look singular (i.e. no "s") but are actually plural — or vice versa. You may have noticed that Robert Frost's poem speaks of *woods*, in the plural. Why? The answer seems to be that "a wood" is fairly small and covers a limited area, with a defined edge (you can see this implied in the proverbial idiom, "not able to see the wood for the trees" — you can see a lot of trees, but you can't, as it were, get outside them in order to take in the object which is composed of them: the wood). If the trees occupy more space — imagine them perhaps spreading across several hills and valleys, with some clear spaces in between — they become "woods". In fact it is slightly more complicated. In England "a wood" is likely to have a local name, like Black Dog Wood, or Birnam Wood (which plays a famous walk-on part in Shakespeare's *Macbeth*). You can buy very large-scale maps in England which mark and name local features like woods, hills and valleys, and for many people (particularly many nineteenth century poets and novelists) these natural features seem to have individual characters as well as names. But if you want to suggest a generalized scene you will speak of *the woods*. And Robert Frost generalizes the idea even more in the title of his poem: "Stopping by Woods on a Snowy Evening." He drops the article in the title, though not in the poem itself.

Well, you can ignore all this if you wish to, because there is no grammatical problem with the word so long as you don't confuse it with the non-count noun referring to a material (*wood*).

Here, however, are some words that do cause problems.

6.1.2a   Group nouns

Some singular nouns refer to groups of people and can have either singular or plural agreement: *government, jury, committee, army, class, couple, audience, etc.*

A new government *has* been elected.

Our class *are* having a party on Saturday.

The class *meets* on Mondays.

The committee *were* not all in agreement.

The couple *are* having dinner in a restaurant.

At the end of a performance, the audience usually *applaud.*

There are perhaps three points to notice here.

(a) These words can be used to describe *one* group of people; they can then have plural or singular agreement, depending on whether the context seems to stress the individuality of the members or the unity of the institution; in this case, the definite article is often used, even in a general statement such as the last example, about "*the* audience". (I think however *couple* almost always has plural agreement.)

(b) The words can also be used in the plural to refer to several such groups, in generalizing about such groups, or sometimes to refer to something different:

Classes begin on Monday.

(Not a group of people, but "lessons")

Governments sometimes make mistakes.

Any actor will tell you that audiences vary a great deal. No two audiences are the same.

(c) they cannot be used to refer to a single person, e.g. you cannot say "He is an army". To refer to a single person you must add a word like *member* or use a completely different word:

a committee member, a member of the audience, a soldier,
one partner (a couple = two partners)

Note that there may be other features of the context which make it desirable to use, say, plural agreement rather than singular:

His audience *were* concerned about the safety of *their* children.

It would be awkward to use *was* because of the later pronoun, *their*. And probably *its children* will sound awkward, so it is best to use plural throughout.

6.1.2b   Troublesome non-count nouns

Some which cause frequent problems are: *behaviour, information, advice, equipment, news, weather, furniture, slang, jargon, evidence.*

> No news is good news.

(Singular agreement, but in Shakespeare's time it was plural.)

> She studies the behaviour of monkeys in captivity.

(more than one monkey, but behaviour remains singular because it is non-count)

Normally the only grammatical way to quantify such words is by adding another noun like *type, kind, item, piece*:

an unusual type of behaviour
an interesting piece of news
an important item of information

But beware! Do NOT use these extra nouns with count nouns (e.g. it is correct to say *an advertisement*, NOT a piece of advertisement).

6.1.2c   Surprising plural agreement

These are singular nouns with usually plural agreement: *staff, police*

> Our staff *are* trained to be polite to customers.
> The police *are* investigating.

These two, *staff* and *police*, are very widely misused in Hong Kong: *a staff* cannot mean one person, it must mean a group. If you want to quantify these words you should use *member of staff* and *policeman / police officer.*

6.1.2d   Nouns formed from *adjective + the*

Words like *the poor, the wealthy,* and names of nationalities like *the English, the Chinese, etc.* always have plural agreement even though there is no "s" plural:

> The chief problem with the world today is that the rich are getting richer but the poor are not getting any less poor.

> The French are famous for their cooking.

Note however that the words ending in *-an* and some others do have the "s": *the Americans, the Russians, the Norwegians, the Greeks.*

There is also a difference when you use these words for nationality to refer to a single person. With the first group there is usually no indefinite article:

> I am Chinese, she is English.
>
> He is (an) American, she is (an) Italian.

You cannot say <u>an English</u>, and it sounds slightly odd to say <u>a Chinese</u> (though some people do).

6.1.2e Different count and non-count meanings

A great many words have distinguishable general and specific meanings according to whether they are used as count nouns or non-count nouns. Here are just some: *crime, quality, competition, experience, shelter, chance, exercise, opportunity.*

> Crime is on the increase.
>
> (non-count, general term)
>
> If you drive a car under the influence of drink you are committing a crime.
>
> (count, a specific instance)

The distinction in meaning is sometimes very clear, sometimes not so clear. For example, *a competition* generally has a name and rules — you enter it, and if you are lucky you win it and get a prize or a title like "Miss Hong Kong". This is something different from *competition*, which is a key factor in capitalism and one of the reasons why people feel there is a lot of pressure in Hong Kong.

An experience is something interesting which happens to you on a particular occasion; *experience* is what you may need if you want to be considered for a job.

On its own, *chance* means something like *fate* or *destiny*. Some people do not believe that chance governs our lives. With the article, *a chance* is the same as *an opportunity*, and refers to a particular moment when it becomes possible for you to succeed at something:

> I had a chance, but I missed it.
>
> If you get a chance to speak to Eric Clapton, ask him for some tips on how to play the guitar.

As a non-count noun, *opportunity* can be used as an abstract term for being given a chance to succeed, something politicians talk a lot about in modern democratic countries:

> We shall build a society of equal opportunity.

6.1.2f   Similar count and non-count meanings

There are some words which can be used both as count and non-count nouns with very similar meanings. Sometimes the difference is part of an idiom: *trouble, thought, choice, effort, life, society, enemy, success, failure.*

Thank you for taking so much trouble.	Troubles never come singly.
Thought (= thinking) is often painful.	An interesting thought.
You haven't any choice.	There are two choices.
It requires a lot of effort.	He made a big effort.
She enjoys life to the full.	She leads an easy life.

There seems to be a slippery distinction between *trouble* and *troubles*, created by the grammar alone, because the basic sense is more or less the same. Both *trouble* and *troubles* are something you don't want but generally have to accept. But what you do *for* others is *take trouble* (non-count), what you do *to* others is *cause* or *give trouble* (non-count), while what comes to you more or less by chance or fate is *troubles* (count).

Normally you can count your *enemies*; there may be no one, or just one person in the world, whom you consider *an enemy*. But in war enemies seem to become institutionalized, and you speak always of *the enemy*, which behaves like the nouns in 6.1.2a — the agreement can be singular but is more often plural.

6.1.2g Some surprising count nouns

Some words which seem very abstract are used as count nouns with a relatively concrete sense: *a future, a past, a present.*

> I think she has a wonderful future.

> (= approximately, she has a promising career ahead of her)

> He has a shady past.

> (= approximately, he has done something criminal)

These words are not in fact often used as fully abstract non-count nouns, but the above use can be contrasted with *the future, the past, the present* (presumably the definite article because these are relative always to the human speaker — see 6.2.1, 6.2.4).

6.1.2h Usually plural

Some words are usually or often plural: *surroundings, goods (=merchandise), belongings (= possessions).*

> The chameleon changes colour to blend with its *surroundings.*

There is no normal singular form of *goods, surroundings* or *belongings.* If you do ever meet *a good*, it will probably be in philosophical discussion and mean something like "a good thing rather than a bad thing" (nothing to do with merchandise).

6.1.2i Usually plural in one meaning

Some words are generally plural in one of their meanings: *rights, relations, feelings, manners, results, conditions, circumstances, qualifications, authorities.*

Human rights, women's rights.	A right to express our opinions.
Foreign relations, good relations.	Crime bears *a* relation to poverty.
You hurt his feelings.	A feeling of alienation.
In such *circumstances* ...	*An* interesting circumstance
She has good manners.	In *a* strange manner.
Her exam results were good.	*An* important result.

Note that *the authorities* is another way of referring to the government. The singular form, e.g. *the Television Licensing Authority*, seems to be typical of Hong Kong and is relatively unusual in the U.K.

6.1.2j Special plurals

Some words are plural though they seem to refer to a single object: *clothes*, *scissors*, *trousers*, etc.

> Where *are* my clothes?

These are quite well-known and should not cause problems.

6.1.3   *The majority, a majority*

This is plural because it stands for *the majority of (plural noun)*. You might also meet *a majority* as an ordinary count noun (singular) meaning the amount by which the votes or seats of one political party exceed those of the others: "The government had a small majority".

6.1.4   *One of …*

Finally, on the subject of singular and plural, note that the pattern *one of the (noun) / one of the most (adjective + noun)* requires the noun to be in the plural and can only be used with count nouns:

> One of my *friends* says she has seen a ghost.
>
> I believe her, because she is one of the least superstitious *people* I know.

6.2   Grammar and meaning

The interesting point is that a grammatical sub-system like this is creative. Although I said that nouns are either count or non-count, the distinction is not fixed to the word but is part of the way it is used in a particular context with a particular meaning. If you care to look back in this book, you will find that in 2.4.2. I have mentioned *quotation* sometimes with an article and sometimes without. You should be able to work out what the difference is.

Sometimes new meanings can be created by altering the normal count or non-count status of a noun.

For example, there is a tendency for nouns that are common in the technical vocabulary of professional groups etc. to change their status:

> The two subjects exhibited contrasting behaviours.
>
> (*behaviours* = patterns of behaviour, in psychology talk or the jargon of psychology)

Listening to the TV commercials, you can often hear normally non-count nouns used with an article or in the plural:

> What do you expect from *a* mineral water?
>
> (= a *brand* of mineral water)
>
> The nation which is famous for its great beers.
>
> (= its brands of beer)

Similarly, you may come across a singular count noun used without an article (something which I said above is not correct [6.1], except in notes, recipes and other forms of writing where abbreviation is permissible). The effect seems to be to turn the noun into something like a proper noun: e.g. in "Cat goes walking in the night", it seems that *Cat* is a name. You can find examples like this sometimes in poetry.

Another possible effect, of course, is that a non-standard form of English is being represented. Many non-native speakers of English are inclined to omit articles! You might find this in a play or novel, where the character is supposed to be speaking non-standard English. But it will probably be a non-native-speaker form of English because native speakers do not omit articles.

(Yorkshire dialect, however — from northern England — is represented as abbreviating the definite article to the extent that it might sound as if it has not been pronounced: "Put it on't table" = put it on *the* table. You can find other examples in Emily Bronte's *Wuthering Heights*.)

There is an interesting example of a count noun used as a non-count noun in William Golding's *Lord of the Flies*, chapter 4. The boys are trying for the first time to cook meat on a fire, and are not entirely successful:

> In the end they skewered bits of meat on branches and held them in the flames: and even then almost as much *boy* was roasted as meat.

You will notice that *boy*, a count noun, is being used here in the singular as if it were a non-count noun. The effect is to make it sound exactly like *meat* or *pork*, and to give it the meaning of *flesh of a boy*, just as *pork* means *flesh of a pig*.

Another example is the group nouns in 6.1.2a, which you cannot use with an indefinite article to refer to one person: "He is an army" has to be "He is a soldier / an army officer" or "He is in the army". But suppose you come across this:

> She is the committee.

The implication may be either that she is very autocratic and takes decisions without consulting anyone else, or that she dominates the committee she is a member of. Similarly, "He is a good audience" implies that he listens to you with interest and understanding, as actors or public speakers hope the audience will listen to them.

It is worth stressing the relation between grammar and meaning, because otherwise for the learner distinctions like this one between count and non-count are simply extremely tiresome. It is helpful if you can see that they enable different things to be said.

6.2.1   Articles — definite or indefinite?

Whether or not to use the indefinite article depends basically on the count / non-count status of the noun, though this in turn is related to meaning. Whether or not to use the definite article is essentially a question of meaning.

One way to look at the terms *definite* and *indefinite* is to say that they correspond approximately in meaning to *specific* and *general*, terms which are used to describe ideas.

The basic rules for the definite article are:

(1) use *the* before nouns which refer to something unique, as in *the sun*.
(2) Use *the* before something which has been mentioned before: "She bought a dress. *The* dress was...."
(3) Use *the* with a noun, count or non-count, which is made relatively specific by a modifier either before or after it: thus, the general term *industry* becomes **the** *textile industry*, **the** *construction industry*, etc., the general term *manufacture* becomes **the** *manufacture of textiles*, and the general, abstract term *courage* becomes **the** *courage displayed by Sergius*.

This difference between general and specific, signalled by the difference between *a* and *the* can be extremely important for our understanding of a text. For example, in *Arms and the Man*, Act I, Bluntschli describes for Raina's benefit *a* cavalry charge. He tells her how there is usually one man in front, and that man is desperately pulling on his horse because it is running away with him — he does not want to arrive first, alone, and be killed by the enemy. Raina, whose fiancé, Sergius, has just won a battle by leading *the* cavalry charge, is offended by this explanation because it implies that Bluntschli thinks Sergius was not really brave. But this is not what Bluntschli meant. He was not describing *the* cavalry charge (the one led by Sergius), but *a* cavalry charge. He was not speaking of Sergius, but of the leader in *any* cavalry charge. The point hinges here on the difference between *a* and *the*, between general and specific.

Ironically, Bluntschli's theory about cavalry charges is wrong in this case, because Sergius really is the kind of person who would want to arrive first in order to win the battle for his country and gain glory. Bluntschli's view of war and cavalry charges is probably right in general, but he is wrong in this specific instance, because Sergius is an exception to his rule.

6.2.2   Wrong use of *the* in general statements

A common problem is the incorrect use of *the* in generalizations:

✗ The small children need love.

✗ The neglected wives should divorce their husbands.

If these refer to specific cases, they may be true. But the reader will want to know *which* small children you are referring to, and *which* neglected wives. If what you intend is a general statement, the article must be omitted:

> Small children need love.
>
> Neglected wives should divorce their husbands.

Note the difference between these and modified nouns which become specific under my rule 3 above. *Neglected wives* still refers to a whole group of people rather than to specific cases. By contrast, *the textile industry* singles out a particular branch of industry. It is possible however to reverse the status of these two examples. In a report on wives you might divide them into different groups and speak of ***the** neglected wives* as opposed to *the contented wives*, and one might want to say something like "Britain no longer has *an* important textile industry".

Or you might compare the first example above with the following:

> In *Lord of the Flies* we can divide the children into two groups, *the small children*, known as "the littluns", who do not have individual personalities, and the older boys, who are clearly differentiated.

Notice that there is a similar difference between *most* and *most of the* …:

> *Most* first-year students find it hard to organize their time.

You use *most* in a generalization. You would be likely to use *most of the* if you had done a survey and were comparing different groups:

> *Most of the* first-year students complain of having too much work, whereas *most of the* third-year students complain of boredom.

6.2.3   Nouns which can be count or non-count

Nouns like *war* can be a problem. *War* is often a count noun and if the reference is specific you will get something like:

> *The* war lasted five years.

But it can also be a non-count noun, and in a general statement there will be no definite article:

War causes suffering to everyone.

There are a number of nouns like this that occur in literature and linguistics, for example, *dialogue, conversation.*

6.2.4 *The* signifying uniqueness

Another aspect of the meaning of *the* is that it is used to signify uniqueness. It is very difficult however to produce any useful rule about this. A commonly given example is *the sun*, where we use *the* because we generally assume there is only one sun (though astronomers may talk of *a sun*). But often an object seems to be regarded as unique or definite because those to whom it matters know which one is referred to:

> She looked out of the window.
> (She knows which one she is looking out of.)
> He opened the door.
> He won glory on the battlefield.
> She entered the arena.
> She moves so well around the (tennis) court.
> He plays the piano.
> She was reading the newspaper.
> The purpose of comedy is to make the audience laugh.
> (There is only one audience present at a performance of play.)

In some cases the definite article is used because an activity implies an object which is singular (only one of it) and specific so far as the participant is concerned: *moving round **the court***; *playing **the piano***. You might compare *reading the newspaper* with *reading a book*. She is likely to read "the same newspaper" every day, but she doesn't always read the same book. Of course when you think about it, "the same newspaper" means it has the same name, but the newspaper she reads today is not precisely the same as the one she read yesterday or there wouldn't be much point in reading it!

It is worth noticing that these sentences are perfectly grammatical with the indefinite article, though it tends to give them special meanings: "He opened *a door*" seems rather likely to be metaphorical; "she is *playing a trombone*" suggests a situation where someone has just said, "What is that strange instrument she is playing?" rather than "How beautifully she plays!"

6.2.5   *The* with institutions

The definite article is also used with institutions like *the army*, *the government*. Similar, perhaps, is *the arts*, which is used to refer to literature, music, the fine arts and so on all together.

6.2.6   Definite and indefinite article as clues in literature

You may find it quite illuminating if you notice an unusual use of articles when you are trying to interpret a poem. And in all literary texts definite articles may be used in referring to what has NOT been previously mentioned, in order to create the illusion of familiarity, or to encourage us to see the fictitious world through the eyes of the speaker or one of the protagonists:

> He sat in *the* little cafe sipping his beer and thought of *the* woman.

We do not know what little cafe he is sitting in or what woman he is thinking of, but obviously *he* does. This is the way he would refer to them, so we are being encouraged to see through his eyes.

6.2.7   Articles in idioms

Idioms are usually defined as expressions which do not follow normal grammatical rules. This often means that their parts cannot be altered separately. The nouns in them therefore tend to remain unchangeable: always singular or plural, with or without article, etc.

For example, in the idiom *kick the bucket*, which is old-fashioned slang for *die*, only the verb can change. The following are impossible, except as a joke:

✗ They all kicked buckets.

✗ He was about to kick a bucket.

Some other examples:

to lose face

✗ They lost their faces.

to take shelter

✗ He looked for somewhere to take a shelter.

to take the trouble

✗ He always took troubles to explain it to us.

to lose one's temper

✗ They lost some of their tempers.

to make one's way to

✗ They made their ways back to the city.

Often, using articles or plural with the nouns in idioms like these gives them back a literal sense, which sometimes produces a very strange or comic effect.

6.3 Nouns as modifiers

When you use a noun like an adjective in front of another noun, it is usually in the singular:

> Fred is a collector of *butterflies*.
>
> (= Fred is a *butterfly* collector.)
>
> Jim is an inspector of factories.
>
> (= Jim is a factory inspector.)

Students are sometimes confused by the fact that a noun modifier is sometimes used in spite of the fact that an adjective form of the same word exists:

The Education Department
An educational programme.

Sometimes there is no difference in meaning, but here there is. *Educational* contains positive evaluation: it refers to something which has a good effect; the *Education Department* is merely the department which is concerned with education, its name does not try to tell us whether the measures it adopts are successful or not.

Where there is a difference in meaning it will generally be similar to this: the noun will be used to avoid the descriptive, emotional, or evaluative associations of the adjective. Compare:

a horror movie, a horrible movie
the construction industry, a constructive proposal

Sometimes the same kind of distinction between evaluative and non-evaluative can be made between two similar adjectives:

an economic policy

(= a policy for managing the economy)

an economical shopper

(= a shopper who cleverly does not waste money)

6.4   Miscellaneous problems

6.4.1   Certain nouns and adjectives commonly get confused

confidence (noun)
confident (adjective)

There are many other *-ence / -ent* pairs like this. Learn just one of them, with a suitable context, and check against it when you use any of the others.

6.4.2 Many words have more than one noun form

Often one of them refers to a more general or abstract concept, while the other refers to a specific example:

poem / poetry, image / imagery, scene / scenery, symbol / symbolism

> If you want to study *poetry*, you should first read *some poems*.
>
> If you think the imagery of the play is important, you should start by identifying all the images and then consider how they relate to the play's theme or themes.
>
> Shakespeare's plays have many changes of scene, but the Elizabethan theatre made very little use of scenery.

Notice that the more general and abstract word has no plural.

Sometimes the more abstract of two related nouns is derived from a verb, as in the case of *portrait* and *portrayal*:

> Dickens paints a vivid portrait of life in nineteenth century London.
>
> Dickens' portrayal of life in nineteenth century London may be exaggerated but it is essentially true.

A *portrait* is a picture or representation, whereas *portrayal* refers to the technique used in portraying, describing or representing something.

Another pair which causes problems is *character / characteristic:*

a character (1) the distinctive personality of a human individual; (2) the fictitious representation of a human individual.

a characteristic one particular feature or trait of an individual's character.

6.4.3 Some nouns have special plurals

phenomenon, phenomena (plural), *criterion, criteria* (plural).

The word, *media*, is plural, but nowadays people often treat it as if it was also singular (strictly speaking, the singular is *medium*). Uncertainty arises because of the word's meaning: *the media* is a collective term, meaning newspapers, magazines, TV and films. It therefore tends to have both plural and singular agreement like *government*. (6.1.2a)

6.5   Agreement problems in sentences

6.5.1   Mistakes of agreement occur with many of the nouns in 6.1.2

e.g. *police*, which has plural agreement.

6.5.2   Mistakes also occur because the verb is made to agree with the wrong noun in a sentence

✗ The structure of both poems <u>are</u> carefully designed.

✗ The language of the two poems <u>are</u> carefully chosen.

The verb ought to agree with the head noun of each phrase, *structure* and *language* respectively.

But compare …

The rhyme schemes of the two poems are quite different.

This raises another difficult question: when a noun applies to two or more things (like *structure*, *language* and *rhyme schemes* in the above sentences), should it be singular or plural?

As the examples show, there is no fixed answer. It depends on the meaning. If what you are saying is that the two things are *different* in respect of some feature, then it becomes logically uncomfortable to use the singular: that is why I wrote *rhyme schemes*. However, this principle cannot apply in the case of a word like *language*, or you would get:

✗ The languages of the two poems are different.

This could only mean that one poem is written, say, in English, the other in Chinese. It may help you to understand this if you spend a moment thinking about the difference between the words *language, structure* and *rhyme scheme*; for example, *structure* could be singular or plural, because we can think of both poems having *structure* (non-count) or each poem having *a structure* (count).

Similarly, the first of these seems all right, but not the others:

> The backgrounds of the two speakers are quite different.
>
> The childhoods of the two speakers are filled with joyfulness.
>
> The images of the mothers are similar.

In cases like this, where you feel there is an awkwardness that will not go away however much you think about it, the solution is to practise what I can only call linguistic agility; you turn the sentence around till the problem disappears:

> In both cases, the childhood of the speaker is filled with joyfulness.
>
> The image of the mother is similar in both poems.
>
> The rhyme scheme is different in each poem / Each poem has a different rhyme scheme.

You will find that you need to do quite a lot of this turning things around when you are comparing two things.

6.5.3 Notice that *each, everybody / everyone, nobody / no one, anyone* all have singular agreement

> Everyone *knows* this, but nobody *likes* it.

It is however possible to use the plural pronoun (*they, their*) to continue sentences like this to avoid upsetting feminists by using *he, his*.

Usually *what*, in the following type of sentence, also has singular agreement, even when it is followed by more than one noun, phrase or clause:

> What I want to know *is* who she is and where she comes from.

Sometimes *what* can have plural agreement when it represents a number of quite concrete items, but many people still would use singular:

What the little girl found when she came home *was / were* three bears.

6.5.4 There is sometimes a problem deciding whether a noun complement should be singular or plural

They all washed their faces.
They all took the examination.

There's no problem here: they all washed different faces and they all took the same examination. But what about these?

They all had dinner.
They all went to the cinema.
They all played the piano.

They may have all eaten the same dinner, gone to the same cinema and played the same piano, but not necessarily. There seems to be a tendency for the noun to remain singular when it is part of an idiomatic expression, especially one which represents a common activity, e.g. *have dinner, play the piano, go to see the doctor, etc.*

6.6 Nouns followed by prepositions

Nouns often combine in phrases which link two nouns with a preposition:

*the manufacture **of** electronic goods*
*an objection **to** the proposal*
*discrimination **against** foreigners*
*a comment **on** the style*
*a review **of** the play*

What preposition should you use? First note that in all the above the first noun is related to a verb. The general rule to follow is that the preposition will be the one that would follow the related verb; if the verb would have no preposition, then use *of*:

I shall carry out an analysis of the poem.

(= I shall analyse the poem.)

She published a critique of the poem.

(= [approximately] She criticized the poem.)

She wrote a review of the play.

(= She reviewed the play.)

In her discussion of *Macbeth*. ...

(= When she discussed *Macbeth* ...)

a summary of the speech. ...

(= to summarize the speech)

a survey of the subject. ...

(= to survey the subject)

Note that when no preposition is used with the verb, the noun phrase tends to have *of*. When the verb has a preposition (*object to*, *discriminate against*), the noun phrase tends also to use that preposition:

She raised an objection *to* the proposal.

Discrimination *against* women still exists.

There are exceptions however:

The author satirizes the political establishment.

The work is a satire *on* politics.

In his speech he delivered a fierce attack on his critics / he attacked his critics.

Where the noun is not related to a verb things are less clear:

An essay on man

A poem on / about love

An advertisement for toothpaste

A diatribe against money-lenders

A note on the language of the play

Another noun with which the *on / of* problem occurs is *impression*. In this case the problem relates to two quite distinct meanings and structures:

The book made a deep impression *on* me.

My impression *of* your essay is that it was written in a hurry.

(= I have the impression that your essay was written in a hurry.)

Impression of refers to an impression (*an idea*) that you *have*, whereas *impression on* is an impression (*an effect*) that something or someone makes on you.

6.7   Views and points of view

Students sometimes confuse these expressions. A *point of view*, often synonymous with a *viewpoint*, is really a place where you stand in order to look at something. A *view* can be two things: (1) *an opinion* (2) what you see when you stand on a mountain top (assuming there is no mist!).

The difference between *view* (in its first meaning) and *point of view* is really quite straightforward:

I asked her for her view(s) on the proposal.

(= her opinion)

She may have different views, because as a woman she has a different point of view. (i.e. she sees things from a different angle.)

Her point of view is different (she looks at the question in a different way) but it is also possible that her view or views may be the same (she may have the same opinion or make the same judgement.

This difference in meaning is maintained in the introductory phrases, *In my view* …, and *From my point of view* …:

In my view this question is not important.

(= I think that …)

I can see why you say the question is important. But from my point of view it's not worth discussing it now because I only have a week left before the exam.

In the second example, the speaker does not say other people should not discuss the question; it is only *from her point of view* that it is not worth discussing.

Note that in this meaning of *view*, similar to *idea*, it is often used in the plural: "I would like to hear your *views* on this".

The second meaning of *view* may also occur in writing about literature and is followed by a different preposition:

> This picture is a view *of* Victoria Harbour.
>
> The critic, W. Carp expressed his *view of* Shakespeare's late plays in an essay published in "The Critical Review" in 1977.

It may seem that there is very little difference between *a view of* and *someone's views on*. It is perhaps best to think of *a view of* as meaning *an interpretation of*.

Viewpoint is also the technical term used in analysing narrative: *omniscient viewpoint, first-person narrative*, etc. (see Appendix A.1)

7

DESCRIPTION AND ADJECTIVES

Finding words to describe to others what we see or feel plays an important part in our use of language. It is a particularly literary use of language. Poets describe the world and their feelings, novelists describe the characters and settings of their stories. Critics writing about a text try to describe certain aspects of the text and their response to it.

Description is also involved in a number of more practical or everyday activities: in travel writing, for example, in journalism of all kinds, including writing about food and fashion, and in everyday conversation.

A look at the language of description will lead us naturally to consider some problems with adjectives and adverbs. And although it is often said that a good writer does not use too many adjectives, some of the pleasure we derive from a good piece of writing is undoubtly related to the writer's ability to find good adjectives.

7.1 Describing people

Consider first some of the questions about people that might ordinarily be asked:

(a) What is Carmen like?
     (Describe her character or personality)
(b) What does Carmen look like?
     (Describe her general appearance)

(c) What does Carmen do?
     (What is her job?)
(d) How does Carmen act / behave?
     (Describe her behaviour)
(e) How does Carmen react when she's teased?
     (Say what she does or says in response to teasing)
(f) How does Carmen look?
     (Say what you think of her costume, make-up, hair-style, etc., at this
     particular moment, or say what you can deduce about her health)

Note the difference in structure between "*What* does she look *like?*" and
"How does she look?" (the meaning is similar, however).

The answers might be something like this:

(a) She is attractive. She is impulsive. She has a friendly nature.
(b) She is blonde. She has blue eyes.
(c) She works in a tobacco factory. She is a worker.
(d) She is very kind to her parents. She works hard.
(e) She gets angry.
(f) She looks great.

Notice that the word *pair* is not usually used with *eyes* etc. The *number* of
eyes people have is taken for granted, unless, like the giant Polyphemus in
The Odyssey, they have only one!

Notice the difference between "What does Carmen do?" and "What is
Carmen doing?" The former is of course limited to questions about some
regular aspect of Carmen's life — most often her job, though if she is not
employed it would have to involve any other ways in which she regularly
spends her time. It is however possible to ask about her work using the
present continuous.

> What *is* Carmen *doing* nowadays? I haven't seen her since she
> resigned from TVB.

As the example suggests, this usually implies that Carmen is someone you
know, but haven't seen lately.

(In a particular context "What does Carmen do?" can have other meanings.

For example, in a classroom discussion of a character in a story, you might ask "What does Carmen do when she finds her husband has been unfaithful to her?" But when there is no other context we will tend to interpret the question as being about Carmen's job.)

7.1.1 *Have* and *is*

To describe people's features and qualities there is usually a choice between related adjectives and nouns (sometimes there is also a noun which on its own describes a person with a particular feature or quality):

> She has blue eyes. She is blue-eyed.
>
> She has blonde hair. She is blonde. She is *a* blonde.
>
> She has charm. She is charming.
>
> She has good manners. She is polite and well-mannered.
>
> He reveals his cowardice. He is cowardly. He is *a* coward.

There are two things worth noticing about this. First, it is an aspect of the apparently random nature of language systems that there may or may not be a noun corresponding to the adjective or vice versa. For some reason English does have common nouns for people with different-coloured hair, *a blonde*, *a brunette*, *a red-head*, but does not have equivalent terms for people with eyes of a certain colour or noses of a certain size and shape.

Secondly, the choice among the forms (*have + noun*, *is + adjective*, etc.) is not completely free because you will often find that one of the forms is much more commonly used than the other, or that the different forms are not exactly equivalent in meaning. For example, "She has charm" makes a definite statement about a particular quality she has that makes people like her or feel attracted to her. On the other hand, "She is charming" says rather less; it is more or less an equivalent of "She is nice, I like her."

7.1.2 *With* and *in*

Notice that physical features which are something people *have* can be added to a description using *with*. Details of dress are usually added with *in*:

> A girl *with* long legs. A man *with* a big nose.

A girl *in* a red dress. The man *in* the grey suit.

7.1.3   *Features, appearance, outlook, expression* **and** *nature*

On its own, the word *features* is often used to refer to someone's face:

> She has very good features.

(Usually this means that her nose, mouth, eyes, etc. are considered to be well-shaped or well-proportioned)

> She has regular features.

Appearance is the word for the way someone looks, and *expression* (technically referred to as *facial expression*, but in ordinary language just *expression*) refers to "the look on their face", which expresses their feeling or emotional state:

> Her appearance was charming.
>
> There was an expression of amazement on her face.
>
> Her expression was a mixture of relief and disappointment.

But beware of *outlook* which has a completely different meaning. It refers to a person's attitude towards life or way of looking at things. It can also refer to a situation and the way you think the situation is going to develop in the future:

> She has an optimistic outlook.
>
> The outlook for Asian and Pacific countries is very hopeful.

You might expect someone with an optimistic outlook to smile rather than frown, but in fact *outlook* tells you nothing directly about a person's appearance.

Nature refers to something more permanent in a person's character, as of course we know from the expression *human nature*. The word itself is not often used in descriptions, except in the following:

> She has a friendly nature.
>
> She is good-natured.

(= she is friendly and easy-going.)

Adjectives can be formed quite freely on the pattern of *good-looking*, to describe appearance:

a fierce-looking dog, a strange-looking man, an angry-looking woman

This is only necessary when it is felt that the appearance may not reflect the true nature of the person or thing described, i.e. a fierce-looking dog is not necessarily fierce, it merely looks fierce.

7.1.4 Body

The word *body* is not normally used in describing people. It is taken for granted that *slim*, *fat*, *plump*, *strong*, etc. refer to people's bodies. There are also a number of other expressions that writers use when they want to be specific about the body:

He was of a strong *build*. He was well-built.

He had a strong *physique*.

She had a wonderful *figure*.

(This implies shape, and depends of course on fashion.)

Her *stature* was classical.

(This suggests she is tall.)

7.1.5 Age

Someone's age can be conveniently given through the hyphenated adjective form or joined to the noun with *of*:

a five-year-old boy, a twenty-five-year-old man, etc.

a boy of five, a man of twenty-five

If a complete sentence is used, the word *age* is usually omitted:

He is twenty-five (years of age).

Journalists often try to save space and time with phrases like:

Twenty-five-year-old housewife, Mrs Maureen Jones …

Mrs Maureen Jones, twenty-five, a resident of Plumtree Villas …

7.1.6   Combining features

Students get into various difficulties, especially when they want to combine descriptions of different features, some expressed by nouns and others by adjectives:

✗ She was with blue eyes.

(She *had* blue eyes.)

✗ She was blonde and blue eyes.

(She was blonde and *had* blue eyes.)

✗ She had experience and hard-working.

(She had experience and *was* hard-working.)

✗ She was tall and carrying a Gucci handbag.

(She was tall and *was* carrying a Gucci handbag.)

The last of these is not really wrong but it is awkward because the verb *to be* is not really the same in "*to be* tall" (*be* + *adjective*) and "*to be carrying* a handbag" (*be* + *tense*). However, the trick of treating two different uses of a verb as if they were the same, can be used for comic effect (and has a technical name: zeugma).

7.1.7   Order of adjectives

When descriptive phrases are placed after the noun, the main principle is to organize them so that ones combined in the same way (e.g. using *with*) come together:

> He was an old man, of heavy build, with a fair, shaven face and large eyes. There was something childish in those eyes, though it was not the childishness of senility. (E. M. Forster, *A Room with a View*)

Adjectives which come together before the noun often have to be placed in a certain order: closest to the noun and inseparable from it are words which combine with the noun to narrow down its meaning (often these are noun modifiers, like *office* and *garden* below). In the following, pairs of words under 1 cannot be separated, so further modifiers have to be placed on the left, as under 2:

1	**2**
office furniture	*well-designed office furniture*
a garden chair	*a white garden chair*
an old lady	*a grey-haired old lady*
a little girl	*a shy little girl*

Notice how the expressions in column 1 represent a special class of things or people. A garden chair is a different kind of chair, often made of metal; a little girl is not so much a girl who looks small as a girl below a certain age.

You can see this better by comparing *a wild party*, where the word *wild* is really descriptive, and *a wild animal* where it is used to classify a particular set of animals. Adding adjectives, you might get *a **wild** all-night graduation party* and *a big dangerous **wild** animal*. Notice the different positions of *wild*: near the beginning when it describes, close to the end when it classifies.

If there is a word to describe the material of which something is made, it comes next nearest to the noun:

*well-designed **stainless-steel** office furniture*
*a white **wrought-iron** garden chair*
*an ugly pink **plastic** doll*

Colours are likely to be towards the left of the phrase. Also towards the left-hand end will be the really descriptive words, the ones that you would not easily guess, and on the extreme left are words that have an evaluative function or express the speaker's emotional attitude towards the thing or person described:

a funny little old lady
beautiful stainless-steel office furniture
a dear little white wrought-iron garden chair
a poor neglected old man

The common evaluative words include *big, great, little, tiny, poor, funny, old, young*, etc.; the literal meaning of such words is often blocked in phrases of this kind (see 7.3.2).

7.2   Describing characters

Authors of fiction do not always give detailed physical descriptions of their characters, and in any case behaviour and personality are more important evidence for an analysis of the characters than their appearance.

When you analyse a character you often have to deduce more or less permanent *characteristics* from the relatively accidental features that the author tells you about. So, for example, you might read in a story, "She was wearing an orange pullover and a purple skirt" and in your analysis you might write something like: "She likes bright-coloured clothes", or even "Her taste in clothes is terrible / She has very bad taste." The use of the present tense here shows that you are producing a generalization from the specific information provided by the author. What you are trying to describe is not just her appearance at a given moment but her *characteristics*, her *character traits*, her *characteristic features*.

Of course the example just given may depend partly on what kind of clothes *you* like and *your* view of good or bad taste. But not entirely. The author will almost certainly convey what he or she thinks by indicating other characteristics or features which reinforce the impression caused by the clothes. Such characteristics may be conveyed by the character's actions or ways of speaking.

There are some possible problems with the words used in connection with describing character. The word *character* itself can be used in two ways.

7.2.1   Character as personality

Everyone has *a* certain *character*. This means that they behave in certain *characteristic* ways. You can describe *someone's character* by saying how he or she behaves.

In this first sense, *character* can also be a non-count noun. Psychologists are also interested in the study of *character* (non-count, no article), or in the study of *personality* (also non-count), which is very similar to this meaning of character and is both count and non-count:

> Lucy has *a* friendly, outgoing personality.

> Lucy's personality is quite different from Charlotte's.

You can also state *the characteristics* of a person or thing or situation. This means stating what is important or unique about this particular person, thing or situation. *Characteristics* is usually plural, but you can if you want refer to one specific *characteristic* of a person, thing or situation:

> His outstanding characteristic is obstinacy.

Other words which can be used in approximately the same way as *characteristics* are *traits*, *features* (which can also be physical, 7.1.3), *qualities* and *attributes*:

> Honesty and realism are Bluntschli's main *traits*.
>
> In Forster's view, snobbishness is one of the most unpleasant *features* of early twentieth century English society.
>
> Raina has many (good) *qualities*, but modesty is not one of them.
>
> Lucy has many pleasing *attributes*.

The word *quality* generally implies *good feature*; you cannot really use it for an unpleasant characteristic or a bad feature.

You can also talk about different *aspects* of someone's character or personality. A particular aspect of someone's character is often called *a side of their character*:

> As soon as Raina goes out, Sergius reveals a different *side of his character*.

7.2.2 Characters in a story

In its second meaning, *character* refers to *a character in a story*. The two meanings are so closely related that they tend to get mixed up, and no great harm is done. Consider this exam question:

> Discuss the character of Miranda in *The Collector* and say whether you think she is in any way responsible for what happens to her.

You are perhaps being asked to say what Miranda's character is or what sort of character she has. But Miranda, of course, *is a character* herself, so you are also being asked to discuss Miranda *as a character* in the novel, that is, to discuss her function in the novel. Fortunately the two things are so nearly the same, or so closely related, that the slight confusion is unimportant.

7.2.3   Nouns in character description

Speaking of someone we know we are liable to use sentences of the form "She is very attractive", rather than saying "She is an attractive lady." You can treat the characters in a story as people you know. It sounds quite awkward if you say:

>   ✗ Lucy is a straightforward lady.

It is much better to write this as:

>   Lucy is straightforward.

The problem with the first version is that the noun generally only tells us something we know already, i.e that Lucy is female. If the point were to tell us that Lucy has, by nineteenth or early twentieth century standards, the qualities of a lady, i.e. that she is not coarse and ill-bred, or lower-class, then what you want to say is:

>   Lucy is a lady.

Notice how here the meaning "Lucy is a female" is blocked because it would be a tautology — something which is obviously true and not worth saying. Other aspects of the meaning of *lady* (good manners, high social status) therefore come into play.

All the general nouns which can be used for referring to people have distracting connotations, though we can say approximately that the most neutral forms are as follows:

girl   young female

woman   older female

old lady / old woman   elderly or aged female

boy   young male

young man / man   older male

old man   elderly or aged male

But note that the following must have special implications, since their purpose cannot be just to tell us about someone's sex (which is already conveyed by the pronoun):

> She is a (real) lady!
>
> She is a woman!
>
> (depending on context this may imply fickleness, emotional instability, sexual attractiveness or any other stereotype)
>
> She is just a girl!
>
> (She is immature, innocent, etc.)
>
> He is a gentleman! He is such a gentleman!
>
> He is only a boy!
>
> (immature, innocent, etc. In Shakespeare's time to call someone a boy could be an insult.)
>
> He is a real man!
>
> (tough, brave, or any other stereotype)

Certain other word choices, like *kid* versus *child*, and *fellow*, *bloke*, *chap* versus *man*, tell us something about the speaker rather than about the person referred to. For example, *kid* is very informal and would probably not be used in formal writing except humorously.

7.2.4 The right word: good and bad connotations

Finding the right words for describing a character is important and quite difficult. It reflects not only your control of vocabulary but also the sensitivity of your reading. You will frequently find that the words which spring first to mind are too strong or not strong enough. You will also have to pay close attention to the favourable and unfavourable associations of adjectives.

Here are some examples of good and bad associations or connotations:

Good	Bad	Neutral or either
brave, courageous, daring	*foolhardy, rash*	*audacious*
cautious, prudent,	*cowardly*	*timid*
careful, circumspect		
self-confident	*boastful, conceited*	*proud*
innocent	*naive*	*simple*
gentle	*weak, feeble*	–
firm, decisive	*obstinate, pig-headed*	*persistent*
persevering, tenacious,	*stubborn*	*inflexible*
principled, constant		

There are reasons for caution however in accepting this kind of classification. In many cases the associations are not entirely fixed, and it is possible that a writer will redefine the term. Secondly, a writer may use the word ironically — often this means it is the word that is used or would be used by some other character in the story, whose judgement the writer does not endorse (*endorse = accept, agree with*). For example, in *A Room with a View*, Forster writes:

> Lucy, who had not yet acquired decency, at once rose to her feet, exclaiming: "Oh, oh! Why it's Mr Beebe! Oh, how perfectly lovely!...."

Our interpretation of the story as a whole will lead us to interpret Lucy's lack of "decency" as something more like pleasing innocence and naturalness of behaviour. Only the middle-class English whom Forster is satirizing would equate decency with not expressing true feelings.

Another point to notice is that some adjectives have much *stronger* meanings than others: for example, *feeble* is stronger than *weak* and implies stronger disapproval.

7.2.5 Support

In writing about literature, descriptions often need to be linked to evidence. There are many ways to do this but here is an example:

> Lucy is friendly and spontaneous. When Mr Beebe enters the dining-room she greets him excitedly.

The link can be made closer by changing the full-stop to a colon:

> Lucy is friendly and spontaneous: when Mr Beebe enters the dining-room, she greets him excitedly.

The description and the evidence for it can be linked in one sentence:

> Lucy's romantic nature *is reflected* in the way she opens the windows in her room.
>
> *It is typical* of Lucy's friendly, trusting nature *that* she opens the window and enjoys the view, whereas Charlotte ...

7.2.5a *So ... that ...*

Providing evidence sometimes coincides with describing consequences, using the *so ... that ...* pattern. Students, however, have a tendency to over-use *so ... that ... / such a ... that ...*; they use these constructions when really they want to focus on the description, not the consequences:

> Charlotte is a cautious, suspicious person. The first thing she does is search her room in case someone is hiding there.
>
> Charlotte is *such a* cautious, suspicious person *that* the first thing she does is search her room in case someone is hiding there.

The first of these is preferable when the focus is on description of character and there is no special need to emphasize the consequences. The second would be more appropriate if you were summarizing the plot, since it tells us what happens (Charlotte searches her room) together with the reason why it happens (because she is such a cautious, suspicious person).

7.2.6 Discussing characterization

Generally the purpose of discussing the characters is to comment on the author's skill in creating them, which is also known as *characterization*.

There are some basic terms which apply to this. Characterization, for example, can be *true to life*, *lifelike*, *realistic*, *convincing*. Characters can also be described with any of these words, and they can also be *lively* or *vivid*, and *rounded* or *flat*. A rounded character is one who seems to have some complexity and depth. A flat character is one who never changes and never says or does anything surprising. Flat characters may also be called *types*, or *stereotypes*.

The author's work is sometimes described in terms that normally apply to painting or sculpture: words like *portray* and *depict* are used, and it is possible to talk of how the author *shapes* the characters.

You can present a character from the reader's point of view, or from the author's point of view:

> Lucy strikes us as …
>
> Lucy appeals to us because …
>
> We are interested in Lucy because …
>
> We are told that Lucy is …
>
> The author depicts Lucy as … (portrays, presents, describes)
>
> Lucy is depicted as … (portrayed, presented, described)
>
> Lucy is shown to be …

There is a slight difference between

> Charlotte is narrow-minded and hypocritical.
>
> Charlotte is portrayed as narrow-minded and hypocritical.

The latter stresses the author's intentions and technique:

> In *A Room with a View*, Forster attacks the life-defeating qualities of the English middle class. Charlotte, for instance, is portrayed as narrow-minded and hypocritical.

Note also the frequent use of *as* in these sentences: *depicted **as**, portrayed **as***.

7.3 Adjectives

There are a number of problems with adjectives. One of the most basic is knowing the difference between nouns and adjectives, or verbs and adjectives and using the right one at the right time.

There are for example times when you might use either of these:

> Charlotte is a hypocrite.

Charlotte is hypocritical.

But if you want to use more than one descriptive word, it is easier to make them the same part of speech:

Charlotte is narrow-minded and hypocritical.

Sometimes the problem may stem from the *have / is* distinction (see 7.1.1):

The girl in this story is supposed to *have* good powers of observation but in fact she *is* not observant at all.

She wants her boy-friend to become a publisher. It is unlikely he would *have* much *success* in this business because he knows nothing about it. He is much more likely to *be successful* in the wine trade.

A great many adjectives are formed from verbs with the past participle (*-ed*) ending or the present participle (*-ing*) ending:

She is not a very relaxed person.

The experience was quite frightening.

These *-ed* forms and *-ing* forms cause a lot of confusion.

7.3.1   Adjectives describing emotion and experience

The basic difference between *-ed* forms and *-ing* forms is that the former generally describe your emotions or sensations, and the latter apply to what causes them:

I was very excited when I heard the news.

(The emotion I felt was excitement.)

The news was very exciting.

(The news was the cause of my excitement.)

One way to explain the distinction between *-ing* adjectives and *-ed* adjectives is to consider a basic sentence like "Horror movies excite me" and its passive form "I am excited by horror movies." The *-ed* adjective is really a past participle, related to the passive: "I am excited" implies that I am excited *by* something; the *-ing* form is active and applies to the thing that excites me:

> Horror movies are exciting. Horror movies excite *me*.
>
> *I* am excited *by* horror movies. Watching horror movies I feel excited.
>
> Watching horror movies is exciting.

Often the *-ed* adjectives have a human subject and the *-ing* adjectives have a non-human subject:

She is …	**It is …**
excited	*exciting*
interested	*interesting*
bored	*boring*
frightened	*frightening*

It is possible though for the *-ing* adjectives also to have a human subject:

> He is bored.
>
> (He feels boredom.)
>
> He is boring.
>
> (He causes boredom, he makes me bored.)

It is possible, but unusual, to use these *-ing* forms with a first person subject. It may produce some quite unusual meanings. Bearing in mind that the *-ing* forms mean something like "causes X to other people", a statement like "I am interesting" would sound almost impossibly boastful; "I am boring" suggests a rather disturbing lack of self-confidence; and it is doubtful if even Count Dracula would say "I am frightening."

There are some other related adjectives which describe emotions, sensations or behaviour and which divide into two groups:

understanding	*understandable*
ashamed	*shameful*
satisfied	*satisfactory, satisfying*
–	*painful*

If you say a person's behaviour is *understandable*, you mean that you can understand their behaviour; if you say a person is *understanding*, you mean approximately that the person understands you:

> If you're in trouble, go and talk to Eleanor. She is very understanding.
> She is a very good listener.

It would be more accurate however to say that *understanding* is nearly a synonym of *sympathetic*.

Similarly, if you feel *ashamed* about something you have done, you may have to admit that what you did is *shameful*.

Unfortunately if you try to make a list of such adjectives, you will find it is not neat and symmetrical. For example, *painful* means *which causes pain* and has no equivalent to describe what the human subject experiences. It is wrong to say "I was painful" and there is no adjective which can be substituted. The best you can do probably is to say "I felt a lot of pain" or "I was in great pain". Otherwise you must give up the attempt to start your sentence with "I", and say instead, "It was painful", which normally must imply that something was painful to the speaker.

On the other hand, some adjectives, like *hopeful*, can be applied to both the subjective feeling and the situation which produces it:

> The chairman said he felt very hopeful.
> The chairman said the situation was very hopeful.

The moral is that you need to be careful to check exactly how to use any of these adjectives which deal with emotions, sensations and behaviour.

7.3.2 *Poor, little, old*, etc.

There are a number of adjectives which, when placed before the noun, have a purely evaluative function, with no literal meaning: they include *poor, dear, little, great, old, young*.

When they are placed after the verb, as verb complement, they tend to have their more literal meaning:

> Poor Angela!

(I feel sorry for her.)

She is poor.

(She does not have much money, NOT I feel sorry for her.)

Dear little Ivy!

(Ivy is my friend, I like her.)

The goods are dear.

(They are not cheap, NOT I like them.)

I have known old Charles for years.

(He is my friend.)

Charles is old.

(He is not young.)

These words appear in certain set combinations that are clichés commonly used conversationally or in personal letters:

a dear little cottage, a great big kiss, a lovely great prize, a funny little person, a silly old fool

Sometimes an evaluative note is introduced by an adverb applied to one of the adjectives.

*an **exquisitely** carved wooden coffee table*
*a **beautifully** balanced artistic composition*

It is the carving which is exquisite, rather than the table itself, and the balance which is beautiful rather than the composition.

7.3.3   *It is difficult* etc.

There are a number of adjectives like *difficult, important, useful* and so on that are often used in impersonal expressions with *It is ...*, and which cannot usually have a human subject:

It is difficult to learn Russian.

Russian is difficult to learn.

What you cannot say is, "She is difficult / easy to ...". If you really need to include some reference to a human actor, you must do it differently:

> It is easy *for her* to learn Russian, because she has a Russian grandmother.
>
> *She finds* it easy to learn Russian.
>
> *She finds Russian* easy to learn.

Notice that the simple infinitive is used after these adjectives. Students tend to use a passive infinitive (see 5.4.5a):

> ✗ The meaning of this poem is difficult <u>to be grasped</u>.

You will see why this is wrong if you assume that *difficult* here means *difficult for someone*, even when this is not made explicit:

> The meaning of the poem is difficult (for anyone) to grasp.

If you do come across the *is + adjective + infinitive* construction with a human subject, the meaning is rather different:

> She is difficult to please.
>
> (It is difficult [for other people] to please her.)
>
> She is difficult.
>
> (She is not an easy person to live with or work with.)

There are however a few similar words that can have a human subject without a change in meaning (*likely*), and some which can only have a human subject (*eager, willing*) or usually have a human subject (*liable*):

> He is likely to come.
>
> She is liable to do it.
>
> He is eager to come.
>
> She is willing to do it.

Examples such as these are often used by linguists to prove that apparently identical structures can in fact be quite different:

Pronoun	is + adjective	verb infinitive
She	is willing	to go. (*She* will go.)
She	is difficult	to please. (I find it difficult to please *her*.)

7.3.4   Colours

Note that colours in English have their own names, which can be noun as well as adjective, so there is no need to use the word *colour* with them:

> Her dress was pink and her shoes were green. She wore a purple hat.
> I prefer beige to pink.
> She nearly always wears dark blue.

7.3.5   Adjective phrases

Notice that adjectives can head descriptive phrases in the same way as participles can:

> We are looking for a person *interested* in fashion and *aware* of the latest trends, *willing* to travel, and *capable* of working independently.

In particular the words I called non-verbs in 5.7 (e.g. *aware*) are quite often used this way, which may be one reason why students often use them incorrectly as main verbs without *to be* (see 4.1.2b). Here there is no need for *to be* because the sentence already has a main verb and *interested*, *aware*, *willing* and *capable* stand in place of a relative clause: "*who is* interested … etc."

7.3.6   Using adverbs to strengthen or weaken adjectives

Adjectives can be qualified or emphasized by adverbs, some of which are more colloquial, while others are more formal:

> She is *very* lazy.

Informal   incredibly, unbelievably, extraordinarily, fantastically, awfully, dreadfully

Neutral or formal   very, extremely, exceedingly, exceptionally

She is *quite* lazy.

(Note the spelling of *quite*).

Informal pretty, fairly

Neutral or formal rather, somewhat, relatively, comparatively, a little

This does not exhaust the possibilities. You can also qualify adjectives to add a critical sense:

too, excessively, frighteningly, disgracefully, absurdly, shockingly

There is also a set of adverbs, neither informal nor formal, with the sense of *completely*:

completely, totally, thoroughly, altogether, entirely, etc.

Note however that not all adjectives can be qualified, or rather, there are adjectives which in careful writing should not be qualified, because their meaning is emphatic or absolute:

This setting is perfect.

(= it could not be better)

The environment is ideal.

(= it could not be better)

It was an appalling sight.

(*appalling* = *very* bad)

If you come across something like *rather perfect*, or *rather impossible*, it will be in representations of informal speech and the intention is probably humorous.

7.3.6a *A little bit*

Note that there is something a little childish about the use of *a little **bit***, which is popular with students. The more adult and formal version is *a little*.

Feeling a little tired, she decided to have an early night.

7.3.7   *So*

So used in the sense of *very* has a strongly emotional tone and is expressive of excitement or exaggerated enthusiasm, mainly in speech. You should not use *so* in writing, unless you are very sure there is good reason for it. Basically, the formal use of *so* is to emphasize that something has a consequence:

> He was so frightened (that) he locked himself in his bedroom and wouldn't come out.
>
> He wouldn't come out because he was so / too frightened.

Because of its subjective, emotional tone, *so* is a word that can be used in fiction to suggest viewpoint: "She was so beautiful. Would she ever love him?" (We are sharing *his* thoughts). But if you are trying to write in an objective tone, for example in summarizing a plot or discussing the characters in a story, this sort of use of *so* should be avoided. (See 4.2.6 and 4.5.7)

7.3.8   Verbs which can be followed by an adjective

After a verb you normally expect an adverb. But after the verb *to be* you can use just an adjective:

> Lucy is straightforward.

(In 7.2.3 I suggested that this is the normal way of describing someone, rather than saying "Lucy is a straightforward lady.")

A limited number of other verbs can replace *to be* in such a statement (see 5.8.5):

> Lucy seems / appears naive.

These verbs often have the effect of qualifying the statement: "Lucy is naive" admits no doubt, but "Lucy seems naive" allows the possibility that she may not really be naive.

Verbs connected with sense perception (*sound, look, smell, taste*) can be used in this way, with a following adjective rather than adverb:

> She sounded tired on the telephone.

> She looks happy.
>
> It tastes strange.

Another case when you find a following adjective rather than an adverb is after *find* or *consider*:

> They consider the Emersons inferior.

This is similar to saying, "In their view, the Emersons *are* inferior." You can compare it with "They treat the Emersons unkindly", where *unkindly* is an adverb describing *the way they treat* the Emersons.

The same grammatical construction (verb followed by adjective rather than adverb) occurs with verbs like *stay, keep, remain* and with *feel*:

> Small children find it very difficult to keep quiet and stay still.
>
> She wanted to keep her marriage secret.
>
> Miranda feels desperate.

This is more or less the same as saying "Miranda is desperate" (see 5.8.5 for problems with *feel*).

Adjectives also often occur after *make*:

> "You make me very happy", he said.

7.3.9 Inventing new adjectives

It is worth noting that compound adjectives (consisting of two words joined by a hyphen) can be formed from verb phrases or relative clauses:

behaviour which gets attention = ***attention-getting*** *behaviour*
an economy which is growing fast = *a **fast-growing** economy*
a cake which was made at home = *a **home-made** cake*

You will notice that the second part is either a present participle or a past participle. Many of these expressions tend to be associated with specific nouns in conventional phrases: e.g. *a law-abiding citizen*, meaning a person who obeys the law. Some such expressions become fashionable as soon as they are formed and then go out of fashion: *sick-making violence*, for example is at present quite common, but *epoch-making*, meaning "important, sensational", which was once greatly used by the Hollywood movie industry in advertising movies, seems to have rather gone out of fashion.

7.4   Describing emotions and tone — adjective or noun?

Since stories and plays are generally centred on emotional conflict, identifying the emotions of the characters often plays a part in writing about literature. Words for emotions also have to be used for describing tone in poetry.

Note that emotions can generally be named with either nouns or adjectives:

angry	*anger*
excited	*excitement*
sad	*sadness*
annoyed	*annoyance*

There is no need to use the word emotion in conjunction with these: e.g. *sad emotion, angry feeling*:

> Fred describes his anger after Miranda has tried to seduce him.

However, you can speak of either *an angry tone* or *a tone of anger*.

There are some occasions where the noun is more useful than the adjective. This is particularly so when you want to focus on defining the emotion, tone, attitude, or whatever:

> Her attitude towards her husband is one of respect, but not of blind obedience.
> What she feels towards him is calm love rather than violent passion.

Generally it makes little difference whether you say "I was angry" or "I felt angry". However there are a few words which can be ambiguous: for example, *guilt* can be a subjective feeling, or it can refer to the objective fact that someone is proved to have done something wrong.

If you speak of the subjective feeling you use the following:

> He felt guilty after losing his temper with her.
>
> He had a sense of guilt.
>
> He suffered from guilt.
>
> He had a guilty conscience.

Describing the facts:

> He was guilty of many crimes.
>
> He was found guilty.
>
> His guilt was established beyond all doubt.

Normally then we would take "He *was* guilty" to mean that he is known to have committed a crime, and "He *felt* guilty" to mean he had a sense of guilt.

7.5 Adverbs

Adverbs should on the whole be used sparingly. In particular there is a range of adverbial phrases like *in a loud voice*, *in a soft voice*, *at a fast speed*, which are very unidiomatic in English. It is much more normal to use a single adverb: *loudly*, *softly / quietly*, *quickly*. In good literary style it may well be better to express these meanings by choosing a good verb, e.g. *shout*, *whisper*, *race*.

Adverbs are useful for qualifying statements. A generalization like "Chinese University students attend many lectures" can be qualified, for example:

> Chinese University students generally / often / usually attend many lectures.

Be careful, however, with the word *always*, which is sometimes untrue and often unnecessary. (see 5.1.1a)

Here are some other problems with adverbs.

238 The Language of English Studies

7.5.1 *-ly* adjectives

If an adjective ends in *-ly*, it cannot conveniently be made into an adverb:

fatherly, leisurely, friendly, cowardly, lively

You have to find various strategies for dealing with the problems this causes. For example, you can use a phrase like *in a fatherly way*. It may, however, be better to use a different word altogether:

> Forster's *description* of this scene is very *lively*.
> Forster *describes* this scene very *vividly*.

(There is, however, a growing tendency to use *leisurely* as both adjective and adverb, and occasionally you might meet *friendlily* in semi-humorous style.)

7.5.2 Adverbs with same form as adjectives

Some common adverbs have the same form as adjectives:

fast, straight, direct, hard, late, early

> a fast car
> she works fast.
> a late meeting
> she is working late.

Note that *hardly* exists, but means "scarcely", *directly* exists, but in a sentence like "I shall go directly" tends to mean something like "immediately", and *lately* exists, but means "recently".

7.5.3 *Detailed*

Another commonly used word which has no adverb form is *detailed*:

> The author gives a detailed description of the scene.
> The author describes the scene *in detail*.

The same is true for a number of other *-ed* adjectives / participles. There normally is an adverb form of *-ing* adjectives/participles, but it may not convey the meaning you want.

7.5.4 *Totally*

Similarly, although *totally* exists, it is a synonym of *completely* and should not be used to mean *in total* or *the total number*:

> The village was *totally* destroyed by the earthquake.
>
> A *total of* two thousand people lost their homes.
>
> *In total*, two thousand people were made homeless.

7.5.5 Doing something *a number of times*

Note that no preposition is needed for saying how many times something happens or is done:

> I have been to Canada three times.

The common mistake is to use *for*, which should not be used with "number of times". It is only correct to use *for* in discussing the time something lasts or the time that must pass before something happens. (see 8.3.2)

> ✗ She revised her assignment <u>for</u> five times.
>
> ✔ She sat up writing her assignment *for* five hours.

Possibly, however there may be confusion with the following:

> She only agreed to marry him when he asked her *for* the third time.

This of course also implies that he asked her *three times*.

7.5.6 Adverb or adjective?

Apart from the special verbs discussed in 7.3.8, one expects a verb to be followed by an adverb, not an adjective. Occasionally, however, adjectives are used after a verb because the meaning applies not to the verb but to the subject of the sentence:

> The rain fell, heavy and unrelenting.

> The day dawned grey and ominous.

According to these, the rain itself is heavy and unrelenting, rather than the manner of its falling; the day is grey and ominous, rather than the manner of its dawning.

Sometimes it can be useful to be able to use an adjective or participle like this, because there is no available adverb. For example,

> "What was that?" she cried, *frightened* by the sudden noise.

It is not very normal to make *frightened* into an adverb (*frightenedly*), though you could use *nervously* instead. But the participle phrase, "frightened by the sudden noise", has the advantage of expressing both her fear and its cause.

PRONOUNS, REFERENCE

WITHIN THE TEXT AND TIME

Pronouns are used in English to reduce repetition; they enable you to go on talking about a topic without constantly repeating the noun phrase which names the topic. They play quite an important part in connecting sentences to each other (producing cohesion) because the meaning of a pronoun usually cannot be understood without relating it to something in an earlier part of the text. Students are generally quite familiar with this because in comprehension exercises and tests they are often asked to identify the reference of pronouns.

8.1 Personal pronouns

There are a number of problems students have with personal pronouns.

8.1.1 Consistency

One of the main problems is remembering who you are talking about; that is to say, you must use the appropriate pronoun to refer back to an earlier noun, and you must not change to a different pronoun unless you have introduced a different noun.

The problem usually arises not when you are writing about specific people or things but when you are making generalizations. If you make a general statement about human behaviour using an active verb, you have to find a subject for it, even when you have no individual person in mind. Suppose for example you are going to write something about studying at university and your aim is not just to describe your own experience, but rather to make some more general statements:

> *Students* have to spend much of *their* time in the library. *They* need to consult reference books and search for information by *themselves*.
>
> *A student* is *someone* who pursues learning. *He or she* knows that the purpose of university education is not just to acquire a practical skill, but to train *his or her* mind.

In each of these examples there is an opening statement followed by an elaboration or reason. In order to elaborate an opening statement or provide support for it or continue it in any way at all, you will need to use pronouns; otherwise you would have to keep repeating the original noun subject. So long as you get the following pronouns right, it makes no difference whether you say *Students* or *A student*, except that nowadays, through the influence of feminism, there is a tendency to prefer the plural form: the plural saves you from having to choose between *he* and *she*, or having to write *he or she* — and also, of course, *his or her*.

When you make statements that apply to your readers in general you can use *we*, *you* or *one*:

> *We* should take better care of *our* environment.
>
> *One* should not blame other people for *one's* own shortcomings.
>
> *You* should remember that *you* cannot learn without making mistakes.

In some contexts *we* may be preferable because by using it you unambiguously include yourself in what you are saying, instead of adopting the position of someone giving instructions. But do not forget that *we* is plural, so it is very awkward to say something like "As *a student*, <u>we</u> have to attend many lectures."

It is particularly appropriate to use *we* in writing about literature. (see 1.4.1)

You will notice however that in these notes I am constantly using *you*. Well, this is because I *am* trying to give instruction, and because I am addressing *you*. It seems more honest and direct therefore for me to use *you*.

To some extent *you* is ambiguous (but this is not a problem) because it can also be used in general statements which apply to the speaker as well:

> If you want to travel, you need money.

By this I mean that *anyone* needs money to travel; *I* need it just as much as *you* do.

One is less popular than it used to be. It can sometimes sound old-fashioned to use *one* a lot, except as a joke. It can also be awkward to continue or elaborate sentences with *one* as subject, because of a difficulty with the pronoun used for further references to the subject:

> One should not count one's / his chickens before they are hatched. If one / he does, one / he is liable to make a fool of oneself / himself.

British usage favours the repetition of *one / one's*, while American usage favours the use of *he / his*. Either can be awkward, unless you intend a humorous effect. The example above suggests a faintly humorous intention.

(In the comic novels of P. G. Wodehouse, written in the 1930s and 1940s, you will find characters who frequently use *one* when they mean *I*, along the lines of "*One* doesn't want to presume, but may *one* be permitted to ask why *one* has not been invited to the party?".)

Let me repeat, however, that the really important point about pronouns is consistency. It is essential to check your work to make sure that you have not changed pronouns in mid-sentence (the writer's equivalent of changing horses in midstream, proverbially said to be dangerous).

8.1.2   *Someone* and *some people*

Notice that *someone* cannot be used in a generalization, though *nobody / no one* can:

> *Nobody* likes being told off by their boss, but *some people* resent it more than others.

If you say "*Someone* resents it more than others", it means that you are referring to a particular person but don't know his or her name or do not want to mention it:

> "*Someone* has been eating my porridge", Father Bear said.

Beware of starting a sentence with "Someone says…." This can be correct only if you have one particular person in mind — a person whom you could name if you wanted to, or if you could remember who it was. What you probably mean is "Some people say…."

8.1.3   Possessives

Generally the possessive form of the pronoun (*his*, *her*, *its*, *etc.*) is preferable to *of him, of her, of it, etc.*

> ✗ Amanda scolds Tom because she does not like the smoking of him.
>
> (Rewrite as "… does not like *his* smoking.")

> ✗ The education system in Hong Kong puts great pressure on students. This hinders the learning of them.
>
> (Rewrite as "… *their* learning")

8.1.4   *Self: oneself* etc.

There are differences here in English and Chinese usage that cause problems. In English *himself, herself*, etc. cannot stand alone as subject:

> ✗ When Cleopatra learns of Antony's arrival, herself goes to meet him.

You can, however, use it *with* the subject pronoun: "She goes to meet him herself", or "She herself goes to meet him."

The same problem occurs in the following:

> ✗ She thinks herself is superior to every other woman.

This ought to be "She thinks *she* is superior to every other woman."
The following, however, is correct:

> ✔ She thinks herself superior to every other woman.

Here *thinks* is not followed by a clause but by *herself* as object.

Secondly, *-self* with an object pronoun refers back to the *nearest* subject noun or implied subject. This can often be the subject of a subordinate clause or the implied subject of an infinitive construction:

> The host invited his guests to help *themselves*.
>
> The host asked his guests to help *him*.

You could not use *himself* in the second example because the implied subject of the phrase is not *The host* but *guests*.

Note that the preceding subject has to be exactly the same; it cannot just be something connected with the same person:

> ✗ Her secret marriage brings <u>herself</u> a bad reputation.
>
> ✔ Her secret marriage brings her a bad reputation.

It is wrong to write *herself* because the subject is "marriage".

8.1.5   Pronoun referring to countries

It is somewhat old-fashioned to use *she* in referring to countries and wrong to use *she* in referring to a government. A government can be either *it* or *they*. If you feel uncomfortable about using *it* to refer to a country, simply repeat the country's name or turn the sentence round so that the country is not subject or object, or in some cases use *they*:

> Hong Kong lacks recreation facilities and sports grounds. This is because Hong Kong does not have enough land. / This is because land is too scarce in Hong Kong.
>
> China is modernizing very fast. Soon *they* will catch up with other advanced economies.

8.2   Reference to what you have said or what you are going to say

Pronouns and other expressions perform the function of allowing you to use previously mentioned ideas without repeating them word for word. But if pronouns are not used carefully they can make your meaning unclear.

8.2.1   *It* or *this*?

If you want to refer to what was said in the preceding sentence or paragraph, use *this*. Only use *it* when there is an identifiable singular noun to which *it* refers:

> Hong Kong children seldom enjoy learning for its own sake. *This*
> (= the fact that HK children seldom enjoy learning for its own sake)
> is because they have no time to think of anything except exams.
> Education in Hong Kong is not a process of enlightenment. *It*
> (= Education) is a kind of force-feeding.

It would be wrong in the first example to write *It is because* ... since there is no noun *it* can refer to, but in the second example the reference is to *Education*, a singular noun.

An exception to this rule, however, is that having used *this* to refer back to something previously said, you use *it* for later references to this same idea:

> Hong Kong children seldom enjoy learning for its own sake. *This* is
> because they have no time to think of anything except exams. *It* is also
> due to the fact that parents see education as a way to gain material
> advantages and put too much pressure on the children to succeed.

In this case, *It = This = the fact that Hong Kong children seldom enjoy learning for its own sake.*

8.2.2   *It is because*

In fact any sentence beginning *It is because* is very likely to be wrong. Generally *because* is used to join sentences (i.e. with no full-stop):

> Hong Kong students are not independent because they are not en-
> couraged to be independent.

When the sentence answers a question it is possible to begin with just *Because*:

> Why are Hong Kong students not more independent? Because they are
> not encouraged to be independent.

It is likely that some students have been taught to say *It is because* in order to answer a question with a complete sentence. The habit of answering questions with complete sentences is quite unnatural and should NOT be taught unless there are very good reasons for doing so. It involves unnecessary repetition, which is not good for your written style.

You will, however, meet *It is because* when it refers forward to a noun clause (stating the result) that comes after the *because* clause (giving the reason):

> It is because she loves her children *that* she criticizes them so much.

This may sometimes appear another way round:

> If she criticizes her children a lot, it is because she loves them.

8.2.3   *This* or *these*?

Use *this* or *all this* rather than *these* even when more than one previous idea is referred to:

> Hong Kong children are subjected to pressure from the examination system, from their teachers and from their parents. They have to study in a second language. They grow up in a society increasingly dominated by material values. *All this* makes it difficult for them to view learning as a process of joyful discovery.

Here *all this* means something like "what I have just said", or "everything that I have just said."

8.2.4   Substitute nouns

If you feel that using *this* to refer back to a series of ideas, as in the example in 8.2.3, is too vague, the alternative is to find a suitable substitute noun:

> *All these circumstances* make it difficult for them to view learning as a process of joyful discovery.
>
> *These features of their environment* make it difficult for them to …

Nouns like these (*circumstances, features*) are very general. They can include and sum up ideas that you have developed in whole preceding sentences or paragraphs. They can be very useful in linking a new paragraph to a proceeding one. It will help you in writing if you have a good selection of such nouns at your disposal. Here are some others:

factor, situation, influence, phenomenon, aspect, quality, view, trend, tendency, development, process, event, etc.

But make your own list, and make sure you do not use *aspect* and *phenomenon* all the time, because they tend to be overused.

8.2.5   *This* in introductions or explanations

When you introduce someone, you say to the other person: "This is my friend, Paul". You do not say, "It is my friend, Paul." Similarly, when you refer to something in a heading, or a preceding quotation, or an immediately preceding item in a list, you use *This*:

> "Love is flower-like." *This* is a simile, comparing love to a flower.

8.2.6   *Such* or *this*?

Students tend to overuse *such* for referring to something previously mentioned. If you do use it, remember it must be followed by the indefinite article or a plural noun (e.g. *such a situation* or *such situations*), unless the following noun is non-count:

> It is difficult to know what to do in *such a* situation.
>
> Such people find it hard to make friends.
>
> Such behaviour is unusual.

(*behaviour* is a non-count noun)

Do not use *such* when you merely want to refer back to something previously mentioned. Use it only when you want to generalize a previous example, that is, when you want to make a general statement about *all similar* cases:

> ✗ *The Glass Menagerie* begins with an introduction by Tom, who explains the play's setting. <u>Such an opening</u> is followed by a scene in which the family are shown at dinner. (Rewrite as "*This* opening is …").
>
> ✔ *The Glass Menagerie* begins with an introduction by Tom, who explains

the play's setting. *Such an* opening would not be possible in a more realistic kind of play.

Notice that *such* is correct in the second example because it is used to make a generalization. For *Such an opening* one could substitute *An opening like this*, without any change in the meaning. Note that when you use *like* in this way to produce a general statement, the preceding noun cannot have a definite article:

✗ The image like "sea of life" is very effective because it expresses a number of meanings simultaneously.

Even when you are referring to a particular image in a specific poem, as here, it must be *An* image like "sea of life", because *like* turns your reference into a generalization. *An image like this* and *such an image* both mean "this and any other image like it", so they are not synonymous with *this image*.

8.2.7   *Such* and *this kind of*

You can generally substitute *This kind of* for *such*. But do not use them both together. *Such* and *this kind of* are alternatives, and such kind of is wrong:

This kind of opening would not be possible in a more realistic kind of play.

(Such an opening …)

This kind of word is known as a function word.

(Such a word …)

Notice that the noun following *this kind of* … is generally singular; the second example above is a generalization, and is equivalent to saying "All *words* of this kind *are* known as function *words*".

8.2.8   *One, ones*

Usually *one* substitutes for some fairly concrete count noun, and is probably more useful in conversation than in writing:

Your typewriter ribbon is worn out. You should use a new one.

> Your shoes are worn out. Why don't you get some new ones?

Students overuse *one*. It is not, for instance, needed after *another, the former, the latter,* or after a possessive in comparisons:

> Your typewriter ribbon is worn out. Why don't you get another?
> Susan's computer is faster than Jennifer's (one).
> My essay is longer than his (one).

It is also better not to use *one* in the following choice between two things:

> A: We have two proposals to consider.
> B: *Which* (one) is the more likely to succeed?
> A: I don't know, but Jennifer's (one) is the more straightforward (one).

8.2.9   *The former, the latter*

These words are quite difficult to use correctly. It may be best not to use them at all unless you really have to. They are needed when a previous sentence contains two noun phrases of equal status so that it would be very ambiguous to use the simple pronoun, *he, she, it.*

> Robert Frost's *Stopping by Woods* is quite a traditional poem, whereas the poem by e.e. cummings is extremely unconventional. The former contains no unusual grammatical structures, whereas the latter seems to violate every grammatical rule.

(e.e. cummings was an American poet who always wrote his name like this without capitals.)

Obviously you couldn't use *it* here. There is no problem about using *the former*, which refers to the Robert Frost poem (mentioned first in the preceding sentence), and *the latter*, which refers to the cummings poem (mentioned last). This is straightforward because the reference is to an immediately preceding sentence, which speaks first of one poem and then of another. If you were to discuss more than two poems or to speak of them separately in various sentences, it could be difficult for the reader to know which one you mean by *the former* or *the latter*.

Note that you do not use *one* with *the former* and *the latter*.

8.2.10 *Respectively*

Similar problems occur with *respectively*, which has to be used with great precision, or not at all.

> I am going to examine two poems, one by Robert Frost and the other by e.e. cummings. I shall consider the two poems as examples of conventional syntax and the violation of normal word-order *respectively*.

This says clearly that you will consider the poem by Frost as an example of conventional syntax, and the poem by cummings as an example of the violation of normal word-order. Without "respectively" it would sound as if both poems might be considered as examples of both features. "Respectively" tells us that the coordinated features "conventional syntax" and "violation of normal word-order" are to be applied separately to the poems and in the same order; i.e. the first-mentioned feature relates to the first poem, the second feature to the second poem.

8.2.11 *Not the case*

This can be quite useful for negating a complicated view of how things are:

> When we read the opening of this story, we imagine that we are dealing with a romantic and somewhat conventional account of the relationship between two ordinary young people, but this is not the case.

It is difficult here to find a simple unrepetitive way of negating what has just been said. According to the sense we might want to say "but it is not". However, that would not be grammatical. According to the grammar we should say "but we are not". It is not clear, however, what that means. We can avoid this problem by using "but this is not the case". (A virtually synonymous expression is "This is not so".)

8.2.12 Verb substitution

Generally *do / does, did, am / is / are, has / have*, etc. can be used to avoid repeating a verb. Which you use depends on the tense you want:

> I wanted him to pass the exam and he did (pass the exam).
>
> I was hoping she would pass the exam and she has (passed the exam).

> I wanted to know if he had passed the exam. He told me he had (passed the exam).

It is important to distinguish between the verb *to be* and other verbs and to use the appropriate form:

> He wanted her to be happy and she was (happy).
> He wanted her to marry him and she did (marry him).

Note that the auxiliary is stressed, as it always is when it occurs last in the sentence, and cannot be abbreviated:

> He asked if I was going and I am (not I'm).

8.2.12a *And so am I*

Problems sometimes occur with the *and so* form (= *also*) used in comparisons, which requires subject–verb inversion:

> She is eighteen and so am I.
> She likes swimming and so do I.

Note the inversion and the usual *am/do* choice. All the other tenses are also possible (e.g. *so was I, so did I, so would I*).

8.2.12b *Do so, did so*

Problems also occur with the use of *do so*. This implies compliance with a previously stated request, but there must also be an exact match between the two sentences:

> She asked him to post a letter for her. He *did so*. (= posted the letter)

It has to be possible to turn *do so* into a verb phrase which can be found in the previous sentence. We could rewrite the example as: "What she wanted was that *he would post the letter*. He *posted the letter*."

The following, however, is wrong:

> ✗ She wanted a letter posted. He did so.

The first sentence is equivalent to: "What she wanted was that *the letter would be posted*." The subject of the italic phrase is *letter*, so it does not correspond to "<u>He</u> did so." A more appropriate continuation would be:

> She wanted a letter posted. He posted it for her / He did it for her.

8.2.13 *The following, the above*

Students are rather fond of using *the above*, but in fact it is often unnecessary, and may make your writing sound too much like an official announcement. Certainly it is better to avoid ending your essay with some statement like: "The above are my views on the subject of capital punishment." Such a sentence tells us nothing because we must know by now that you have been giving your views on capital punishment.

References to preceding ideas can usually be made with *this* or *this + a suitable substitute noun* (see 8.2.4).

If you do need to use *the above*, note that it has no "s" even when it refers to more than one thing, and the verb agreement is usually plural:

> *The above are* just some of the commonest arguments that are used to support this idea.

Note that you can use *above* as a simple adverb of place, in which case no preposition is used (just as no preposition is used with *here, there, where,* etc.):

> The metaphors in the passage are listed *above*.

It is sometimes convenient to refer to what you are going to say, using *the following* or *as follows*:

> My reasons are *as follows*: ...
>
> *The following* are some of the points that could be made.

Again, note that there can be no "s" on *the following* although the verb agreement is plural. Also there is no way of changing *as follows* in which the verb agrees not with *reasons*, but with *what* follows.

8.2.14   Reference forward to what you are going to say

Before starting an explanation which is going to be complicated, it is sometimes helpful to provide your reader with some forewarning of what is to come:

> There are two points to be made about this. First....
>
> There are a number of reasons for this. One is that....
>
> This helps to capture the reader's attention in several / various ways. To start with it....
>
> The introduction serves several purposes. In the first place ...

Note that these introductory sentences are meaningful if you use *several* or *various* in them, but not if you use *some*:

> ✗ The poet's use of similes serves some purpose.

This is virtually meaningless, because just about everything in the world serves *some* purpose. If you say *various purposes*, you are saying that it serves more than one purpose — which is worth saying, especially when it prepares the reader for an explanation which will include more than one purpose.

If, on the other hand, you can only think of *one* purpose, or *one* point to make, then do not use this kind of introductory sentence at all.

You could in fact say:

> The poet's use of similes serves some purpose, but I can't figure out what it is.

But this would probably be unwise in an academic essay!

8.3   Reference to time

I have dealt with time under verb tenses (5.1) but here I shall consider adverbs and adverbial clauses, which also cause some problems.

8.3.1 Time clauses

Time clauses can be used to relate two events to each other in terms of time. The effect of doing so can also be emphatic, or dramatic, particularly in narrative, because it may draw attention to the speed with which things happen, or to the suprising coincidence of things happening simultaneously.

8.3.1a *When* and *while*

Students sometimes confuse *when* and *while*. It is true they are often interchangeable:

> When / While I was waiting in the queue, a man came along and started telling jokes and performing conjuring tricks. Such a person is known as a busker.

However, *while* cannot be used for things which happen quickly or when the main clause refers to something which could not have been going on at the same time as what happens in the time clause:

> *When* the bell *rang*, everyone *rushed* out of the classroom.

If you used *while* here, you would be insisting that they had all left the classroom before the bell stopped ringing (not very likely?).

> *When* Martin Lee *went* to London, he *spoke* to the British Prime Minister.

You could only use *while* if the Prime Minister was also on the plane and they talked while they were on the plane (of course, for this meaning you would probably change *went* to *was going* or *was flying*). You must however use *while* in the following:

> Please wait while I get my coat.
> You keep him covered, while I take his gun.

8.3.1b *Once*

This can be used in place of *when* to introduce a time clause. It should not be used together with *when*:

Once the bell rang, everyone *rushed* out of the classroom.

(As soon as the bell rang, everyone rushed out of the classroom; Everyone waited till the bell rang before rushing out of the class-room.)

You will remember it *once* you *have understood* it.

(You have to understand it first in order to be able to remember it.)

As you will see from these examples, *once* can have various implications. (Don't confuse this use of *once* with "story-telling *once*", which can be followed by *when* as in: "Once, when I was young, I met a famous writer." See list of time-expressions in 8.3.2.)

8.3.1c   *The moment …*

This is useful for stressing the rapidity with which one event follows another and also is used without *when*:

The moment he *walked* through the door, I *recognized* him.

(As soon as he walked through the door I recognized him)

The moment the bell *rang*, everyone *rushed* out of the classroom.

8.3.1d   *No sooner … than …*

This also shows the rapidity with which one even follows another, and is synonymous with *as soon as*, but slightly more emphatic. It requires subject–verb inversion:

No sooner *had he put down* the receiver than the phone rang again.

The word order perhaps creates a slightly dramatic effect.

8.3.1e   *Hardly … when / before …*

This is very similar but even more emphatic:

Hardly had he left the room when / before everyone started criticizing him.

The implication is that they started criticizing him almost *before* he left the room.

8.3.1f *By the time (that)*

This emphasizes the amount of time elapsing before some event. It may be a suprisingly short time, or an unpleasantly long one:

> *By the time* she was thirteen she already had a university degree in mathematics. (surprisingly short)
>
> *By the time* I see you again, we may all be quite different. (unpleasantly long)

Notice that the simple past is very seldom used in the main clause with this:

> By the time they had caught ten fish it *was getting* dark.
>
> By the time they had caught ten fish it *had got* dark.

The main clause has to describe some continuing process or something which happened over a certain period of time, not a sudden event.

8.3.1g *Until (till) / not until*

This seems to be one of the most difficult expressions in English, especially when it is used negatively:

> He did *not* come home *until* midnight.
>
> (= He came home at midnight but he ought to have come home much earlier)
>
> I shall wait for you *till* nine o'clock.
>
> (= I won't wait after nine).

The problems seem to be in the first example that the negative form tells you when he came home but focuses on the fact that before that time he was *not* home; in the second example that the positive form is in no way an equivalent of *when* or *at*:

> Don't do it until ten o'clock. Start doing it at ten o'clock.
>
> Do it until ten o'clock. Stop doing it at ten o'clock.

The two sentences in in the first example go perfectly well together: there is no contradiction between them. But they contradict the sentences in the second example.

Generally it is possible to reverse the order of negative and affirmative:

> "Until I met you," he said, "I didn't know what true love is."
>
> "Not until I met you," he said, "did I discover what it really means to love."

Note that if you start with *Not until*, there must be subject–verb inversion in the main clause.

8.3.2   Time expressions

A number of expressions (typically adverbs or adverbial phrases) combine with verb tenses to convey a variety of time references that are obviously important in narrative but may also play an important part in everyday arrangements.

There are quite a number of problems with time expressions: they involve a bewildering variety of prepositions; they may carry quite complicated implications; there are often restrictions on the tenses they can occur with.

Many time expressions are useful for starting a sentence with, because they tend to structure your ideas by providing a contrast with some other time or aspect of time:

> *On weekdays* she has to get up before seven. But *on Sundays* she stays in bed till nearly lunchtime.

The following expressions can all be found in a good English dictionary or dictionary of English idioms, but students often do not take the trouble to check, and so misuse them. I list them here, therefore, to encourage you to pay more attention to their precise meaning.

after all   (1) in its main use, this is not really a time expression at all, but a connective, implying that something is known already but may have been forgotten:

We should not be too ready to dismiss Gorbachev. After all, it was he who initiated the reforms.

Students should not complain too much about their workload. After all, it is in their own interest to study hard.

(2) *after all* can have another meaning which is related to time when it is not used at the beginning of the sentence:

He didn't go to Paris after all. (implying that he was supposed to go to Paris but, suprisingly, he didn't go)

The important point is that *after all* cannot be used to mean "after every-thing was over". Instead you should use *in the end, at the end of the story, etc.*

(Do not confuse this however with the use of *after* followed by *all + noun phrase*: "After all the effort he put into training for the Olympics, he was ill and could not participate.")

after all that   this implies that someone has made a lot of preparations to do something, but in the end did not do it:

After all that! What a waste of time!

This use tends to be quite colloquial, but it can be used in a formal con-text:

Representatives of the two sides have met repeatedly to discuss the issue and there have been a number of attempts to mediate by third parties. After all that, it is disappointing to note that no progress seems to have been made.

after a while   synonymous with *by and by, after a little while*; also in some contexts with *as time went by*:

At first she was very shy. But after a while she grew used to him and would fly down from her cage and eat from his hand.

after this / that   you would use this in a past-tense narrative if you wanted to emphasize the result of a preceding event:

The king had learnt his lesson. After that he didn't ask his courtiers to flatter him any more.

Beware of *since then* which cannot be used in this kind of context (see below).

at   used as follows with time of day and week-ends:

> The show begins at 7 o'clock.
>
> Let's meet at lunchtime.
>
> I'll be there at noon/midday.
>
> She handed in her paper at the last minute.
>
> At the eleventh hour they announced their willingness to accept the conditions. (= at the last possible moment)
>
> What are you doing at the week-end?
>
> (In American usage however "on the week-end" occurs.)

at last   this causes many problems. It has an emotional tone and a subjective viewpoint and is used more in speaking than in writing (unless fiction). It expresses relief when something you have impatiently waited for finally happens:

> A. At last! Where have you been all this time?
>
> B. I'm sorry, I was caught in a traffic jam.

It would not be very appropriate for example in the following:

> If you keep on trying, in the end you will succeed.

It is best also not to use *at last* in an objective summary of a story:

> Hamlet hesitates a long time before eventually / finally killing his uncle and avenging his father's death.
>
> She took the driving-test many times. *Eventually* she passed.

Nor should it be used to mean "at the end of the story":

> At the end of the story they get married.
>
> The story ends with their marriage.

In fiction, however, it may be used to suggest the viewpoint of a character:

> At last she had passed her driving-test. Now she could drive the children to school.

(= she is feeling very relieved, we are sharing her feelings)

It can also be used to imply the writer's emotional involvement in a view he or she is expressing:

The government has at last decided to do something.

This implies that we have been waiting a long time for them to do something.

at once   synonymous with *immediately*.

at present   this refers to the speaker's present and suggests a contrast with the future. More or less synonymous with *at the moment*.

Note that *presently* has a different meaning, more or less synonymous with *after a (little) while*, *in a while*, *a little later*. There is a modern tendency to use *presently* for *at present*, but many people would say this is incorrect:

✗   I am presently studying Japanese.

The standard meaning can be illustrated by

I shall do it presently.

at that / the time   this can substitute for *then* when it is used to contrast with something that happens later:

I had no idea *at that / the time* how difficult it was going to be.

The implication is that later you realized.

It is advisable, however, to be suspicious of *at that time*, because it often comes from Chinese translation and pops up in quite inappropriate places. You cannot use it for instance with an action or an event that only lasts a short time, or in narrative or plot summaries:

✗   She dropped her handbag in the middle of the street. At that time she felt very embarrassed.

Probably English, with its tense systems, has less need than Chinese to specify time in contexts like this.

at the moment   always refers to the speaker's present, potentially contrasting with what may happen in the near future. For example, a famous tennis player after winning a tournament says to the press:

> I am playing very well at the moment.

He knows that his winning streak may not last. If he said, "I am playing very well now", the contrast would more likely be with the recent past (he wasn't playing so well last year). If you reported this in the past, it would become *at that time*.

At the moment is nearly synonymous with *right now*.

by   this is one of the most frequently misused time prepositions. The problem lies partly in the fact that, referring to the past, it describes a state of affairs, not an action:

> In 1950, he died.
> By 1950, he was dead.

In the sentence with *by*, you could not use the simple past. Another part of the problem is that *by* adds an implication not present in the meaning of other time prepositions like *in*, *on* or *at*:

> By the nineteen fifties it was obvious that Britain was no longer a world power.
> By the nineteen fifties it had become obvious that Britain was no longer a world power.

The implication, more explicit in the second sentence because of *become* and the past perfect, is that this is the result of a process which had started earlier. There may therefore be a further implication: it was probably true before, but people did not become aware of it till the nineteen fifties.

Returning to the sentence "By 1950, he was dead", we find that it tells us one of two things:

(1) that in 1949 he may or may not have been dead: the speaker does not know for sure.
(2) that he could not have witnessed or had any influence on some event in 1950, since he had died before that.

Referring to the present or future *by* carries a similiar implication to the first one above:

> You must hand in your work by Friday.

The implication is that you can also hand it in any day before Friday, if you wish, but Friday is the deadline. In this sense it should be possible to add *at the latest*, without altering the meaning.

by and by   used in narration to indicate a lapse of time between the last event and the next:

> By and by he grew used to life in the city and stopped feeling homesick.

Synonymous with *after a while*, *in a little while*, *presently*, though it tends to suggest a somewhat longer time.

by now   this implies that enough time has elapsed for something to have happened:

> It is more than twelve hours since they left. They should be in London by now.

Used in a past tense narrative, it has the effect of making us share a character's viewpoint:

> He had been walking since morning. By now he was thoroughly exhausted.

by the hour etc.   this has two meanings:

> Part-time workers are paid by the hour. (= for each hour's work)

> The situation was getting more desperate by the hour. (= very fast)

by this / that time   more or less synonymous with *by now*, but more neutral. It might be used, for example, in objective past tense narrative:

> In April the king dissolved parliament. By this time popular indignation had grown so strong that thousands of people took to the streets in protest.

It means always that something had already happened before the time referred to. It should not be confused with *at this time*.

day after day   this stresses the repetitiveness of something and is nearly synonymous with *endlessly, continuously*. The same pattern can be used with other time words like *month, week, year*, etc.

> Day after day it rained. They began to think the sun would never shine again.

An equally emphatic and nearly synonymous expression is *for days on end*.

day by day   this stresses the gradual steady development of something. The same pattern can be used with other time words like *month, week, year*, etc.

> Day by day he grew stronger again after the accident.

eventually   this refers to something which comes after a long wait, but it does not have the subjective point of view of *at last*:

> If you keep on trying, eventually you will succeed.

It is possible to use *eventually* with past or future, but not with the present tense (except in retelling a story — 5.1.1c) or the present perfect — see *finally*:

finally   very similar in meaning to *eventually*, but with less sense of having waited. It can be used, as *eventually* cannot, with the present perfect or present tense:

> We have finally succeeded.
> We are finally here.

It is also used in a different meaning, generally at the beginning of a sentence, to introduce a final point.

for   Time expressions beginning with *for* can have two meanings.
(1) they can refer to the amount of time you spent somewhere or doing something, or the amount of time you are going to spend:

> We were neighbours for ten years.
> I am going to Beijing for three weeks.
> We went to Thailand for ten days.
> I shall be working in London for the next two years.

Notice that this often describes something like an intention, and it can be a past intention as well as a present one: i.e. we went to Thailand with the intention of spending ten days there.

It helps to clarify the situation when you describe how a plan was changed:

> We were going to go for ten days, but we all got sick so we came back after two days.

(2) they can refer to the amount of time which must elapse before something happens or has elapsed since something last happened:

> I am not going to Beijing for another three months.
> You needn't hand in your assignment for another three days.
> I haven't see her for ten years.

for a moment   this generally implies "temporary", and in the past refers to something contradicted by reality: "For a moment I thought I was going to die." (but I did not die)

It can also refer to the future:

> Can you wait (for) a moment?

You can generally substitute *for a (little) while.*

Note that *not for a moment* is used, at the beginning of a sentence with subject–verb inversion, in a completely different sense:

> Not for a moment did I imagine that I would win.

This is an emphatic negative and often expresses surprise.

> He's handed in his assignment on time for once!

The implication is that he usually hands it in late.

for the moment   definitely implies that something is only temporary:

> For the moment I'm living with my parents, but as soon as I can I shall get my own flat.

It refers to some present situation which will continue into the future, but not permanently.

Synonymous with *for the time being*.

for the / his / her time   this implies some contrast between an idea or event and the time when it appeared or occurred:

> X's theories were very advanced for the time.

for the time being   synonymous with *for the moment*, with a very clear sense of something temporary.

for years   when the number of years is not specified, the meaning is "for a very long time". It may well be used with the present perfect:

> I haven't eaten anything as good as this for years.

Often this is hyperbole or exaggeration. Another way to say this would be "It's years since I ate anything as good as this".

Even more emphatic are *for years on end* and *year after year*, both of which would normally be used to describe something which happened repeatedly for a very long time. Any of them can of course be used with any appropriate time-period: *days, weeks, months*, etc.

from day to day   this stresses change. It can be used with other time expressions, *week, year*, etc.

> The situation changes from day to day.

Note also:

> We shall deal with problems as they arise, on a day-to-day basis.

from now on   this announces the start of something, and often implies the importance of a change from what happened in the past:

> I've been letting you off very lightly so far, but from now on you're going to have to work harder.

It is often synonymous with *in future*.

from time to time   more or less synonymous with *occasionally, now and then*.

immediately   (1) referring to the future this is synonymous with *at once, right now*:

> I want you to do it *immediately.*

(2) in the past it implies "after something else":

> He felt better immediately.
>
> (for example, after taking the medicine)

in   used with months and years:

> She was born in June.
> He was born in 1950.

(But use *on* when the day of the month is specified: *on June 4.*)

Somewhat informally, *in* is also used with the same meaning as *for* in the following:

> I haven't see her in years.

in a moment   (1) referring to something in the past, this implies that it happened very quickly:

> It was all over in a moment.

Near synonyms are *in a flash, in an instant, instantaneously.*

(2) referring to the future, this implies that something will happen soon but not immediately:

> I'll do it in a moment.

Probably this means you cannot do it immediately because you are busy *at the moment.*

in (the) future   with the article this tends to be synonymous with *one day* in its future sense:

> In the future we will get all our power from the sun.

Without the article it tends to be used to announce some change to the present arrangements, and is synonymous with *from now on*:

> In future you will hand in your assignments on time, please.

in the end   also very similar to *eventually*. Not likely to be used when referring to the present. It may imply that something did not turn out as expected:

> Several plans were proposed, but in the end we accepted none of them.

in the near future   this is synonymous with *soon*:

> We are expecting a breakthrough in the near future.

There is another version of this, which must have originated as a slightly humorous paraphrase: *in the not so distant future*:

in the meantime   similar to *for the time being*, but it implies also that you are waiting for something else. A sports commentator might say:

> We will return to live coverage as soon as the rain stops. In the meantime we are going to show you a recording of yesterday's match.

in those days   this refers to the past and to something that was the case at some time in the past:

> In those days I was just a foolish young man with no experience of the world.

This is similar to *At the time*, but more conversational, more personal.

in time   (1) doing something *in time* means not doing it too late:

> My taxi was caught in a traffic jam, but I got to the airport just in time.

(in other words, you did not miss the plane)

> I arrived in time to catch the plane.

In this sense, *in time* cannot be used at the beginning of a sentence.

(2) it can also mean something like "as a result of time passing":

> At the moment you are very unhappy, but in time you will forget.
> In time even the worst memories fade away.

Another way to say this would be *with the passing of time*.

in (Shakespeare's) time   same meaning as *at the time*, only this allows you to specify what particular time you are referring to:

> In Shakespeare's time, boys played the women's parts on the stage.

If you want to express this meaning in relation to a historical period it may be more normal to use *during*:

> During the Elizabethan period, women's parts were played by boys.

in times to come   more or less synonymous with *in the future*, *one day* (in its future sense).

in X years(' time)   this usually refers to the future:

> In ten years' time, I hope to be earning a big salary.
> In a hundred years' time, the world will be a very different place.

This is a synonym of *X years from now*.

> A hundred years from now, the world will be a very different place.

If used in the past, "time" is usually omitted, and it refers to the amount of time it took for something to happen:

> In only ten years he had become one of the most successful artists of his era.

This is approximately synonymous with *within X years*, but note that the two expressions cannot be combined: you cannot say, "within ten years' time."

last Friday **etc.**   no preposition is used with *last*, *next* and *this*:

> I saw him last Friday.

next Friday **etc.**   as with *last*, no preposition:

> I shall see him next Friday.

now   (1) can refer to the speaker's present, in which case it generally implies some contrast with the past or the result of something in the recent past:

> I used to play three times a week, but now I don't play at all.

> My secretary left last week. Now I'm looking for a new one.

(2) At the end of a positive sentence or after an imperative, it contrasts with *later*:

> He's going to do it now.
>
> (= not later)
>
> Do it now.
>
> (= don't put it off)

(3) In a past tense narrative, it has the effect of making us share a character's viewpoint:

> She had passed the exam. Now she must find a job.

It can also be used in something like a running commentary for successive events or actions:

> … now he's running with the ball, now he shoots.

This effect is also found in poetry and fiction.

now and then   more or less synonymous with *occasionally, from time to time*.

nowadays   synonymous with *now* so long as it refers to a generalization:

> I'm playing very well nowadays.

But you cannot substitute it when *now* refers to a unique event:

> ✗ I've just lost my secretary and <u>nowadays</u> I'm looking for a new one.

You cannot use *nowadays* for the second and third senses of *now*. *Nowadays* is particularly useful in describing trends:

> Nowadays Hong Kong is becoming more and more prosperous.

on   is used with days of the week:

> Let's have a barbecue on Saturday.
>
> We get paid on the last day of the month.

once upon a time   this is the traditional introduction to a children's story:

> Once upon a time there were three bears.

once   (1) this can be used as an abbreviated form of *once upon a time*:

> Once there was a poor girl called Cinderella.
> I once met the author of *A Room with a View*.

It is worth noting that *once* counts as an expression indicating a time in the past, so you cannot use the present perfect with it: "I <u>have once lived</u> in Thailand" is incorrect.

Nor can you use *once* when you are quoting a character in a text

> ✗ As Miranda <u>once</u> says, "I'm so superior to him." (see 2.4.1)

You can however use it when you are quoting a real person:

> ✔ As Marx once said,...

(2) *Once* can also be used to imply a contrast with *now*, referring to a state of affairs which has changed:

> Once I played three times a week, but now I don't play at all.

More or less synonymous in the last sense are *in the past, formerly, in the old days, in bygone days*.

one day   referring to the future, this is more or less synonymous with *in the future*:

> One day we will get all our energy from the sun.

This does have a slightly special sense, which can perhaps be captured by paraphrasing it as:

> A day will come when we get all our power from the sun.

Referring to the past, it is an introduction to a story or a new stage in a story:

> One day Gregory Samsa woke up and found he had changed into a cockroach.

In this sense it implies narrative, even if immediately followed by a continuous tense:

> One day he was sitting outside enjoying the cool breeze, when he saw a stranger walking up the road towards the house.

There is a traditional story-telling form, *one fine day*:

> Well, one fine day the three bears came home and found something had happened in their house.

on time   easily confused with *in time*. To do something *on time* is to do it at the set time:

> Even if you didn't hand in your paper *on time*, you should still hand it in. You may still be *in time* to be given a grade.

It cannot stand at the beginning of a sentence.

over the years   this emphasizes something which has been happening, often some kind of change, during a long period of time:

> Over the years we have seen a gradual erosion of traditional values.

presently   synonymous with *after a while* etc.:

> Please take a seat in the waiting-room. The doctor will see you presently.

It is sometimes used to mean *at present*, but many people still consider this incorrect.

right now   generally synonymous with *at the moment*, but it also can be used for *immediately*, *at once*, as in:

> I want you to do it right now.

since then   this is used when the time base is present tense:

> Joseph and I had a quarrel last week. Since then I haven't seen him.

In a past tense narrative it can only be used when the writer is adopting the viewpoint of a character:

> She had quarrelled with Joseph the week before. Since then she had not seen him.

so far   this describes what has happened up to the present but implies that things may change:

> We're doing all right so far.

(but our success may not last)

> So far so good.

then   (1) the commonest meaning is something like "next".

(2) It can mean something like "at that time in the past" if it is placed after the verb, or at any rate not first in the sentence. Compare the following:

> *Then* I was twenty-one.

(next step in the story — I came of age)

> I was *then* twenty-one.

(this is the age I was at the time of the events)

Often in the second sense there is an implied contrast with "later on":

> I had no idea *then* how difficult it was going to be. But later I began to understand the full seriousness of what I had taken on.

Beware, however, of overusing *then* if you are trying to write a narrative. It is a conventional expectation that in narrative one event follows another, so there is generally no need to mark this connection. It seems to be useful to do so mainly after there has been some break either in the regular sequence of narrative steps or in the situation they describe:

> For six months I saw her on the station platform every day. Then one day she was no longer there.
> For a long time I thought of her. Then I forgot her.

this Saturday etc.   as with *last* and *next*, no preposition:

> The party is this Saturday.

Even native speakers are quite often confused about the difference between *this Saturday* and *next Saturday*, though all would agree that the former is closer in time. Generally you use *this* to refer to a day within the same week.

this once   this is hard to define, but is generally used to describe doing something which normally you would not do; it implies that you are making an exception:

> She decided to indulge herself just this once.

throughout   this stresses that something happens continuously during a certain period:

> Throughout the years I worked for them they never gave me a raise.

(in modern) times   these expressions that refer to the present or present trends (*in recent times*, *in these times*, *in modern times*) usually have *times* in the plural.

until (recently)   this describes a situation which has now changed:

> She disappeared ten years ago, and until recently I had no idea what had happened to her. Then suddenly last week I got a letter.

until now / up till now   this is approximately synonymous with *so far*, but it does not have the same implication that things may change:

> She disappeared ten years ago. Until now, I have no idea what happened to her.

> (= I still don't know)

A synonym in this context would be *to this day* which stresses the long time that something has lasted.

within   this has two uses with time expressions. It is used like *in* referring to the past, in order to stress that something happened quickly, in a very short period:

> Within ten years he had become the leading artist of his era.
> Within seconds she had vanished.

It is also used in setting a deadline or time limit in the future:

> You must hand in your revised paper within the next week.

APPENDICES

A. *SOME TECHNICAL TERMS IN LITERATURE*

A.1 Narrative

a narrator the person who tells a story. The "I" in a first-person narrative.

a narrative (count noun) = *a story*

narrative (non-count noun) = a general term for a kind of writing defined by its purpose: to recount events, generally chronologically (in the order in which they occurred). It can also be defined by its opposition to other kinds of writing, such as *description, argumentation*, etc. Since many art forms recount events (real or imagined), the word can be applied to other things than writing, for example films, plays, TV serials.

narration the act of narrating:

> Fred's narration of the kidnapping is so matter-of-fact that at first we remain unaware of the full horror of what he is doing.

narrative (modifier) e.g. *narrative technique*.

first-person narrative a first-person narrative (count noun) is a story which is *told in the first person*. There is a narrator who uses the pronoun *I* and takes some part in the story. An author who uses first-person narrative (non-count) tells his story through a narrator who is a character in the story:

> John Fowles uses first person-narrative in *The Collector*.
>
> The first part of the story is told in the first person by Fred.
>
> The narrator of the first part is Fred.
>
> The second part is also first-person narrative, but it represents Miranda's diary; it is as if Miranda was talking to herself.

viewpoint (or *point of view*) the term used in discussing how a story is told, whether as a first-person narrative, or from the point of view of one of the main characters, or from the point of view of several characters. With *omiscient point of view* or *an omniscient narrator*, the narrator speaks to us directly and can tells us what is going on in the minds of any of the characters.

A.2 Poetry and verse forms

Poetry   all poetry has rhythm. When the rhythm of *a poem* falls into regular repeated patterns, it has *metre*. A poem may or may not have *rhyme*. A poem will almost certainly have other effects which depend on the sound of the words: *alliteration, assonance, onomatopoeic words*.

A poem can be (written) *in rhyme, in rhyming couplets, in iambic pentameters, in blank verse, in free verse*, etc.

Stanza   a poem may be divided up into *stanzas*, which are approximately the equivalent of paragraphs in prose. There is one important difference however: stanzas often contain a large amount of repetition. In some traditional types of poem, for example, there may be a line or two lines (or more) repeated at the end of each stanza, or at the end of every second stanza. This can be called *a refrain*.

Rhyme   if rhyme occurs at the end of the line it can be called *end-rhyme*. If two words in the same line rhyme, this is known as *internal rhyme*. If every two lines rhyme, the poem is written *in rhyming couplets*. A poem may be written with a more complex *rhyme scheme*. Rhyme schemes are generally described by using letters of the alphabet: *The rhyme scheme is abba, cddc*, etc.

> Pope's *The Rape of the Lock* is written in rhyming couplets.
>
> A lot of modern poetry is in free verse.

A poet can *use rhyme* or *use a complicated rhyme scheme*. A poet may also use *half-rhyme*, or *eye-rhyme* (the spelling is the same but the pronunciation is different) or *not use rhyme at all*.

> Shakespeare *uses* rhyme in his sonnets, but his plays are mostly *in* blank verse, which *has* a regular metre but *does not rhyme*.

Notice the use of *rhyme* as a verb:

> The first poem rhymes; the second does not.
>
> In rhyming couplets, the first line rhymes *with* the second line, the third line with the fourth, and so on. Each two lines *rhyme*.

Note that if you say two lines *rhyme*, it must mean they rhyme *with each other*, so there is no need to say so.

Metre   English metre is defined by the number of stressed and unstressed syllables in each line of verse. In traditional metre a line contains a fixed number of *feet* (between one and six) and each foot normally contains two or three syllables of which one is stressed.

Metres are classified according to the number of feet in the line and the order of stressed and unstressed syllables in the foot. A pentameter, for example, has five feet, and in a regular iambic pentameter each foot contains an unstressed syllable followed by a stressed syllable: *ti-tum ti-tum ti-tum ti-tum ti-tum*.

The names for metres are sometimes used as count nouns and sometimes as non-count nouns: "This poem is in iambic pentameters" / "This poem is in iambic pentameter."

It is worth bearing in mind that you are not likely to find any poem which is in a completely regular metre throughout: the effect would be too boring. So a statement like "This poem is written in anapaestic tetrameter" (four feet with the pattern *ti-ti-tum*) means that the *predominant* pattern is anapaestic. Shakespeare writes in iambic pentameter, but you will find many variations in his verse.

blank verse   the form of verse typically used by the Elizabethan playwrights, with no end-rhyme. Shakespeare writes his plays in blank verse, though he sometimes ends a scene with a rhyming couplet, and sometimes uses prose, particularly for comic scenes.

free verse   much modern poetry is in free verse, which means that it has neither rhyme nor regular metre.

A.3 Drama

Drama   is usually a general term and therefore non-count. The equivalent count noun is *a play*:

> Students who study drama ought to go and see some plays performed.

Plays can be of various kinds and the terms describing them, *tragedy*, *comedy*, *farce*, *melodrama* are both count and non-count:

> Hamlet is a tragedy.
> There are various definitions of tragedy.

Acts and scenes   plays are usually, but not always, divided into *acts* and *scenes*. In English drama there is no precise definition of these terms. However, the division into acts may be related to changes in time: for example, the second act may show something that happened the day after the events of the first act. The division into scenes may be related to changes in the characters on stage, or changes in place.

Stage directions   stage directions are the instructions the author gives to actors and director, describing the setting or explaining the appearance or behaviour of the characters. In stage directions the verbs are mainly in present tense.

Performance   another noun which is both count and non-count:

> It is always helpful to see a play in performance.
> A good performance can help you understand much more.

In the performance of a play the actors *come on* and *go off*, or *enter* and *exit*. While they are *on stage*, they must have something to do; that is, they must move about, or sit, or stand and their actions must be motivated. Above all, they must interact with any other actors who are on stage.

A.4 Irony, satire, criticism

These terms are both hard to define and hard to use, but they are essential. First we must distinguish between *irony* and *sarcasm*, both usually non-count nouns.

Sarcasm, sarcastic

Approximately one can say that while *irony* is a literary device, *sarcasm* is only used in speech. If someone says to you, "Oh, she's so perfect, isn't she?" and you know they don't like her, they are being *sarcastic*. Sarcasm can be quite offensive, and it is possible to say to someone, "Don't be so sarcastic," whereas you would not normally say "Don't be ironic."

Note, however, that sarcasm is very frequently used among friends or brothers and sisters in a friendly way.

Irony, ironic

Irony is a great deal more complicated because there are various different kinds of *irony*. What most kinds of irony have in common is that they have some kind of hidden or non-literal meaning. I do not want to define irony here, but to show how the word is used. I shall be mainly concerned with *linguistic irony*, rather than *dramatic irony* (irony of situation).

It is fairly simple to draw attention to the presence of irony in a work:

> Forster constantly uses irony in *A Room with a View*.
> Forster's novels are generally filled with / full of irony.
> There is a great deal of irony in this work.
> Irony occurs frequently in this work.

Irony is generally associated with *tone*:

> Forster's tone is ironic throughout the book.
> Forster uses an ironic tone.

Both people and situations can also be ironic:

> Forster is being ironic when he says that Lucy "had not yet acquired decency".
> The situation is intensely ironic, because Alan does not understand the true significance of the old man's words.

There is clearly some difference of meaning here: while the second example describes some aspect of the situation, the first describes Forster's intention, which I think is why it uses the present continuous.

Note that intentional, linguistic irony generally has a persuasive purpose of some kind; that is to say, by using irony the writer is trying to make us see things from a certain point of view and to some extent is *criticizing* or *making fun of* someone or something:

> Forster's irony is directed at the narrow-mindedness of the middle-class British tourists.

Dramatic irony is a technical term normally used to describe the situation when a stage character (in a play) is unaware of something that the audience are aware of.

The word *irony* also occurs in the set phrase *an irony of fate*, which refers to a situation in which good or bad luck comes to someone in what seems a particularly appropriate or inappropriate way.

Satire, satirical

Satire (non-count) is a particular type of writing, or literary *genre*. Satire attacks or criticizes some aspect of human behaviour by making it appear ridiculous, or more precisely, by portraying characters who are ridiculous. There is also a count noun, *a satire*, which refers to a particular work and a non-count noun, *satire*, which refers to the genre or type of writing:

> Satire is always negative.
>
> Jonson's *Volpone* is a satire on human greed.

Mostly you will need to use the non-count noun, or the equivalent adjective and verb:

> The satire in *Volpone* is very obvious.
>
> Jonson is a satirical writer.
>
> In *Volpone* Jonson satirizes human greed.
>
> Swift's intention in *Gulliver's Travels* is satirical.

There are relatively few literary works which can be described as *satires*, but there are a great many which *contain satire*, or which *satirize* some aspect of human behaviour or society. A work is not necessarily "a satire" just because it contains satirical elements or satirizes something.

Strictly speaking, satire is only involved when the writer's aim is to correct some fault or exaggeration by laughing at it. If the intention is only to make us laugh, we can say the tone is *humorous* or that *humour*, rather than satire, is involved in the work.

Any of the following verbs can be used to describe satire, or a satirical intention:

to laugh at, to ridicule, to make fun of, to mock, to pour scorn on, to hold up, to ridicule / scorn, to attack

> In *Gulliver's Travels* Swift laughs at / ridicules / attacks / satirizes all forms of human pretentiousness.

Criticism, criticize

It is slightly confusing that the verb *to criticize* is generally not used in a neutral sense but has the meaning of *to find fault with.*

> The job of a literary critic is to analyse and evaluate works of literature.
>
> She criticized the author for failing to acknowledge all his sources.

Notice the construction: *to criticize someone for something. Criticize* is one of the verbs that cannot be followed by a *that* clause:

> ✗ She criticized that the author had failed to acknowledge all his sources.

If the proper construction does not fit easily into what you want to say, use a neutral verb; most probably the meaning of what you are reporting will show that it is adverse criticism:

> ✗ She criticized that the book failed because the characters were unconvincing.

Rewrite as

> She argued that the book failed because the characters were unconvincing.

In more everyday situations, the verbs *complain* and *object* are useful alternatives which can be followed by a *that* clause.

B. BIOGRAPHICAL DETAILS

A number of grammatical mistakes occur very frequently in writing about people. I shall deal here with some of the expressions that crop up in people's biographies.

B.1 Being born

The first chapter of Dickens' *David Copperfield* is entitled, "I am born". As the narrator says:

> To begin my life with the beginning of my life, I record that I was born (as I have been informed and believe) on a Friday, at twelve o'clock at night.

Grammatically, the point to remember is that *born* is not by itself a verb and must have some form of *to be* with it. But it is interesting to notice also how the present tense is used in Dickens' chapter heading, a convention which is followed in all the chapter headings of this novel I think, though the story is told in the past tense, as you would expect.

Another point about being born is that there is no active equivalent. That is to say, a woman gives birth to a child, there is no form of the word *born* which can be used. In very old-fashioned, literary language, you might read of a woman *bearing* a child, or *being delivered of* a child: e.g. "She *bore / was delivered of /* a handsome male child." But in ordinary language, people nowadays would say: "She had a baby", or, if you already knew she was going to have a baby and were mainly interested in the sex, "She had a boy/girl."

B.2 Dying

There is an important distinction between the *state* of being *dead*, and the *event* of *dying*:

The victim was already dead when he reached the hospital.
He died on the way to the hospital.

If you get this wrong you can produce some surprising meanings:

✗ She was dead when she went to her daughter's funeral. A sniper's bullet killed her.

The writer did not mean to say that she attended her daughter's funeral as a ghost. What she meant to say was "She *died* when...."

B.3 Marriage

This is a relationship which is constantly referred to in literature. It is often the climax of traditional stories and comedies. It is therefore worth getting the terms right:

Cynthia didn't want to work, so she *married* a rich man.

Janet didn't want to *get married*; she wanted a career.

Janet *is not married*. Cynthia *is married to* a rich man. Cynthia *married / got married* in June last year. Her *marriage* is very successful. She enjoys *married life*.

Henry and Cynthia *were married* in June last year.

One important point to notice is that *marry* and *get married* refer to an event, whereas *to be married* refers to a state. It is important to keep this distinction in mind, because referring to the state with something like "She hasn't got married" is quite odd. What you would normally say is "She is not married."

Notice also that the preposition *with* is not used. You use *to* when referring to the state: "She is married *to* a rich man." You do not use any preposition when you refer to the event: "She married a rich man."

The main difference between *to marry* and *to get married* is that the latter is a little less formal. Mostly they can substitute for each other. Either is relatively unusual in the negative, for obvious reasons. Here is an example of the relatively unusual case in which *get married* is used in the negative:

> She did not get married on Sunday, because the bridegroom did not turn up.

Normally when someone decides to get married, they do it. It is only when you are talking about the *state* of *being married* or *not married*, that the negative is equally likely.

If people are old-fashioned and formal enough to *get engaged* before getting married, this expression is used in the same way, with the same distinction between *being engaged* and *getting engaged*. But you get engaged *to* someone:

> In the first chapter of part two of *A Room with a View*, Lucy *gets engaged to* Cecil.

And if the marriage breaks up, the couple *get divorced*. The only difference here is that there is not usually an equivalent to "married to a rich man". I don't think "She is divorced from a rich man" is impossible, but we just don't usually think of saying it!

Instead of getting divorced, a couple may decide just *to separate* or *agree to part*. They then achieve a *state* of being separated:

> She is separated from her husband.
>
> She and her husband are separated.

We might as well consider here the verb *part* (meaning *separate*) here, which is often confused with *depart*, which simply means to leave:

> Romeo *parted from* Juliet.
>
> After killing Juliet's cousin, Romeo *departed from* Verona.
>
> The *parting* of the lovers was very sad.
>
> Romeo's *departure* from Verona was hasty.

B.4 Love and falling in love

Note that *love* is a stative verb and carries no sense of beginning and ending. To describe love's beginning, you must normally use *fall in love*:

Romeo falls in love with Juliet when he meets her at a ball in her parents' house.

You might however meet something like "He loved her the moment he saw her." This is an emphatic way of saying it, almost seeming to imply that he had always loved her, even before he met her.

Used as a noun, *love* can be *love of* (food, life, etc.) or *love for* (a person), and you *make love to* a person:

What is attractive about Lucy is her love *of* life.

Romeo declares his love *to* Juliet (i.e. he tells Juliet he loves her). Later he tells his friends about his love *for* Juliet.

The same preposition, *for*, is used after some other words with similar meaning, regardless of what follows:

a liking for, a passion for, a craze for, a craving for, an appetite for, hunger for, thirst for, a feeling for

Her thirst for adventure got her into trouble.

Notice that any of the words above could be used here without any change, but if *love* is substituted it becomes *love of* adventure.

If you want to refer to a more luke-warm feeling than love, you might choose *interest in*. For a stronger feeling you might use *infatuation with*, *obsession with*.

Moving to verbs, in approximately increasing order of strength:

He is attracted to her, he loves her, he adores her, he pines for her love, he dotes on her, he raves about her, he is infatuated with her, he worships her, he is obsessed with her.

Some of these have special connotations: *infatuated* implies that he is foolish, *raves about* means that he tells everyone how wonderful she is, or *sings her praises* all the time; *pines for* implies that he does not get her love, that he is suffering from *unrequited love* (a favourite expression in synopses of traditional stories).

B.5 Relations and relationship

In one of its commonest colloquial meanings, *relations* means members of the extended family and is synonymous with *relatives*:

He wrote to all his friends and relations.

She's a relation of mine, not a girl-friend.

Its more general meaning is something more like *connection* and in this sense it is often in the plural, for no clear reason, and does not refer to a family connection:

Foreign relations, trade relations, relations of friendship

It is important to *have good relations with* your neighbours.

(= It is important to *be on good terms with* your neighbours.)

A family connection could be referred to as *a relationship*:

What is your *relationship to* the accused?

(= How are you related to the accused?)

He is my brother, sir.

A *relationship* (singular count noun) is also used to imply something like a close friendship:

They have a very good relationship.

(= they know and understand each other well, they can disagree and still remain friends, perhaps even they are in love with each other — *they* probably refers to two people, rather than two countries or institutions)

They have very good relations.

(they do a lot of business with each other, they help each other — *they* probably refers to two or more companies, countries or institutions)

Either term can be used of both people and institutions. However, when you say, "We must build up a good relationship between our two companies," you might seem to be humanising the companies. And if you were to say

"Relations between me and my wife are not good at the moment," you might seem to be comparing your marital situation to international affairs.

B.6 Friends

There are a number of useful expressions for referring to friendly relations between individuals:

> We're good friends. We're great friends. We're old friends.
>
> I get on very well with her. We get along fine.
>
> I'm on very good terms with her. We're on excellent terms.
>
> We hit it off. (colloquial)

The expressions for initiating a friendship or referring to a specific past occasion are slightly tricky:

> We became friends when we were at the summer camp together.
>
> I made friends *with* her when we were at the summer camp together.
>
> The moment I met her, I knew we were going to be friends.

Notice that *friends* in *to be friends with*, *to make friends with* is plural.

If you say of someone, "She's always been a good friend to me," you generally mean that she has helped you in some way.

There is the well-known reply given by film-stars and the like when asked about their relationship with someone of the opposite sex: "We're just good friends." This is supposed to mean that there is no love relationship between them, but is often not believed.

B.7 Knowing people

The verb *know* is stative (see 5.5.3) and has no sense of beginning and ending. The following example should explain this:

> Yes, I know Martha. I *met* her at John's party.

You could not normally say "I <u>knew</u> her at John's party." It is however idiomatically possible to say something like "I knew her the moment I saw her." But in this case, *know* means *recognize*: what you probably mean is that you did *not* know her (you had not met her before) but you had seen her picture in the paper. (This follows the general rule in our understanding of language that when the normal meaning for an expression is blocked we assign some different meaning.)

The other possibility for turning *know* into an act with a beginning is to use the expression *get to know*:

> I got to know him very well when we worked together on the trade mission.

If you have heard someone's name, or heard people talking about them, but have not met them, you may want to say, "I have heard *of* her" or "I know *of* her."

B.8   Keeping in touch

Having got to know someone, you may want to *keep in touch* with them:

> Here is my address. Please keep in touch, and let me know if there is anything I can do for you.

You can even use this convenient expression as a way of saying goodbye: *Keep in touch!* or *We'll be in touch!*

Be/get in touch with are synonymous with *contact* (note that *contact* as a verb is used without a preposition):

> Please get in touch with our sales representative when you get to London.
> Please contact our sales representative when you get to London.
> We shall be in touch (with you) later.

The last of these is commonly used as a way of ending an interview (especially a job interview) without making any commitment to the candidate.

B.9 Being educated

Depending on the context, you might say:

> She was educated at St Teresa's College and the Chinese University. (formal)
>
> She went to St Teresa's College and the Chinese University. (normal, conversational, or semi-formal)

With regard to graduation there is a slight difference between British and American English:

> She was graduated with honours from the Chinese University in 1989. (American)
>
> She graduated with honours from the Chinese University in 1989. (British)

This difference is unimportant, but I mention it because students sometimes ask.

B.10 Experience and qualifications

Note that the count and non-count uses of the word "experience" have different meanings. *An experience* is a particular event:

> My trip to Europe was a fascinating experience.

As a non-count noun, *experience* refers to the kind of thing employers look for when they advertise a job:

> We are looking for someone with good qualifications and two years' experience in the field.

While *experience* is necessarily singular (as a non-count noun), *qualifications* is generally plural in this sense.

C. SOME USEFUL VERBS

These are verbs which may be useful in writing because they help in analysing ideas or making connections between ideas.

C.1 Saying what something is

(a) X is a whole made up of parts: *X consists of ...*

consists of, is made up of, is composed of, is / can be divided into, contains, comprises

> A sonnet *consists of* fourteen lines with an elaborate rhyme-scheme. The Shakespearean sonnet *is divided into* three quatrains and a final couplet, whereas the Petrarchan sonnet *is divided into* an octave and a sestet.

It is useful to draw a distinction between features that are inherent and those which you define for the purpose of your analysis; that is to say, some features are obviously present in the object or, as in the example above, are defined by rules, and some features you deliberately choose to see in the object:

> The story *is* divided into three parts.

> (The author divided it this way, and they are perhaps numbered in the text, Part 1, Part 2, etc.)

> The story *can be* divided into three main parts.

> (The author did not divide it this way, but you see it as having these parts.)

(b) If you want (to do) X, you need (to do) Y: *(Doing) X involves (doing) Y.*

involves, means (we must), requires (us to), depends on

Understanding the story *involves* close attention to the ending.

Success in business *requires* constant hard work.

Analysing a poem *means* paying attention to the sound of the words as well as their meaning.

(c)   The subject / theme of X is Y: *X is about Y.*

is about, is concerned with, deals with, examines, discusses, looks at, has to do with

This story *is about* a young girl who thinks she is going to be a great novelist because she is going to have her first novel published.

This poem *is concerned with* the cruelty of war.

Mostly these expressions can refer to either the subject (the story, the things which happen in it and the kind of people they happen to) or the theme (what you think the story really means).

But it is important to distinguish between what a text is *about* and what a text *is*. For example, if you are asked to analyse an advertisement, do not say "This text is about an advertisement." What you should say is, "This text *is* an advertisement."

An alternative way of saying what a story is about is "The theme of this poem is the cruelty of war." You should not try to combine them, however; you should not say "The theme is about ..."

Notice that you can personify the text, i.e. you can say "This story examines the relationship between two people." You can also of course say, "In this story, the author examines the relationship between two people." What you should not say is "In this story, it examines ..." because then there is nothing which *it* refers to.

(d)   The main part of X is Y: *X focuses on Y.*

concentrates on, focuses on, is centred on, centres on, the focus ... is on

The story *focuses on* the relationship between the two protagonists.

The focus of this story is on the relationship between the two protagonists.

It is often useful also to point out what something does NOT focus on:

> The story focuses not, as we might expect, on the Japanese, but on the dialogue between the girl and the boy.

(e) X describes Y as ...:

describes, depicts, portrays, represents, characterizes, presents (us with), provides us with a picture of, paints a picture of

> Shaw *portrays Higgins as* arrogant and insensitive, but also rather shy.
>
> The author *represents* Tom as desperately wanting to escape.

The first five of these will all be followed by the same construction: *describes someone / something **as** adjective, noun or participle.*

C.2   Describing purposes or intentions

The purpose of X is Y: *X is intended to Y.*

aims at / to, X's aim is to, is designed to, is intended to, is supposed to

> Shaw's play *is intended* to make us think.

This would be slightly ambiguous if you used *supposed to*, which could imply that it does not succeed.

A number of adverbs are useful: *on purpose, intentionally, deliberately.*

> The author deliberately leaves this question unanswered.

These contrast with: *accidentally, unconsciously, sub-consciously.*

C.3   Describing origins and connections

X is caused by Y, X is related to Y:

comes from, results from, is due to, stems from, is caused by, is based on, is produced by, lies in, is created by, is a result of, derives from, originates in / from, can be put down to, can be ascribed to, can be explained by, can be blamed on, is related to, is connected to / with, is something to do with, etc.

> Our sense of mystery *stems from* the use of images of darkness.
>
> The interest of the poem lies *in* its imagery.

These kinds of expression are particularly useful in accounting for the effects of language. The last three in the list are very much qualified; that is to say, they only suggest a connection or cause, without implying that you fully understand it:

> Our sense of horror is something to do with the way the author uses animal imagery.

C.4 Relating evidence to conclusions

X shows that Y:

proves, demonstrates, establishes, convinces us (of), tells us, signifies, means, confirms, indicates, shows (how), illustrates + noun, reflects + noun, points to + noun, suggests, implies, leads us to suppose

> Liza's use of non-standard English reflects her lower social status.

Note that *reflects* is followed by a noun rather than a *that* clause. It seems to combine this sense with the one in C.3: the example can mean that Liza's non-standard English (1) shows she has lower social status and (2) is a result of her lower social status.

The last four are particularly useful because they are less assertive:

> The vagueness of this metaphor *suggests* that perhaps the writer was not sure herself what she meant.

The order of evidence and conclusions can be reversed by using a passive:

Y is shown by X:

is reflected in, is revealed by, is shown by, is suggested by, is implied by, can be deduced from

Liza's social background *is indicated by* her use of non-standard English.

C.5 Relevance of further evidence to an existing view

X supports / does not support the view that Y:

agrees with, accords with, reinforces, confirms, echoes, chimes with

This fact reinforces our first impression that the writer is not particularly concerned with social questions.

contradicts, does not agree with, calls into question, casts doubt upon, is hard to reconcile with, does not accord with

This fact casts doubt upon Raymond Carp's view that the writer is not particularly concerned with social questions.

C.6 Referring to the process of analysis

There are several ways in which it can be useful to refer to what we are doing when we analyse a text:

When *we examine* the text *we find* that …

When *we look at* / *consider* / *analyse* what is actually said,…

We *can find* several examples of … in the text.

At first sight this appears to be … But a closer look reveals …

Notice that you *find* things in the text, you do not *find them out*. It is assumed that the process of textual analysis only makes explicit what readers already know. *Find out* suggests uncovering a secret. The meaning of a text is not a secret but something which is presumed to be available to every careful well-prepared reader.

D. DANGEROUS WORDS

D.1 An alphabetical list of problem words and structures

This is a very limited list of some of the words and structures which very commonly cause errors. You need to add to it by making a list of your own to include the words with which you have trouble. You should keep your own list beside you when you write in order to remind you to be careful when you use these words and to look them up if necessary.

care for, care about

Care is a word with several related meanings, but as a verb it cannot be followed by a noun without a preposition:

> I don't much care *for* Charles.
>
> (= I don't like Charles.)

> Mother Teresa has devoted her life to caring *for* the sick and dying.
>
> (= looking after the sick and dying)

> She doesn't care *about* his feelings.
>
> (= She doesn't pay attention to his feelings.)

The preposition is only absent in this idiomatic use:

> I don't care what you say.
>
> (= I don't mind what you say.)

There is also a use of the noun, *care*, which frequently corresponds to the meaning of *careful*:

> Electrical appliances should be treated *with care*.
>
> *Take care* when you cross the road.

The noun is also used with the meaning of *look after* in the idiom *take care of*:

> Young children should not be left at home with no one to take care *of* them.

(= with no one to look after them)

casual, causal

Casual means "informal":

> Casual conversation differs from stage dialogue in that it is unscripted and has no specific purpose.

Causal means "related to cause and effect":

> There is a causal relationship between deforestation and flooding. If you cut down the trees you lose the topsoil, and there is nothing to soak up heavy rainfall.

common, ordinary, normal

Care must be taken with *common* because it can have a derogatory sense. If you say of someone, for example, "She is just a common person", you are insulting her. If what you intend is a neutral statement, you should say:

> She is just an ordinary person.

The equivalent neutral statement about an event or situation is:

> This is quite a normal situation.

Again, if you use *common* in front of a non-human noun, it will produce a different effect:

> This is a common occurrence.

(= this happens *often*)

> This is a common error.

(= an error people often commit)

There is a further meaning of *common* which is expressed unambiguously in expressions like *to have something in common* (= to share something).

What do the words "rough" and "stuff" have *in common*? They both end in the sound / f /.

This meaning can also be conveyed however by *common* on its own, without the preposition, in which case there may seem to be ambiguity:

What is the common element in "rough" and "stuff"?

I say there may *seem* to be ambiguity, because in fact it would not make much sense in this context to interpret *common* as meaning *frequently occurring* or as *vulgar*.

concern, concerned about, concerned with, concerning

This might be called the number one source of errors in English for contemporary Hong Kong students. *Concern* can be both verb and noun, and has a number of different (but more or less connected) meanings. For convenience we can group them under two headings:

(a) *concern* (non-count noun) = *anxiety, worry*
     be concerned about
     to concern (transitive verb)

> Thank you for your concern.
>
> (= for showing sympathy)
>
> I am rather concerned about my grades.
>
> (= worried about)
>
> This is a matter of concern.
>
> (= something to be worried about)
>
> The patient's condition concerns me.
>
> (= worries me)

The last example is ambiguous, and could also have the next meaning, if the context were right:

(b) *concern* (count noun) = *business, company, affair*
     to concern (transitive verb) = *to "be the business of", to be concerned with*

a concern = business / a business

> Any problem which affects the company's image concerns her.

> (= is her responsibility, is a problem she must deal with)

> Her job is concerned with public relations.

> (= deals with, is involved with)

> What she does is no concern of mine.

> (= is no business of mine)

Notice that in either sense it is very unusual for *to concern*, the simple verb in the active voice, to have a human subject. So you should know immediately that a sentence like the following is wrong:

> ✗ She <u>concerns</u> her son too much.

There is a further meaning of *concerning*, equivalent to the preposition *about*:

> I wrote to you previously concerning this matter and I still have not received a reply.

This usage is somewhat pompous and it is generally preferable to use *about*. But note that you do NOT use both *concerning* and *about* together: they are alternatives.

conscience, consciousness

No doubt it is largely due to the very difficult spelling that these words are so often confused.

conscience   the part of the mind which worries about whether something you do is right or wrong. If you *have a guilty conscience*, it means you think you have done something wrong. You may say of someone you disapprove of that "she has no conscience."

consciousness   your mind and its ability to be aware of what is happening; your awareness of yourself. If you faint, you *lose consciousness* or *become unconscious*, and when you *regain consciousness* (in everyday language, *when you come round*), you probably will not know what has happened to you. According to psychological theories, you also have ***an unconscious*** (note here the adjective is used as a noun) which motivates some of your actions without your being aware of it.

context, text

A *text* is a passage or piece of written language. *The context* is that part of the text which surrounds (which precedes and follows) some piece of the text which you are commenting on. It can also be the physical surroundings in which actions or words occur. *Context* is a rather fashionable word in language studies or language teaching, which is perhaps why students tend to use it when all they mean is *text*.

doubt

This verb often does not mean what people want it to mean.

> We doubt that / if her words reveal her true character.

(= we think her words do NOT reveal her true character)

> We suspect that her words reveal her true character.

(= we think her words DO reveal her true character)

To convey the idea that you are not sure about something you need something like this:

> We wonder if her words reveal her true character.
> We are uncertain whether her words reveal her true character.

effort

No problem with the meaning but the usage is slightly idiomatic:

> We must *make every effort* to solve this problem.
> She puts a great deal of effort *into* her work.
> Her efforts to improve the company's situation were rewarded.
> We shall need to make a big effort.

Note that there is no way to use the verb *to pay* in connection with effort.

-ence forms and *-ent* forms

There are many words with these endings, so it is worth learning that *-ent* is the adjective ending:

> She is very confident.
> She is full of confidence.

glance, at a glance

The best way to use *glance* is as a straightforward verb:

> He glanced at the table in the corner.

It is probably best to use the verb, but if you do want to use noun, *a glance*, be careful about the verb you use with it: *pay*, *have*, and *make* are all wrong. The only possible ones are *give* and *take*:

> She gave him a quick glance.

Other expressions with *glance* are:

> He saw at a glance that she was angry.
>
> (= quickly, easily)
>
> At first glance, the poem seems simple. But a closer examination reveals that it is actually quite complex.

good for, good to, good of

The different prepositions produce different meanings:

> The Protestant work ethic says that work is good for you.
> Ginseng is supposed to be very good for you.

Good for means you benefit spiritually or physically from it.

> Be good to your wife and don't beat her!

Good to means being kind to someone, behaving nicely towards them.

> It was very good of you to come when I needed help.

Good of is what you say when someone else is being kind.

hard-working and hard work

You write *hard-working* with a hyphen, and it is an adjective. The noun equivalent is *hard work*. The common mistake is to use *hard-working* as if it were a noun,

> ✗ He quickly rose to the top because of his <u>hard-working</u>.

Rewrite as any of these:

> He quickly rose to the top because he is so hard-working.
> He quickly rose to the top because he works so hard.
> He quickly rose to the top because of his hard work.

ignore, be ignorant of, innocent, naive

To be ignorant of something, simply means not to know it. *To ignore* something is to pay no attention even when you are aware of it:

> Many people are ignorant of this fact.
> He ignored my advice, so I'm not surprised he got into trouble.

You do not often speak of someone ignoring a fact, because a fact is something you either know or do not know. It is possible however to *overlook* a fact (meaning that you forget about it).

Used on its own the adjective *ignorant* is strongly critical, since it implies that a person has no education or does not know things they ought to know. It should not be confused with *innocent* or *naive*:

> Small children are innocent.
> Although she's over 21, she's very naive.

human

This is an awkward word. It is normally an adjective, and its meaning is sometimes quite hard to distinguish from *humane*, which means something like *kind*:

> It is only human to make mistakes.
>
> It is not humane to keep children always indoors.

The negative forms, *inhuman* and *inhumane*, are often very close in meaning.

As a noun, *a human* can occasionally be used instead of the more correct form *a human being*, meaning an individual member of the human race. Either way, you are using a count noun, and there must be an article or plural form:

> Humans / Human beings are distinguished from animals by the ability to laugh.
>
> A chimpanzee is very like a human.

So it will generally be wrong to write something like "Human being *is* ..."

indulge, self-indulgent, self-indulgence

The simple verb used transitively without a preposition is quite rare. It really means something like *to allow yourself to do something that you perhaps ought not to do*:

> Every time he comes to Hong Kong, he indulges his passion for eating.

Similarly, *self-indulgence* is more or less the opposite of *self-restraint*, or *self-discipline*, and *over-indulgence* generally means eating or drinking too much. All uses of the word have negative connotations:

> She knew it was bad for her, but she decided to indulge herself, just this once.
>
> Heart disease is the price you pay for over-indulgence.
>
> That child behaves badly because her parents indulge her.

To *indulge in* does not have these negative connotations but is little more than a fancy way of saying *to have*, *do or practise* something:

> He occasionally indulges in a glass of wine.

(= has a glass of wine)

> She indulged in a lot of criticism at my expense.

(= She criticized me.)

The mistake students make is to use *indulge* in the sense of being *absorbed in* something:

> ✗ Amanda does not notice, as she is <u>indulged in</u> her memories.

This can be rewritten with *absorbed*, *lost* or *engrossed*, or even *immersed*.

initiative, initiation

Two words that are commonly confused but which are actually quite different in meaning: the word usually needed is *initiative*, which has a range of meanings connected with the idea of acting positively and independently:

> She showed great initiative in solving the problem on her own.
> We should not wait for the other side to make a proposal; we should take the initiative and put forward our proposal first.

Initiation is a noun form of the verb *initiate*, meaning to begin or to introduce someone to some new situation. It is well worth looking both words up in the *Cobuild* dictionary.

involve, to be involved with / in

These can be often be substituted for *to be concerned with*:

> She is involved in public relations.
> Her job involves trying to improve the company's image.

With this meaning there cannot be a human subject for the verb in the active voice. But as a synonym of *implicate*, *involve* can have a human subject:

> She involved the President in an extra-marital affair in order to blackmail him.

lack

Do not confuse the various constructions all with more or less the same meaning:

> Tom feels that his life *lacks* adventure.
>
> Tom feels that his life *is lacking in* adventure.
>
> Tom hates his life because of *its lack of* adventure.

lay, lie

Two verbs easily confused. The main point is that *lay* is transitive and *lie* is intranstive:

> She told him to lay his cards on the table.
>
> He wanted to lie on the beach all day, doing nothing.

Unfortunately (for students) the past tense of *lie* is *lay*, which obviously adds to the confusion even for native speakers, who often use *lay* when they mean *lie*: "Get up! You can't lay in bed all day doing nothing!" This is not acceptable standard English, however.

like

Do not confuse *to like* (similar to *to love*, *to have a liking for*) and *to be like* (a non-verb — see 5.7 — meaning *to resemble*):

> He *likes* his mother better than his father.

(the sort of thing Freud called the Oedipus complex?)

> He *is more like* his father than his mother.

(= he resembles his father)

literary, literal

A clear difference in meaning:

literary = relating to literature
literal meaning = not metaphorical

loss, lost

There seems to be special confusion between these two which are noun and adjective / past participle respectively:

> The company made a loss this year.

> We will try to make up the lost ground next year.

This seems to be a case of the final "t" problem; students either panic over words ending in "t" or else assume that every English word ought to end in "t".

Perhaps it all boils down to a problem of pronunciation.

nature

This is a very dangerous word, especially for students of English literature, because it is well known that many poets write about *nature*. In this sense it may or may not have a capital letter, but it must have no article. This is of course simply a rule of English; it is not one of *nature's laws*.

The second problem occurs in phrases like *human nature* (also with no article). This is a very abstract concept and it is not very easy to say what it means.

> It is human nature to be jealous.

(= It is natural to be …)

> Human nature is very complicated.

(= The way people behave etc.)

See also *human*, another dangerous word.

pay

Even in its ordinary meaning the grammar is a little difficult:

> Have you paid the telephone bill?
> Have you paid Bill?
> Have you paid *for* the tickets?
> Have you paid Bill for the tickets?
> She paid two hundred dollars for the tickets.

Note that you pay money, a bill, and a person directly, without a preposition, but you pay *for* the goods or services you get in return for your money.

There are some other, idiomatic uses of *to pay*:

> to pay a visit
>
> to pay one's respects to someone
>
> to pay attention (to someone or something)

More importantly, note that it is not used in other expressions: *to **put** effort into*.

pity, to feel sorry for

The emotion of *pity* is well understood, but not the ways of talking about it. The word itself is rarely used, either as verb or noun, in describing the way you feel about someone:

> She has had a very hard time. I *feel extremely sorry for* her.
>
> He is very hard-hearted. He *showed no sympathy* when she became ill.

If you do use *pity*, it often has some negative connotations and can even be used as an insult:

> "I pity you!" she said, contemptuously. "You're such a small person."
>
> People who are disabled do not want pity, they want help.

There are two adjectives, *pitiful* and *pitiable*, with slightly different meanings. *Pitiful* is generally insulting:

> The government's attempts to cover up its mistakes are pitiful.
>
> (= useless)
>
> His present situation is pitiable.
>
> (= to be pitied)

Note that the count-noun, *a pity*, is only used with an idiomatic meaning:

> It will be a pity if it rains on the day of the picnic.
>
> (= it will be unfortunate, we shall feel disappointed)

portray, portrait

The verb is *portray*; *portrait* is a count noun:

> Shakespeare *portrays* Hamlet as indecisive.

Greene's narrator paints an unflattering *portrait* of the girl.

The students' mistake is to use noun for verb. A case of the final "t" problem, perhaps. If you fail to pronounce the final "t" it is quite likely that you will fail to distinguish in your mind between the two words.

pretentious

This does not mean the same as *deceitful, false, untruthful.* It is not an adjective having the same kind of meaning as the verb, *to pretend.*

It can only be applied to someone or something you think is claiming to be more important than he, she, or it, really is:

She's very pretentious: she always behaves as if she knows everything.

pursue, pursuit

The verb is *pursue*; *pursuit* is a non-count noun, rarely used on its own, or a count noun meaning something similar to *a hobby.*

The police pursued the robbers into the building.

The robbers fled, with the police in pursuit.

We pursued the enemy to the edge of the forest. After that, pursuit became impossible.

Some people think stamp-collecting is a fascinating pursuit.

You may recall a number of other phrases where a non-count noun follows *in*: *in haste, in trouble, in sickness or in health.*

The usual mistake is to use noun for verb. Another case of the final "t" problem?

put forward, put forth

Put forward is associated with proposals:

The committee put forward a proposal for solving the problem.

Put forth is a somewhat literary or biblical expression, describing what plants do:

> Spring is a time of rebirth, when all the plants put forth new shoots.

In Hong Kong however proposals are being "put forth" all the time; perhaps Hong Kong administrators are like trees.

raise, rise

Two verbs which are easily confused because they are very similar in meaning. But *raise* is transitive, while *rise* is intransitive. There is therefore often a choice to be made between *rise* or the passive of *raise*, both grammatical, but slightly different in meaning:

> Prices are likely to rise this year. Bus fares will probably be raised.

A *rise in* prices is not likely to be the result of anyone's deliberate action, so the intransitive verb is best. But a *rise in* bus fares is the result of the bus company's decision: they will *raise* the fares.

refer to

There should be no problem with this, but students tend to use it quite unnecessarily in the passive.

> "Gentlemen callers" *refers to* Amanda's suitors.

(not is referred to)

refuse, reject, refute

If someone offers you something you don't want, you *refuse* it. If someone proposes something you don't like, you *reject the proposal*. If someone accuses you unfairly you *reject* the accusation.

If someone asks you to do something you don't want to do, you *refuse*.

If someone asks permission to do something undesirable, you *refuse permission*, or *refuse to give permission*.

If someone applies for a job and doesn't get it, he *is rejected*. Speaking somewhat informally, if someone asks permission to do something undesirable, he *is refused*.

If you offer proof showing that a theory or an accusation is wrong, you *refute* the theory or accusation.

response and respond

Response is a noun. The confusion may stem from the fact that it can be used in verb phrases like *make no response* (= *not reply, not respond*), *give an unfavourable response to* (= *reply to unfavourably*). If a verb is needed, it has to be *respond*:

> We are still waiting for them *to respond* to our proposal. So far we have had *no response* from them.

rid

This can be a verb. King Henry II of England, when angry with Thomas à Becket, is supposed to have said, "Who will rid me of this troublesome knight?" But students usually use it in the idiom *get rid of*. The point about this is that the subject stays where he is and the unwanted object is removed. It is not really appropriate in situations where the subject runs away or escapes:

> ✗ She decided to get rid of him by going to another country.
> ✔ They got rid of the president by sending him on a diplomatic mission.

Often where it is used incorrectly the verb needed is *avoid*.

shame, ashamed, shameful

The basic emotion of *shame* is understood well enough. The problems come with the adjectives. The common way of describing the state of someone's mind when he *feels shame* is to say he *is ashamed*:

> When he thought about how he had treated her, he felt / was very ashamed.
> "You ought to be ashamed of yourself," she said.

The adjective *shameful* describes not emotion but behaviour viewed from the outside:

> His behaviour was shameful.

(= *disgraceful, shocking*)

The noun, *shame* (non-count), is not used very often, but does occur sometimes in the negative:

> He showed absolutely no shame.
>
> He seems to be completely without shame.

The count noun, *a shame*, is only used with an idiomatic meaning:

> It will be a shame if it rains on the day of the picnic.
>
> (= *a pity*)

subject to, subjected to

There is a transitive verb, *to subject someone to something*, meaning something like "to force someone to undergo something". This must not be confused with the invariable form *subject to*, which means something like *liable to* but is followed by a noun phrase rather than a verb:

> The weather is subject to sudden changes.
>
> (= is liable to change suddenly)
>
> These proposals are subject to the committee's approval.
>
> (= may be changed if the committee does not approve of them)

totally, in total

In standard English, *totally* is a synonym for *very, completely*. It does not have its apparent meaning of *altogether*.

> Altogether twenty prizes were given out.
>
> A total of twenty prizes was / were given out.

(*A total* is singular, but it tends here to work like *a number of* which is followed by a plural noun and usually has plural agreement.)

underlie, underline

To underline is more or less synonymous with *to emphasize*:

The chairman underlined her commitment to a progressive policy.

To underlie is to lie underneath, usually in a metaphorical sense:

Fred's underlying motive is probably envy.

used to be and be used to

Do not confuse these two different meanings and different constructions:

Amanda used to be rich and popular.

(but now she is not)

Amanda is used to poverty now.

(Since her husband left her, life has been a continual struggle — she is accustomed to it.)

It is best to regard *used to be* as a kind of tense with the same meaning as *was once, was formerly*.

widespread

This is an adjective and there is no exact noun eqivalent; the nearest is *spread*:

Corruption is widespread.

We must take measures to combat *the spread* of corruption.

INDEX

weather
 non-count noun, 6.1.2b
what ... is only ...
 better replaced by *All ... is ...*, 4.5.12
when
 compared with *while*, 8.3.1a
whether
 indirect question, no *that*, 4.2.5
while
 requires subject and verb in clause, 4.2.2a
 compared with *when*, 8.3.1a
widespread
 Adjective not noun, Appendix D
wish
 often with past tense, 5.1.5
with
 compared with *have* in descriptions, 7.1.2, 7.1.6
within
 use with time expressions, 8.2.3
wonder
 self-questioning, compared with *doubt*, 5.8.3
wood
 count and non-count, singular and plural, 6.1.2
wording
 non-count, collective, compared with *word*, 2.5.4
written by
 when to omit, 2.1.2
work
 a work / works of, 2.2.1
worth
 non-verb, needs *to be*, 5.7
would
 rather than simple present in offers, 5.1.1
 overuse of, 5.1.4
 not with *hope*, 5.1.5

yet
 with present perfect, 5.1.2c
 contrast connective, not followed by comma, 4.6.1